A Hard Pounding

A Hard Pounding

Politics and Economic Crisis
1974–1976

Edmund Dell

OXFORD UNIVERSITY PRESS
1991

Oxford University Press, Walton Street, Oxford OX2 6DP
Oxford New York Toronto
Delhi Bombay Calcutta Madras Karachi
Petaling Jaya Singapore Hong Kong Tokyo
Nairobi Dar es Salaam Cape Town
Melbourne Auckland
and associated companies in
Berlin Ibadan

Oxford is a trade mark of Oxford University Press

Published in the United States
by Oxford University Press, New York

© Edmund Dell 1991

All rights reserved. No part of this publication may be reproduced,
stored in a retrieval system, or transmitted, in any form or by any means,
electronic, mechanical, photocopying, recording, or otherwise, without
the prior permission of Oxford University Press

British Library Cataloguing in Publication Data
Data available
ISBN 0–19–828394–6

Library of Congress Cataloging in Publication Data
Dell, Edmund.
A hard pounding : politics and economic crisis, 1974–1976 / Edmund Dell.
Includes bibliographical references and index.
1. Great Britain—Economic policy—1945 2. Great Britain—Politics and government—
1945 3. Great Britain—Politics and government—1964–1979.I. Title.
HC256.6.D477 1991   338.941'009'047—dc20   91–13709
ISBN 0–19–828394–6

Typeset by Pentacor PLC, High Wycombe, Bucks.

Printed in Great Britain by
Bookcraft (Bath) Ltd,
Midsomer Norton, Avon

For Susi

Preface

The Labour Government elected in 1974 faced the most difficult economic and political baptism of any post-war British administration except that of Attlee, and it was not well prepared. Nor was the Treasury. The interest of the period arises from the unfortunate conjunction of a new government lacking a secure base in the House of Commons, with a major international economic turning-point signalled by the breakdown of Bretton Woods and the 1973 oil price hike.

Between March 1974 and the IMF crisis at the end of 1976, the period covered in this book, I was involved in the making of economic policy, first at the Treasury as Paymaster General and Deputy to the Chancellor of the Exchequer, and then as Secretary of State for Trade. Yet no one person, however well placed, could have seen the whole of the game. In addition, therefore, to my own records, and a diary that I kept for much of the period, I have used as the basis for this history the material, both primary and secondary, which is now available. As far as possible I have avoided relying on memory which, at this distance of time, would have been unreliable.

Inevitably my account is biased towards my own perceptions. I hope that bias has been controlled, and where necessary corrected, by the sources listed. One justification for publishing my account now is that most of those who influenced the making of economic policy during this period are still alive and can make their own rebuttals. The principal exceptions are Tony Crosland and Lords Balogh and Kaldor.

Many of those centrally engaged in the conduct of British economic policy in this period have said that the autumn of 1976 was the worst period of their lives, the time that they would least like to live through again. For me, what had to be done had achieved a crystal clarity seldom experienced in public affairs. The irony was that the man burdened with the principal responsibility, Denis Healey, was a great deal less persuaded than I. Fortunately, despite his own doubts and the initial disagreement of the majority of his Cabinet colleagues, he put his outstanding strength of will and intellect behind achieving accommodation with the IMF and was proved right in the end.

I express my particular thanks to Richard Ollard and Sir Leo Pliatzky. Richard Ollard's encouragement and advice have been invaluable, among other things in ensuring that I did bring this work to a conclusion. Sir Leo Pliatzky read successive drafts and I have greatly benefited from his comments and criticisms. My wife, to whom I dedicate this book, has not neglected her usual role as my severest critic. I alone remain responsible.

Edmund Dell

January 1991

Acknowledgements

The author and publisher wish to thank the following for permission to quote copyright material:

David Higham Associates on behalf of Weidenfeld for *The Castle Diaries, 1974–76* by Barbara Castle; the National Institute of Economic and Social Research for the *National Institute Economic Review*; Random Century Group for *Tony Crosland* by Susan Crosland and for *Prime Minister: The Conduct of Policy under Harold Wilson and James Callaghan* by Bernard Donoughue; Copyright Tony Benn 1989, reproduced by permission of Curtis Brown, London, on behalf of Tony Benn. Material from House of Commons debates is subject to parliamentary copyright and that from White Papers to Crown copyright.

Contents

Part I: Introduction

1. Britain in a World without Rules — 3
2. Divisions of Labour — 12

Part II: The Short Parliament: March to September 1974

3. The Economic Team — 23
4. The March Budget — 30
5. The Triumph of Politics — 42
6. Debates on Economic Policy — 54
7. The July Measures — 76
8. The Regeneration of British Industry? — 88
9. A Disorderly Growth of Incomes — 103

Part III: The Mandarins

10. A Problematic Victory — 111
11. The Mandarins Revolt — 119
12. The Mandarins Retreat — 131
13. Industrial Policy: The Excitement Fades — 139
14. The Social Contract on the Brink — 145
15. The Battle for a Statutory Incomes Policy — 155
16. Treasury Advice and Cabinet Responsibility — 179
17. Public Expenditure: The Fight for Control — 183
18. The Current Account: Forecasting a Crisis — 193

Part IV: Catharsis

19. Sterling in Free Fall — 203
20. Callaghan's Inheritance — 212
21. The Third July — 225
22. No Alternative to the IMF — 234
23. The IMF in London — 247

24. Accepting the Inevitable 265
25. The Final Assessment 277

References 293
Index 295

Edmund Dell by his colleagues

'That chap is capable of more misdirected intellectual horsepower than anyone I know.' (Barbara Castle)

'He is the most reactionary, obscurantist Treasury man you could find.' (Tony Benn)

'My most formidable ally in the Cabinet.' (Denis Healey)

Part I

Introduction

O·N·E

Britain in a World without Rules

Labour did unexpectedly well in the February 1974 general election. It became the largest party in the House of Commons.[1] The country had rejected the policies of the Heath Government that had led to the miners' strike and the three day week but had certainly not endorsed those of the Labour Party.

Though it fell thirty-four seats short of an overall majority, Labour was invited to form a government. It had now only one objective, to gain an overall majority in the further election inevitable later that year. Yet, despite the endeavours of the new Government, the electorate remained sceptical. In the general election the following October, Labour gained only the barest overall majority. It was the unfortunate consequence that, at a critical time in the economic history of the UK, short term party political considerations were more than usually insistent as an element in policy formation. The course of policy selected by the Government led straight to the encounter with the International Monetary Fund in the autumn of 1976.

Britain in the eyes of the International Monetary Fund

The IMF will play one of the major roles in this history. Its staff had a responsibility for identifying potential weak points in the international economy. It could hardly have escaped them that the UK had its problems. In studies made in the mid-1970s, responsibility for these problems was ascribed to the UK's antiquated industrial structure, to low profit margins, high interest rates, high marginal income tax rates, trade union and management practices, together with a low rate of capital formation which contributed to the UK's loss of market share in international markets and prolonged weakness in the external position. There was questioning whether the Public Sector Borrowing Requirement was not too large in relation to gross national product and whether the high proportion of output going to consumption rather than to investment did not suggest underlying structural problems. To the IMF staff, 'it seemed that UK policymakers had been trying to avoid the Scylla of balance of payments deficits and pressure on sterling and the Charybdis of increasingly high levels of under-utilized capacity and unemployment'. Hence there had been 'a series of deflationary policies followed by expansionary policies, so-called stop–go policies'.[2]

This analysis did not provide any new insights. The problems were all long-standing and difficult to correct. The UK economy had long been attempting to sail between this Scylla and this Charybdis. There had never been any shortage of analyses, analogies, or even of attempts at a solution. The significance of the IMF's analysis is only that it shared the widespread concern about the UK economy and about how it would fare in a world without rules that had broken loose from Bretton Woods.

The death of Bretton Woods

By March 1974 the structured world of Bretton Woods, with its fixed, if adjustable, exchange rates, was dead. The Nixon measures of August 1971 had marked the limits of American commitment to an interdependent economic system. In December 1971, at the Smithsonian Institute, Washington, DC, a major realignment of exchange rates had been agreed, the largest for nearly a quarter of a century. Before long, exchange rates were floating. Governments expected that floating would ensure balance in their current accounts and thereby restore some measure of national autonomy to an increasingly interdependent world. With American commitment no longer to be relied upon, American economic hegemony, in any case in decline, had ceased to provide the old guarantees of stability, of social peace, or of mutually supportive economic policy co-ordination.

'Disengagement'

The Heath Government had experimented with a policy of 'disengagement'. It proved to be a perverse reaction to the changing international economic panorama. The disengagement was from the exchange rate of sterling, from the current account, from the Public Sector Borrowing Requirement (PSBR), from the money supply as well as from industrial interventionism. The philosophy behind disengagement was a belief in the unconstrained operation of market forces. Yet it is not at all clear that the Heath Government had much appreciation of what it was doing. To abandon all signposts, to let market forces run entirely free, involved the abdication of economic policy.

It was not appreciated that the loss of one fixed point in economic policy, the exchange rate, made more not less necessary the discovery of alternative signposts by which policy might be guided. If these could not be agreed internationally because of the lack of consensus or the decline of American influence, then signposts would be even more requisite nationally. There could be the money supply, if ways could be found of measuring and controlling it. There could be domestic credit expansion. There could be the PSBR. There could be the current account. There could be some of these in combination. Or there could be, once again, exchange rates rediscovered as the most reliable base on which to build.

The signposts required may change with circumstances or with the objects of policy. There will always be problems of measurement, and the identification of signposts is itself likely to affect the indications provided by them.[3] The only certainty is that, in an open economy, the selection of the signposts, and indeed the policy objectives, must have regard to international opinion. There are limits to the degree to which even the most powerful economies can insulate themselves from the influences of international opinion which often find their most vigorous expression through those very market forces upon which governments seek to impose their will. From an early stage it was the French view that a stable framework of exchange rates was the key to stable international economic relationships.

The 1972 Budget and the abandonment of disengagement

In the Commons on 23 November 1971, Robert Carr, Secretary of State for Employment, lamented the apparent demise of the old and trusted Keynesian techniques. '[T]he sort of measures of demand management which appeared to work, and indeed did work, to control the overall level of unemployment in the past seem now to have lost at least some of their previous effectiveness.'[4]

At the beginning of 1972, the level of unemployment was the highest since the war apart from the exceptionally bad winter of 1947. The Heath Government panicked. Industrial interventionism was reintroduced more lavishly than ever contemplated by Labour.

As the usual quantum of Keynesian penicillin was apparently no longer destroying the economic antibodies, the dose was increased. The 1972 Budget was strongly reflationary. The Chancellor of the Exchequer, Anthony Barber, hoped to add 2 per cent to total output over the following year. He set a target of 5 per cent for the annual rate of growth of output for the eighteen-month period up to the middle of 1973. He stated that 'it is neither necessary nor desirable to distort economies to an unacceptable extent in order to maintain unrealistic exchange rates'. In other words the economy was to be reflated not just by the size of the budget deficit but by export demand stimulated by a depreciation of the currency. This was making a virtue of necessity because Barber's reflation was very likely to undermine international confidence in sterling. In fact, he was soon faced by a massive speculative attack on sterling which had to be met with help from an international support operation.

On 23 June 1972, Barber floated sterling. Sterling abandoned the European 'snake' which it had entered only weeks before. The floating represented an effective sterling devaluation of 7 per cent thereby helping to undermine the Smithsonian agreement entered into the previous December. The UK thus made its own contribution to the breakdown in international economic co-operation. But, for Members of Parliament, floating brought a sense of release from the balance of payments constraint which for so long had dominated policy. Now, it was thought, the UK could compete.

Unfortunately, the technology of the international economic power struggle had changed. The war for national solvency had, under Bretton Woods, been fought under conditions of fixed exchange rates, in which devaluation was an exceptional act which might indeed sometimes win time and enable a deficit country to steal, temporarily, a competitive march on its competitors. But in a world of floating exchange rates the benefits were less certain even than before. It was an illusion for any British Chancellor to imagine that because he was prepared to contemplate a fall in the exchange rate to deal with the consequences for the balance of payments, he could afford a violent explosion in domestic demand.

A Keynesian guide

Yet what the Government was doing had intellectual, not just political, support. For example, this criticism of Barber's policies was not entirely shared by the leading Keynesian commentator of the time, the *National Institute for Economic and Social Research* (NIESR), an institute with strong links to the UK Treasury, whose Journal, the *National Institute Economic Review* (NIER) will be used in this account to provide evidence of what Keynesians were recommending at the time.

The Barber reflation did reverse the rise in unemployment.[5] However the improvement in employment was accompanied by a serious deterioration in the current account. The UK in 1972 had still been approximately in balance on its current account, itself a deterioration as compared with the surplus of 1971. By 1973 a deficit had re-emerged. From then on the deterioration proceeded, to be exacerbated further by the oil price hike of autumn 1973. Did it matter? *NIER*, in February 1973, did not see any necessary inconsistency between improvement in the balance of payments and continued growth in domestic expenditure designed to moderate unemployment, which was still 700,000. There was no imminent 'resource clash'. Immediate and severe deflation was to be ruled out. Better to wait and see.[6]

'Over-heating'

In March 1973 the Chancellor introduced a Budget which he described as 'broadly neutral'. But, only two months later, on 21 May 1973, he was announcing public expenditure cuts estimated to reduce total output in 1974 by 0.5–0.75 per cent.[7] According to some commentators, the economy, boosted by the earlier Barber measures, was 'over-heating', though *NIER* sardonically questioned the term. 'Over-heating is an expression which has gate-crashed the literature, thereby avoiding payment of the entrance fee of a definition, and escaping any critical scrutiny at the door.'[8]

In fact, the inexactness of the term is not greater than that of more sophisticated economic judgements. In November *NIER* was still claiming that the panic about over-heating had been overdone, and that the reflationary policy 'appears . . . to have had almost complete success'. Nevertheless it was itself now forecasting that the current price forecast for the balance of payments deficit for 1974 had worsened from £350 million which it had forecast in August 1973 to £2,100 million. And it was no longer expecting the balance to return to zero by the end of 1974, rather a further worsening in the first quarter of 1974 followed by a 'sharp recovery' thereafter. That forecast was after taking account of the price effects of the November oil price shock but not of any interruption of supply.[9] It took account also of the effects of other commodity prices which were higher than previously forecast and which made their own significant contribution to the UK deficit. Demand was expanding throughout the industrialized world carrying commodity prices up with it.

On 15 January 1974, the Governor of the Bank of England, Gordon Richardson, said:

Last year the current account showed a large deficit which, this year, will be further greatly increased by the rise in the oil price. . . . But even before that factor became important, our balance of payments deficit on current account in the last quarter of the year was running at a rate equivalent to 4 percent of our national product.[10]

Thus, even before OPEC struck, Britain's current account deficit had become a matter of serious concern, to the Bank of England if not to *NIER*. Three days before the February 1974 election, the monthly trade figures showed a £383 million deficit, described by *The Times* as 'the largest monthly trade deficit that Britain has known'.[11]

Inflation

Another sign of 'over-heating' was that the fall in unemployment was accompanied not just by a threatening current account deficit but by mounting inflation. After slowing down through 1971, the rate of increase of average earnings began to accelerate in the spring of 1972. Resistance to inflationary wage claims may thereafter have been sapped by the thought that excessive union demands could now be absorbed by letting the exchange rate depreciate. Indicative is one report of a civil servant saying: 'Oh well, if the unions will insist on excessive wage claims, it won't affect expansion. We'll just let the exchange rate go.'[12] It was soon discovered that a floating exchange rate was not more helpful in dealing with the unions than with the balance of payments. The result was the second stage in the Heath U-turn. A freeze on prices and incomes was announced on 6 November 1972 followed by the development of a full-blown statutory incomes policy. Consistency was not, however, a conspicuous element in the Heath Government's U-turn. Its incomes policy was at odds with its fiscal policy. An overheated economy does not provide a suitable environment for a successful incomes policy.

Nevertheless *NIER* was confident that the policy would hold. 'It is already plain that both Phase 1 and Phase 2 of the present prices and incomes policy have had considerable success on the wages side . . . There is no reason to assume that any additional pressure from further falls in unemployment will be sufficient to break down what appears to be a robust structure.' Thus *NIER* felt able to conclude: 'there is no reason why the present boom should either bust or have to be busted so long as the additional instruments of incomes policy and the floating exchanges are retained.'[13] Phase 3 of the incomes policy was announced on 8 October 1973 effective from 7 November. It incorporated a cost-of-living safeguard if prices rose above a 7 per cent 'threshold', an idea supported by the Labour Opposition.

OPEC strikes

With international co-operation the norm since World War II, the major industrial countries were insufficiently prepared for the unco-operative self-interest of OPEC. There was surprise that an over-expansion of demand could open opportunities to those normally excluded from the circle of international economic policy-makers. 1972 'proved to be the most buoyant year for the world economy since 1966'. An even faster rate of growth in the world economy was forecast for 1973.[14] All the elements were being put in place for the OPEC price shock. OPEC knew that its raw material was the essential basis of others' prosperity. Its members thought of themselves as exploited and underpaid. Yet they could see an opening when it was presented to them. The oil price hike in the autumn of 1973 worsened the balance of payments of the oil-consuming countries by something like $50 billion.[15] In 1974, Britain was paying £2.5 billion more for 5 per cent less oil than had been imported in 1973.[16]

OPEC's strategy was perfectly clear by 7 November, Phase 3's inaugural date. Unfortunately, with the sharp increase in import prices, the threshold formula became a built-in inflation accelerator.[17] Heath may, nevertheless, have felt he had no option but to persevere with Phase 3 and its thresholds.

Four failures

On 17 December 1973 Barber took additional deflationary measures. Severe hire purchase controls were reintroduced, public expenditure programmes for 1974/5 were cut by some £1,200 million, there was to be a surcharge on surtax, and, to control the money supply, the supplementary special deposits scheme was introduced. This scheme is described in Chapter 4. It was to be one of Denis Healey's more useful inheritances.[18] By January 1974, industry's investment intentions had collapsed.[19]

The Heath Government now faced a perilous conjuncture. The international outlook was dominated by the oil price hike. The domestic outlook was dominated by the miners' strike and the three-day week. NIER had changed the earlier rather optimistic note of its commentaries. In an appraisal dated 26 February 1974, two days before the general election, it said: 'It is not often that a government finds itself confronted with a possibility of a simultaneous failure to achieve all four main policy objectives—of adequate economic growth, full employment, a satisfactory balance of payments and reasonably stable prices.'[20] It did not add that it felt any responsibility in the matter. Nor did it consider the possibility that it was no longer feasible to achieve all four objectives simultaneously and that, by its panic attempt to do so, the Heath Government had ensured failure on all four.

Notes

1. It had 301 seats compared with the Tories' 297 seats despite Heath's small lead in votes, 38.2% to 37.2%. Heath tried to negotiate with the Liberals but failed.
2. Garritsen de Vries (1985), 461–3.
3. This is a law attributed to Professor Charles Goodhart. It derives ultimately from Heisenberg's uncertainty principle.
4. HC Debs., 23 Nov. 1971, col. 1259.
5. In November 1983 the National Institute Economic Review (NIER) was to say: 'Only a little over 18 months ago it was considered by many that the then high level of unemployment could not be significantly reduced in the short-term by the usual "Keynesian" remedies which we were advocating.' NIER (Nov. 1973), 4. It was clear that the Review thought such commentators had been proved entirely wrong.
6. NIER (Feb. 1973), 5–6.

7. *NIER* (May 1973), 4. There was to be a net saving in public expenditure in 1974/5 of some £500m. (at 1972 Survey prices). *Economic Trends* (June 1973), p. iii.
8. *NIER* (May 1973), 5.
9. *NIER* (Nov. 1973), 3–4.
10. Quoted by Denis Healey, HC Debs., 11 Mar. 1976, col. 746.
11. Castle 29.
12. Keegan and Pennant-Rea 27.
13. *NIER* (May 1973), 5, 6. Phase 1 was the freeze which extended to 31 March 1973. Phase 2, introduced in a White Paper on 17 January, proposed to restrict pay increases to £1 plus 4 per cent with strict control on prices until the autumn. A Counter-Inflation Bill would establish a Pay Board and a Prices Commission. A Green Paper, *The Prices and Pay Code: A Consultative Document* was published on 26 February and a draft White Paper on Phase 2 on 26 March. For further details see *NIER* (May 1973), 84.
14. *NIER* (Feb. 1973), 57. *NIER* (May 1974), 14–16, comments that the three forecasts, the Treasury, the London Business School, and the NIESR, were all above the outturn and underestimated the extent of the slowdown during 1973, especially NIESR.
15. *NIER* (Feb. 11974), 3.
16. HC Debs., 12 Nov. 1974, col. 242.
17. The danger was noted by *NIER* (Nov. 1973), 3, 4.
18. *NIER* (Feb. 1974), 51. For an assessment of the December 1973 measures, see *NIER* (Feb. 1974), 32–3.
19. *NIER* (May 1974), 14 and 35, table 15. The *CBI Industrial Trends Suvey* published on 9 May showed some recovery in investment intentions. *Economic Trends* (May 1974), p. iv.
20. Healey referred to this comment in his Budget statement. HC Debs., 26 Mar. 1974, col. 282.

T·W·O

Divisions of Labour

Policy incoherence

Major British political parties are inevitably coalitions. The Labour Party has always encompassed both distinct ideologies and people of distinct but pragmatic judgement. It called itself socialist. But for many years 'socialism' had lacked any agreed meaning. It had been redefined to the point of extinction but, apparently, could not yet be allowed to die. At its foundation the Labour Party was primarily the political voice of the trade unions. To a large extent that is what it remained. But radicals of many different kinds had found a platform within it. It was united, if at all, in the search for power. But experience of government in the 1960s had served to exacerbate its divisions. In March 1974 it returned to power. By that time it was so divided that it was difficult even to regard it as a coalition. Due to its divisions, and to different interpretations within it of the experience of the 1960s, it was also unprepared. There is no comparable example of such intellectual and political incoherence in a party coming into office in the twentieth century history of the United Kingdom.

Economic policy

During the time of the Heath Government, there was little discussion of economic policy either in the Parliamentary Party or in the National Executive Committee. The Parliamentary Party's economic committee was largely dormant. Party leaders were engaged in negotiating a Social Contract with the TUC but in that the Parliamentary Party had no part. In the party as a whole there was much more interest in industrial policy than in economic policy. Economic policy constantly appeared to be dealing with a moving target. It was assumed, however, that Keynesian techniques would always be available to control unemployment. There was no controversy that UK economic performance had to be improved. This was to be the role of industrial policy rather than economic policy. The party had, as one common objective, substantially enhanced social provision. Economic policy was seen as making its contribution through taxing wealth, a necessary but somewhat routine activity. It was industrial policy that would be concerned with creating the new wealth that could then be taxed. Industrial policy also contained a strong dose of ideology for those for whom the extension of public ownership remained a principal objective.

Joel Barnett writes: 'If Denis Healey had worked out a plan for a Parliament, I am bound to say he kept it secret from me . . . The real worry was the fact that we had worked out no short-, medium-, or long-term economic and financial policies'.[1] Healey had an excuse if he felt he needed one. Throughout the time he was Shadow Chancellor, the international economic environment was in a process of dramatic change. A plan for a Parliament was beyond the limits of human foresight. It was, therefore, not surprising that Labour was unprepared for the difficult tasks of economic management. The Social Contract was in reality the sum total of Labour's economic thinking before March 1974 and it did not contribute very much except pain in the twelve months thereafter.

The Social Contract

Labour's previous period of office had shown the dangers of inflationary wage demands. At the same time it had generated within the trade union movement deep hostility to statutory incomes control. Trade unions were thought to be very powerful. Labour felt that in its special relationship with them it might possess a key to the electorate's heart. It could perhaps persuade the unions to use their power rather more in the general interest. The Labour Party, after all, was offering little enough otherwise to impress an electorate disillusioned by past experience and by Labour's internal battles. The idea of a Social Contract at once recognized trade union power and established a claim that Labour alone could live peacefully in government alongside that power. Labour could assert a capacity unique among political parties. It could negotiate what would amount to a voluntary incomes policy with the trade union leadership. Labour was the party that could control inflation without conflict.

Economic Policy and the Cost of Living, published by the Liaison Committee between the TUC and the Labour Party on 28 February 1973, embodied the agreement which became known as the Social Contract. Harold Wilson describes it:

> [T]he parties agreed on a comprehensive . . . strategy, covering a wide area of the social and economic life of the nation. This included food subsidies, price controls, housing and rents, transport and a redistribution of income and wealth, combined with a policy for increasing investment in industry. Together with the repeal of the Conservatives' Industrial Relations Act, this would 'engender the strong feeling of mutual confidence which alone will make it possible to reach the wide-ranging agreement which is necessary to control inflation and achieve sustained growth in the standard of living'.

He adds: 'This was widely interpreted as a voluntary agreement to accept restraint in pay demands as part of a wider social agreement'.[2]

This Social Contract had little in common with the social contracts of political theory. It was a bargain with a small, though powerful, section of society. A Labour Government would satisfy certain demands of trade union leaders, made supposedly on behalf of their members. It would concede to the trade union leadership influence over every aspect of government policy. Apart from the repeal of the Industrial Relations Act, various provisions advantageous to union power would be enacted. In his autobiography, Jack Jones recalls a statement in *Economic Policy and the Cost of Living*:

> It will be the first task of the Labour Government on taking office, and having due regard to the circumstances at that time, to conclude with the TUC, on the basis of the understanding being reached in the Liaison Committee, a wide-ranging agreement on the policies to be pursued in all these aspects of our economic life and to discuss with them the order of priorities of their fulfilment.

Jones comments on his subsequent experience with the Labour Government: 'There was a degree of forgetfulness about these words in Government circles.'[3] He was a difficult man to satisfy if he thought there was not enough consultation with the TUC after Labour returned to office.

There were to be many in the Labour Government who believed that to enhance the power of trade unions was good in itself, quite apart from any Social Contract into which the trade unions might enter. It was part of the process of transferring power to working people. That was an objective to which the Labour Party had committed itself. That there was a distinction between transferring power to working people and transferring it to trade unions was not accepted. Those within the Labour Party who could not see the concessions as good in themselves had to be reconciled to them by the thought of the contract against inflation. But if there was to be a contract, there would also have to be regard to the ability of the trade unions to deliver their part of the bargain. Either pay restraint was in the interests of trade union members or it was not. If it was, and was seen to be, there seemed little reason to pay for it by way of political concessions. If it was not, or was not seen to be, it seemed unlikely that consent could be bought by a contract of this kind. Satisfying the ambitions of trade union leaders for political influence has low priority among trade union members.

After one meeting of the Parliamentary Party's economic committee while we were still in Opposition, Healey and I had a sharp exchange as we were walking together down the Committee Corridor of the Commons. I said that the Social Contract was a load of codswallop, or words to that effect. 'That is where you are wrong,' he replied and did not stay for an answer.[4] That optimism was shared by others who were to become senior Ministers in the new Labour Government. Barbara Castle recorded in her diary: 'I do believe that our new concordat with the trade unions is far more hopeful than the arms-length relationship we had last time.'[5]

In fact, in describing the Social Contract as 'codswallop', if that was the word I used, I was understating the matter. The Social Contract was worse than codswallop. A direct consequence was that the Labour Party committed itself to accepting the threshold system which the Heath Government had negotiated. With the oil price explosion many triggerings of the threshold became inevitable unless the threshold system was renegotiated. The Heath Government had not felt able to renegotiate; how much less a Labour Party committed to the Social Contract. Probably Labour's relationship with the trade unions would have left it little choice even without the Social Contract. The contract put the matter beyond peradventure and hence committed the new Government to an inflationary future.

There was also a more philosophical objection to the Social Contract. Here was a party which felt compelled to enter into a contract of this kind with a powerful sectional interest. This could only mean that it should be a major purpose, if that party entered government, to remove the privileges on which that sectional power was founded. Labour had no such intention. Its radicalism on relations with the trade unions had been exhausted by the battle over Barbara Castle's *In Place of Strife*. Labour, in the 1960s, had failed to legislate on trade union power. We were now going to cuddle up to it even closer than before.

Europe

Britain had missed an opportunity in the 1950s when it abstained from participation in the construction of the European Community. If it had joined as a founder member, it might have benefited economically from the faster growth of its European partners. There was always going to be a cost. Europe was built on the basis of the Common Agricultural Policy. But if Britain had been present from the start, there is a possibility that it might have been able to veto a few of those gross absurdities that for decades have consumed two-thirds of the Community budget and have extracted, for the benefit of farmers who did not need it, a super-tax on consumers. In 1973, Britain accepted the cost of an entrenched CAP without the prospect of any economic stimulus.

I had become in the 1960s a supporter of British membership of the European Community. This was not in expectation of great economic benefits but as part of a process of cleansing British policy of its great power illusions. I was the first of Labour's front bench to resign after the Commons' historic decision of principle on 28 October 1971 when sixty-nine of us voted, contrary to a three-line whip, in favour of British entry into the Community. It was probably the most important vote that any of us would cast as Members of Parliament. I resigned the following day. At Harold Wilson's request, Roy Jenkins attempted to persuade me to withdraw my resignation. He did not persist long with his persuasions.

But to many of my Labour associates, Europe represented more than a reorientation of Britain's international priorities. It was a major part of the solution of Britain's economic problems. When Roy Jenkins resigned as deputy leader of the Labour Party, they did not understand my support for Tony Crosland's candidature.[6] Tony had asked my advice as to how he should vote on the principle of European entry. I told him he would lose credibility if he did not vote with the rest of the European 'rebels'. Nevertheless I believed that he honestly held the view that Europe was a question of secondary importance for which it would be wrong to split the party. Therefore when he limited his rebellion against Labour's three-line whip to an abstention, I was ready to understand. I was sufficiently close to him before 1974 to rewrite, at his request, the introductory chapter of his collection of essays *Socialism Now*. His inscription in the copy he gave me offers 'grateful thanks for changing the whole shape of the opening essay, to much advantage'. It was only later when almost all questions which to me appeared important became to Tony of secondary importance that our paths diverged.

The Labour Government of 1974 was deeply split between those strongly for continued membership of the Community despite the terms which Heath had negotiated, and those strongly against. All sections of the party had agreed that a Labour government would 'renegotiate' the terms of membership and that the result of the renegotiation would be submitted to a referendum. That agreement had been necessary for party unity but the two warring sections of the party did not mean the same thing by renegotiation. The opponents of membership wanted to negotiate for a breakdown by attempting to secure terms which the rest of the Community could not possibly then accept. Supporters of membership accepted that there was a limit to the concessions the other member states could then be expected to make.

Industrial policy

Though I had resigned from the front bench, I continued in Opposition to take part in the party's deliberations on industrial policy, standing together with Tony Crosland in joint attempts to avoid committing the party to the follies of Bennery.[7] The greatest division within the Labour Party and Government on industrial policy arose from differences about the role of the proposed National Enterprise Board. The idea of an NEB had emerged from the NEC in a form which could only cause great anxiety. It was to incorporate twenty-five major, newly nationalized, companies. Which twenty-five companies was unspecified, in order either to maximize concern in industry or to demonstrate finally the inconsequential nature of the thinking that had gone into the proposition. It would incorporate also Rolls Royce, BP, and other companies in which there was an existing government shareholding or in which government shareholdings were obtained as a result of providing financial aid. This never became the policy of the party and Wilson threatened to veto it if any attempt were made to include it in the party election programme. But given the balance of power within the party, no one could be sure. The proposal could hardly be taken seriously yet it had to be taken seriously.

I opposed it in speeches, in a letter to the press, and in an article in the *Observer*. In this form it would be, I wrote, a 'dinosaur'. It would be unmanageable and yet more powerful than the government of the day.[8] I did not see the extension of public ownership as the object of the NEB. It was merely to be a useful instrument of industrial policy. It would undertake, with the help of public money, investments which the private sector was spurning for short-term reasons, or would work in co-operation with the private sector where there was a desire on their part to spread their risk. There might also be a role in co-operation with existing nationalized industries. Certainly it should have no powers of compulsory acquisition. Nor should the Government have such powers without, in each case, the most compelling justification and a full parliamentary process. Those in the party leadership who shared this view regarded the 'twenty-five companies' idea as a dangerous diversion from a limited industrial policy purpose.

A sustaining grievance

If there were not too many other sources of unity within the party, at least there was one, commonly held, grievance.

The Labour Party saw itself condemned to the role of crisis manager of the British economy. As Harold Wilson put it, 'It seems to be almost a law of British politics that when Labour becomes the Government, we inherit a record balance-of-payments deficit, and, equally, that we bequeath a record surplus when we go out of office'.[9] Only at a time of crisis could Labour expect to be elected to office. The good times were for the Tories, until the times were no longer so good. When the Tories could no longer conceal their economic mismanagement by Keynesian tricks, Labour governments were returned to face the consequences. Meanwhile the Tories took the waters at some fashionable right-wing ideological spring. Labour always found that, burdened with election promises that had been inadequately thought through, it had been elected to the prior task of clearing up an inherited mess.

This resentful feeling was fostered by repeated experiences. In 1964 the Wilson Government inherited a large balance of payments deficit. Labour had confronted the consequences of Tory mismanagement and Tory extravagance, the devil-may-care, never-had-it-so-good spirit of the Macmillan and Maudling era. Labour, in its first forty-eight hours back in office after thirteen years shaping and reshaping its vision of a better society, had heroically rejected the 'easy' option of devaluation, and found itself instead muddling through a period of import surcharges and harsh deflation. In the end the feared devaluation was not avoided. In the June 1970 general election Labour paid the political price for the subsequent inflation. The electorate did not share the Wilson Government's belief in its own undoubted virtues. Instead, unheeding, it returned the Tories to office. By March 1974, the political cycle had come full circle once again. But, this time, no economic crisis was to be allowed to thrust aside the commitments that were the real Labour purpose in office.

An experienced team

Labour came to office more divided, more ideological, and more closely tied to the trade unions' apron strings than in 1964 or 1966. Wilson proudly claimed that the Cabinet was 'richer in experience than perhaps any incoming Government this century. Fourteen members had sat in the outgoing 1970 Cabinet.'[10] The members of the new government were well known to the Civil Service. Some senior civil servants saw it as an implication of Heath's defeat that the country was becoming ungovernable except with the agreement of the trade union movement. In those circumstances they may even have welcomed the return of such experienced Ministers with such valuable contacts with the real power brokers of modern society. But the experience these Ministers had acquired during their previous years in office was of the good sense of acting 'politically'. They felt that this was a priority they had previously neglected. That neglect had lost them the 1970 general election. To these Ministers now fell responsibility for managing the most perilous economic conjuncture that this country had confronted since the war.

Notes

1. Barnett 15.
2. Wilson (1979), 43.
3. Jones 282.
4. For Denis Healey's views on incomes policy before March 1974 see Castle 18 and 25–6.
5. 6 Mar. 1974, Castle 38/9.
6. Jenkins resigned on the referendum question, another subject on which I was in disagreement with the major body of Labour Europeans. It seems in retrospect odd that the Jenkinsite Europeans, who today are willing to swallow the camel of European federalism, should have strained at the gnat of a national referendum.
7. Hatfield 156–7.
8. *The Guardian*, 6 June 1973, and Hatfield 206–7. For Wilson's account, see Wilson (1979), 30–1.
9. Wilson (1979), 22.
10. Wilson (1979), 17.

Part II

The Short Parliament: March to September 1974

T·H·R·E·E

The Economic Team

Paymaster General

On 5 March 1974, I was asked to go to No. 10 Downing Street to see the Prime Minister. On more than one occasion during the 1964 Labour Government Harold Wilson had apologized to me for not having been able to appoint me to the Cabinet. Tony Crosland had assured me that, despite the fact that I had resigned from the front bench in October 1971, Harold Wilson still had a high regard for me. He told me that Wilson was insisting that this time, unlike 1964, he would be appointing a Cabinet on merit, not on the basis of political deals. Therefore this time it would be a Cabinet that might include people such as myself without political pull. It was in part on the basis of that expectation that, on Tony Crosland's advice, I had refused an indirect approach from the Heath Government to enquire whether I would be interested to be the new, and first, Director General of Fair Trading.[1] In fact Wilson appointed a Cabinet carefully balanced between right and left, with the necessary proportion of trade unionists, and with due regard for geography. In the circumstances, he probably had little choice.

When I arrived at No. 10 I was ushered in to see the Prime Minister. He said:

While we were in Opposition you refused to serve. I assume that that is not your attitude now we are back in government. A lot of people have been asking for you. Even Tony Benn has asked for you. But I told him it would not be a very happy combination in getting done what has to be done in the Department of Industry. I have decided to send you to the Treasury as No. 2 to Denis Healey. You will not have public expenditure. But you will be No. 2 across the board.

I asked who would do public expenditure. He replied: 'You can do it if you want to but I suggest not. I am proposing to give it to Joel Barnett.' I said: 'If that is what you want me to do, that is what I will do.' He said: 'I think the job of Paymaster General is still vacant. I will let you know in due course. Now you can go to the Treasury and make your number there.'

The role of Paymaster General is a loose card, for use as the Prime Minister of the day wishes, in or out of the Cabinet. The Paymaster General does not supervise the operations of the Paymaster General's Office. His first act on appointment is to sign a power of attorney in favour of the Assistant Paymaster General, an official, who then serenely continues with his various functions entirely undisturbed by interventions from his political master. My appointment as Paymaster General continued a precedent set by Edward Heath when he made Maurice Macmillan Paymaster General, and No. 2 at the Treasury, in the winter of 1973/4. In effect it downgraded the role of Chief Secretary. It had not yet become a rule that the Chief Secretary was a member of Cabinet but Chief Secretaries frequently had been so. They had always been No. 2 to the Chancellor. Now the Chief Secretary was to follow in the Treasury pecking order behind a Paymaster General who was not himself in the Cabinet. It was a signal that the Wilson Government, like the Heath Government after its U-turn, would not pay excessive attention to the control of public expenditure.

There were compensations, political and personal, in being Paymaster General and No. 2 at the Treasury, even if not in the Cabinet. The status of a Cabinet Minister may be higher. But the Treasury is, second only to No. 10 Downing Street, the effective centre of government. In practice Treasury Ministers often have more influence than many in the Cabinet. I was joining the Treasury at a moment of great difficulty and would participate in key decisions. I could expect to be at No. 10 more frequently than many Cabinet Ministers. I would often attend Cabinet for particular items of business. Anthony Barber was one of those who kindly consoled me. He reminisced about his own move from Financial Secretary to the Treasury to join the Cabinet as Minister of Health. He had gained in status but lost in real power, influence, and even interest.

There was also the fact that, in his 1974 Government, Harold Wilson, in Barbara Castle's words, 'effectively de-natured Cabinet'. Given the divisions in the Government, this was the sensible course. Wilson could determine the membership of Cabinet Committees much more freely than that of Cabinet itself. Cabinets were kept as brief as possible with agendas as light as possible. Questions were put out to Cabinet Committees of which I was frequently the Treasury member, and it was there that many of the major decisions were taken.[2] In addition to my concerns with economic policy generally, I was to have the specific role of following through the recommendations of the Public Accounts Committee on North Sea oil made when I was Chairman of that Committee. I was to create a new system of taxation, Petroleum Revenue Tax, which would yield to the Government a proper share of the North Sea rent.

Denis Healey

The Treasury team consisted of Denis Healey as Chancellor of the Exchequer, myself as Paymaster General, Joel Barnett as Chief Secretary, and John Gilbert as Financial Secretary. After the October election we were joined by Robert Sheldon as Minister of State. Wilson was fond of saying that it was the best Treasury team ever.[3] However three of the five had never been in government before and Denis Healey had never been responsible in government for any part of economic policy. He had succeeded Roy Jenkins as Shadow Chancellor in the middle of 1972 but his performances in Opposition had suffered from a poor House of Commons manner and his inexperience in the field. Moreover he had lost some respect from his apparent inability to make up his mind about the Common Market. His subsequent mastery of the Commons was acquired only after he had returned to office.

Nevertheless I knew from experience in Cabinet Committees in the 1960s that he possessed the most powerful intellect I had encountered in politics. I was glad, therefore, of the opportunity of seeing him at work in the Treasury. During his years as Chancellor he won increasing respect and affection from his officials. They admired, and were even surprised at, his intellectual stamina, and his ability to take long, difficult, and crowded meetings without flagging. His status among the Finance Ministers of the developed world was exceptional. This did not derive from agreement with his views but from his remarkable command and advocacy. In the early days, I disagreed with him repeatedly and bitterly. Perhaps I did not sufficiently appreciate the immense political difficulties with which he had to contend in a Cabinet blind to economic necessities. Treasury officials probably had more sympathy with his political difficulties having seen the problems faced by other Chancellors.

On arrival at the Treasury, new Ministers are not pushed through a crash course. They are, as in other Departments, given a brief which informs them of their new Department's assessment of its problems and prospects. Apart from that they learn on the job. It is conventionally assumed that they have a policy and that they understand the technicalities of economic management. Whether or not they in truth have a policy when they arrive at the Treasury, they are very soon making decisions which affect economic performance. There is no Department where learning on the job is less advisable and hence where a period of experience on the job would be more valuable. Given our democratic system, this cannot always be arranged. It was not arranged in the case of Denis Healey.

I myself had been a Minister in economic departments throughout the period 1966–70 though never in the Treasury. I had background as an executive in ICI. I was often described as 'cynical' about the economic policies we advocated and then attempted to implement. In 1965, at a meeting of the Parliamentary Party early in my parliamentary career, I criticized the National Plan on a number of counts. There followed a confrontation with George Brown: 'Is Mr Dell saying that we cannot do better than the Tories?' 'Yes', I replied. This was not because I had more confidence in Tory Ministers than in Labour Ministers. On the contrary, it was because of the problems we had inherited from Maudling's over-ambition. I would describe my own attitude not as cynical, not necessarily as pessimistic, simply as realistic.

Healey himself has written:

In a sense, the first year I was chancellor was very much a learning year for me, as I think it is for most chancellors . . . The big mistake the first year was attempting an expansion of the British economy when all our trading partners were restricting theirs. So we were bound to run into a balance of payments crisis.[4]

There could not have been a more hazardous year in which to learn how to manage the British economy. To expand the economy had the attraction of being politically highly convenient. Yet he was not at that stage forcing his ministerial authority on an unwilling Treasury. It was a policy advocated by many of Healey's advisers, official as well as political. Experience is not necessarily a guide when all the familiar contours have suddenly disappeared. It was not only Healey that needed to learn.

Harold Lever

No one was more strongly of the opinion that the correct course was to expand the British economy than Harold Lever. In the winter of 1972 he had suffered a stroke which left him physically handicapped though in no way intellectually diminished. Harold Wilson evidently thought that he was not physically up to the management of a Department of State. Wilson therefore appointed him to the Cabinet as Chancellor of the Duchy of Lancaster with the function of personal economic adviser to the Prime Minister. Harold Lever was one of the kindest people in politics in my time. His wealth, and his generally right-wing views, led some to question whether he should be in a Labour Cabinet. But he had a deep concern for the least advantaged in society, and would always be found on the liberal side of any argument. To this he added a wit and an extraordinary personal warmth that was irresistible.

Throughout nearly five years during which we were in constant contact, and often in vigorous disagreement, I can only remember two occasions when this led to any personal animosity. One was when I tried to force him to stick closely to his Cabinet authority during his negotiations with Chrysler at the end of 1975. This resulted in a bitter attack on me in Cabinet which I, as forcefully, repelled. In the end he apologized. The second occasion was when, during the IMF crisis, I, unwisely, allowed myself to say directly to Harold, in effect if not in words, 'I told you so'. I should not have said it, it was nothing to the point, and when I saw how upset he was, I did not compound my mistake. It was true of Lever that almost everyone loved him however much they might disagree with him. Among those who most warmed to him were journalists. He proudly displayed to Prime Ministers the results of his skill in press briefing. He could evoke support where it was least expected, in the economic columns of the right wing press. But Lever was, not surprisingly, most influential among those journalists who believed that there was a Keynesian solution to every problem.

Unfortunately, with all his qualities went, in my view, a major cost. Lever's charm, his wit, his warmth, his powers of advocacy, his City contacts, his closeness both to Wilson and Callaghan, enabled him to exercise considerable influence over the making of economic policy. But the opinions he held, and the influence he exerted, were inappropriate in the circumstances of 1974.

He took great pride in his ability to conjure 'solutions' for any problem put to him. He was often asked to solve problems in the industrial policy area. They became a personal challenge and, departing from his usual reserved posture on these matters, he would for that purpose readily deploy public money. Some of my colleagues stood in awe of Lever's ability to spend public money in the interest of a politically convenient 'solution' to some lame duck problem. If the expenditure carried Lever's name it appeared to acquire some mysterious value added which would never have been attributed to the extravagances of a Tony Benn. Sir Leo Pliatzky tells us:

> Harold Lever was no believer in hair shirt policies but a man for ingenious solutions rather than hard choices: and Cabinet, impressed by his reputation for financial wizardry in his private affairs, invariably supported his ingenious, even if expensive, solutions for problems of public finance.[5]

The other, and more important, area in which Lever produced solutions was in economic policy. His solutions usually involved borrowing, usually overseas borrowing. His fear of inflation led him to advocate increased subsidies, to be financed out of borrowing, as well as expansionary economic measures which would, he hoped, serve to cement relations with the trade unions. No message could have been more dangerous in 1974 but, if his persuasiveness needed any help at all, it could be found in the fact that the Government was looking for easy options, and Lever's options were usually the easiest. In Tony Benn's view, 'Harold Lever . . . had moved from being a growth man to being a straight gambler'.[6] It must be assumed that the Prime Minister, in appointing Lever as his personal economic adviser, was aware of his character and aware too of the value of his 'solutions' in winning the coming election.

Lever's support included the Left. They were surprised to find him so frequently in the role of saviour of their public expenditure programmes. Barbara Castle reports on a meeting of the Cabinet on 10 April 1974: 'Harold L. . . . did not agree with Denis's basic assumption that the balance of payments gap must be closed and there must be a rapid shift to exports. We needed a much clearer definition of public expenditure and an early discussion of basic economic strategy.' A proposal for 'an early discussion of basic economic strategy' has always been an encoded attack on the Treasury. Such views were attractive to many in the Cabinet who believed that the Treasury was no friend to their policies and believed that it should be made to be. They did not realize how unorthodox much of the Treasury had become.

Harold Lever had no more faithful supporter within the Treasury than the Chief Secretary Joel Barnett. Barnett was no expenditure cutter at this stage in the life of the new Government.[7] He later wrote:

> I began my ministerial career in the Treasury in 1974 as an optimist . . . after five years in the Treasury I finished as an undoubted pessimist at least as far as Britain's general economic and industrial performance is concerned. Whenever the conversion took place, at the end it was virtually complete.[8]

This then was the ministerial team with which, at the beginning of March 1974, the Treasury got down to managing, or attempting to manage, the British economy. The task is never easy and, at this time, was even more difficult than normal. Fortunately there is a great deal of ruin in a nation.

Notes

1. *The Economist*, 18 Nov. 1978—Dell was offered job of Director General of Fair Trading. Dissuaded with difficulty by Tony Crosland.
2. Castle 376.
3. Wilson (1976), 32–3.
4. *Institutional Investor* (June 1987), 66.
5. Pliatzky (1982), 123.
6. Castle 141.
7. Castle 81.
8. Barnett 1.

F·O·U·R

The March Budget

The Budget: time and chance

Denis Healey decided that Budget Day would be 26 March. This allowed well under three weeks to make the Budget judgement and to prepare the necessary tax changes which would make it possible to meet Labour's electoral commitments, and yet reduce the PSBR.

At an early meeting of the new Cabinet Healey apprised his colleagues of the seriousness of the economic situation. The balance of payments was in serious deficit and threatening worse. Inflation was likely to surpass 15 per cent with the threshold agreements being triggered nine times during the year. There would need to be increases in the prices charged by nationalized industries. Public expenditure would require strict control with no increases other than the pensions uprating and in those subsidies to which the party had committed itself. Defence expenditure would have to be cut. Concorde should be cancelled.[1] In his Budget statement, he described 'what even before the onset of the three day week was generally regarded as the gravest situation Britain had faced since the war'. Barber had said as much in December. Not the least element in that situation was the fact that 'The balance of payments on current account registered a deficit of £1,470 million on the year [1973] as a whole.'[2]

The current account

Before the Budget, commentators attributed to Healey deflationary views. There was, indeed, some relief on the Labour back benches when these attributions proved to be without foundation. But the relieved

The March Budget

back-benchers were not aware of the route by which Healey had arrived at his Budget judgement. The first position Healey took up was that he wanted the Budget to be deflationary to the extent of about £500 million. This was consonant with his then view that it was vital to move resources into the balance of payments. There were thought to be two elements in the UK balance of payments deficit, that due to the higher price of oil, and the underlying deficit which existed irrespective of the oil price hikes of 1973.[3] It was estimated that the increase in oil prices had added £2.5 billion to the UK's current account deficit. There might be debate about how rapidly that part of the deficit due to the oil price increase should be reduced. But Healey was perfectly clear what must be done about the non-oil part of the deficit. 'This part of the deficit must be reduced. We must therefore achieve over time a large switch of resources out of domestic use and back into the balance of payments.'[4]

In fact, whatever the political convenience of speaking of two deficits rather than one, there was only one deficit. That was the total obligation to foreigners that the UK had to fund. There was debate, in international fora, including the IMF and OECD, as to how rapidly industrialized countries should set out to reduce their deficits. That debate will be considered in more detail in Chapter 6. But it was my view that the new Government, faced with a deficit of the size we had inherited, should place high priority on reducing it. This implied a clearly deflationary Budget, in line with Healey's initial view, even though there was already a great deal of deflation in the system. Whatever we did, there would have to be extensive foreign borrowing. Healey was able to announce, in his Budget statement, a $2.5 billion loan for ten years and that the inter-central bank swap arrangement was being raised from $2 billion to $3 billion.[5] This arrangement was a necessary precaution. But clearly there would be a limit to borrowing depending among other considerations on the vigour of the Government's attack on inflation and the current account deficit.

The Budget judgement

Despite his initial deflationary views, the judgement which Healey eventually made was to introduce a neutral Budget, slightly deflationary, but only slightly. He decided to be content with £200 million. '[M]y judgement is that this Budget should be broadly neutral on demand, with a bias, if any, on the side of caution.'[6] What lay between Healey's initial judgement and the eventual Budget judgement, apart from three weeks of intense discussion in the Budget Committee in the Treasury, 'the most exhausting three weeks of my life'?[7] Healey soon found that, if he was to make the Budget as deflationary as initially had seemed to him necessary, the new Government's expenditure commitments meant that there would have to be larger increases in taxes, particularly in indirect taxes, than he considered politically acceptable.[8] Even to get the minus £200 million he had to raise income tax to 33p in the pound instead of 32p at which initially he had decided to stick. Thus the making of the Budget judgement was done backwards. We arrived at the Budget judgement from the tax changes rather than at the tax changes from the Budget judgement. Even so, Healey was only able to make the judgement he did, and still present his Budget as neutral, because he was given by the official Treasury a gross underestimate of the consequent PSBR.

The Budget and the Borrowing Requirement

Healey thought he was making a reduction of the PSBR to £2,700 million, that is of about £1,500 million as compared with 1973/4's £4,250 million, and of £700 million on the notional PSBR of £3,400 million calculated for 1974/5 on unchanged policies. He declared it to be a principal objective of his Budget that there should be a substantial reduction in the PSBR.[9] There was, however, a logical contradiction between his intention to make a substantial reduction in the PSBR and his declaration that his was a more or less neutral Budget. Such a reduction was itself likely to have deflationary effects. This contradiction was resolved intellectually by making the assumption that the high taxes on high incomes would be paid out of savings rather than out of consumption.

It was Treasury forecasters who led him to believe that his Budget would reduce the PSBR to £2,700 million. Experienced officials might have been expected to suspect this forecast and the massive error revealed later did not increase Healey's confidence in the Treasury. In his Budget statement on 15 April 1975, Healey was compelled to announce that the PSBR for 1974/5 had risen to £7,600 million.[10] The gap of nearly £5 billion between the PSBR forecast of March 1974 and the outcome announced in April 1975 was due mainly to bad forecasting, partly to new decisions, and partly to inadequate control of public expenditure by a government intent on winning votes.[11]

Healey's comment about the gap between the forecast and the actuality is: 'This was the equivalent of 5.4 per cent of that year's GDP. The magnitude of that one forecasting error was greater than that of any fiscal change made by any Chancellor in British history.'[12]

Forecasting errors were, for Healey, a perennial problem during his time at the Treasury. This forecasting error was, nevertheless, exceedingly convenient politically. Healey was bound to describe the economic situation as serious, for so it was. But verbal pain, which could be blamed on his predecessors, was politically much more acceptable than actual pain that could be blamed on him. Some pain he was bound to inflict. The tax consequences of manifesto commitments made that inevitable. But the forecasting error enabled him to limit the agony. The financial world, whatever doubts they had about a Labour government, would be relieved that at least the new Chancellor was announcing a reduced PSBR. At that stage to announce it was more important than actually achieving it. In the longer term, of course, such errors would call in question the reliability not just of Treasury forecasts but of the policies based on them. Meanwhile, Healey could win economic merit while escaping the political costs of actually deserving it. Those who criticize the Treasury for undermining the policies of Labour governments might like to take this counter example into account.

Unkind forecasts

Healey decided to conceal some of the forecasts associated with this Budget. They looked distinctly unkind for a government starting out on a course of collaboration with the trade unions under the Social Contract. Why then, Healey decided, should he say what did not need to be said? No doubt others would forecast the horrors to come. At least such forecasts would lack the authority of the Treasury and could be damned by reference to past forecasting failures. He published no estimate of gross domestic product or of real incomes for the first half of 1975, though such forecasts had been given at Budget time for some years past. Healey's excuse was that the future was more than usually difficult to foresee. The fact that others had made fools of themselves in far easier circumstances did not seem to him an adequate reason why he should do the same in unusually difficult circumstances. Moreover, if the facts turned out as adversely as the forecast suggested, he would, he thought, have the option of changing policy and thereby demonstrate that flexible response could be an element in economic policy-making as well as in defence.

This question of what to publish remained a constant problem. At a discussion on 4 June, we had to consider whether we should release information that would have shown unemployment rising. Healey commented that if he had revealed such information at the time of the March Budget, he would never have got away with it. Treasury officials took the opportunity of emphasizing that it was not they who were secretive about damaging information. It was Ministers.

Arguments derived retrospectively

The Cabinet discussed Healey's Budget, in the usual way, twenty four hours before it became public, and at a time when it was no longer possible to exercise any influence on it. It was in no position, for example, to respond to Tony Benn's unsurprising view that the Budget 'will undoubtedly disappoint the Party and the movement', and had been 'written by the Treasury and not by Ministers'. Lever was more influential. He had access both to the Treasury and to the Prime Minister who would have been consulted by Healey to the degree to which he wished to be consulted. Barbara Castle records Lever as saying in Cabinet: 'This ought to have been a reflationary Budget.' In Lever's view the essence of the Government's policy was the Social Contract. He thought the Budget would inevitably increase unemployment and would lead to trouble with the trade unions.[14] Healey had not gone all the way with Lever but he had moved towards the Lever arguments from his own initial position. Benn was not to know it but things could have been, from his point of view, much worse. Joel Barnett reflects: 'I sometimes wonder how different a Budget it would have been if we had not been preparing it in the knowledge that we would be engaged in another general election before the year was out.'[15]

The course of Healey's future economic management was determined in those first three weeks of rushed decision-making. He realized that it was going to be politically very difficult both to move resources into the balance of payments and to meet the new Government's expenditure commitments. He had begun by believing that the balance of payments represented a priority for his economic management. But, with an election coming, this could involve politically embarrassing sacrifices. He saw that, in justifying policies that were not in the first instance his preferred choice, he must adopt those arguments that were most consistent with them. Lever's arguments, Healey soon realized, were more consistent with his presentation of his Budget as neutral. They were certainly more consistent with the out-turn of his Budget which was very different from his forecast.

There might be those, such as myself, who were telling him that his first judgement had been right, and that the balance of payments must have high priority. But there were others, including Harold Lever and a significant school of Keynesian economists, in and out of the Treasury, telling him that this was entirely the wrong priority, that the problem of the balance of payments could be handled by borrowing, and that he would be wrong to add more UK deflation to a downward spiral in the international economy. Some Treasury economists, but not Treasury economists alone, were afraid, with justification, that the Barber measures of the previous December combined with the current inflation would lead to high unemployment by the end of the year.

And there was a debt Healey owed to fate. If he had actually *planned* a reflationary Budget, and the outcome had been as far from estimate as with his actual Budget, who knows but the IMF would have been buying air tickets to London much earlier.

Debating points and the money supply

Healey, in his Budget statement, drew attention to the rise of 27 per cent in the money supply, broadly defined, in the previous year. He also emphasized that 'price controls and subsidies, even in alliance with the most perfect incomes policy which could be devised, cannot go far towards winning the battle against inflation if fiscal and monetary policy are pulling in the opposite direction'.[16] Monetarist theory suggested that an excessive expansion of the money supply would generate inflation. It was widely accepted that under Anthony Barber there had been an excessive expansion.

There was no need to be a monetarist to be concerned at the rate of monetary expansion under Barber. There was reason for concern whether that rate of expansion was to be regarded as cause, as monetarism would have it, or effect. Barber's record offered Healey an unanswerable debating point. It would have constituted an uncharacteristic surfeit of self-denial for Denis Healey to have refrained from blaming the Barber record for the rising inflation, whether or not he believed monetarist theory. This had positive as well as negative effects. The negative consequence was that the ability to blame others reduced urgency in tackling the inflation. The positive consequence arose from the way in which debating points can help to mould policy. That he had made the debating points, and exploited the political advantages presented to him by the Barber record, helped to place Healey under a compulsion to pay attention to the money supply.

One instrument for this purpose had been introduced by Barber in his measures of 17 December 1973 and was continued by Healey. This was the supplementary special deposits scheme. This was intended to supplement the existing arrangements for controlling the growth of money and credit, and thereby to act as a corset to restrain bank lending. Under this new system of control, banks were to be required to make at the Bank of England special deposits on which they earned no interest if their interest-bearing liabilities rose by more than 8 per cent between October–December 1973 and April–June 1974. The effect was greatly to increase the marginal cost of funds to the banks if they exceeded the 8 per cent guide-line. The banks were, therefore, discouraged from excessive bidding for funds in the money market. The criteria governing the use of this instrument could be varied. It was understandably disliked by the banks who felt that it allowed leakage of funds through other and less reputable lenders not subject to the control. There was debate about its effectiveness, but it did at the time appear to have had significant success in controlling the expansion of credit.

Healey's problem was that his fiscal policy generated a PSBR which was at war with his ambition to control the money supply. He himself had said that Barber's £4 billion PSBR had been 'a powerful contributory force' to the excessive monetary expansion.[17] The burden placed on the remaining instruments available to him, principally the sale of government debt and interest rates, plus such attempts as were made to control the money supply at source, was very great. There were periods when it proved difficult to sell government debt except at high nominal rates of interest. Healey faced manfully the interest rate consequences of his fiscal policy. His early debating points at the expense of the fallen Barber provided a standard against which he knew he would be judged. During his period of responsibility, the growth of the money supply did slow. In 1975, the growth, broadly defined, was under 6 per cent, well below the rate of inflation. Monetarists may claim that it was this decline, rather than the stricter incomes policy adopted in July 1975, that, after some lag, produced a fall in inflation. Other observers were not prepared to rely on better control of the money supply alone to defeat inflation, then approaching 30 per cent.

In monetary policy Healey was freer of interference from his Cabinet colleagues than in matters of public expenditure. A Chancellor's Cabinet colleagues are not normally concerned about the Government's funding policy which most of them probably do not understand. The supplementary special deposits scheme was too intricate a device to provoke informed discussion in Cabinet. Interest rates do occasion debate but only when raised to levels that indicate a crisis which would probably also have its implications for the level of public expenditure. In their neglect of monetary policy Cabinet colleagues may, from their own point of view, have been ill advised. It was an important aspect of policy which was not without influence on what could or could not be done in the implementation of Labour policies.

Nevertheless ignorance kept excessive interest at bay. The Policy Unit at No. 10 attempted but failed to recruit the Prime Minister's attention. It argued that a Chancellor with a free hand in monetary policy had the Cabinet at his mercy. Not till Callaghan had succeeded Wilson did the Policy Unit gain a hearing for their argument that the Prime Minister should explore the implications of monetary policy for the Government's policies in general.[18] So Healey, for the time being, was in a position to manage his monetary policy unencumbered by colleagues' advice and anguish.

The Treasury turns on the Budget

It was soon taken as doctrine, even within the Treasury, that a major fault in this first Healey Budget had been the increase in indirect taxation and particularly the imposition of VAT on some food products. This had a bad effect on the retail prices index in April. Adding to the inflationary effect were the increases in nationalized industry prices. Prices were to be raised to conserve energy but also to reduce nationalized industry deficits. There was much evidence that the Tories had intended to do likewise. This did not stop them, once in Opposition, denying any responsibility either for the deficits that needed to be closed or for the price increases that had to be made. The Tories had an election to win as well as Labour. Why should they alone be honest when dishonesty was in fashion? They had at least this justification for their criticisms. It did seem a little odd that Labour was increasing food subsidies to reduce the cost of living at the same time as it was increasing nationalized industry prices in order to reduce nationalized industry deficits. The inflationary effect of all these Budget measures was multiplied by the existence of threshold agreements. The Budget measures led to three triggerings of the threshold in May.

Company finance

Another inheritance from the Budget was its effect on company finance. The Budget increased the rate of corporation tax to 52 per cent, rather than the expected rate of 50 per cent. To help him meet his PSBR target, Healey had also introduced a surcharge on advance corporation tax (ACT).[19] The information about company liquidity on which the ACT surcharge had been based proved to be seriously faulty. This was a matter about which the CBI warned at the time but, on Treasury advice, their warnings had been neglected. Sir Donald MacDougall, then Chief Economic Adviser to the CBI, has recalled that Healey

said in his [Budget] speech that profits had been doing rather well. Now this was true on a *historic* cost basis . . . but no one seems to have told him that they were doing disastrously badly on a *replacement* cost basis, after allowing for inflation. Nor do his advisers appear to have recognized that the outlook for company *liquidity* was very poor indeed.[20]

These criticisms were unfortunately justified.

On 28 March, there was a meeting at which the CBI leaders emphasized their warning about company liquidity. Tony Benn describes the meeting.

It was just one long moan. Michael Clapham said there was deep disquiet about the Budget; there was no incentive to invest, nor to export; nothing to curb inflation; the remedies were based on the wrong diagnosis; company profits would fall and the investment squeeze would tighten. Large companies were only just maintaining their investment programme. There would be a downturn next year and liquidity would be made worse. The pay crunch would come because the Budget was inflationary.[21]

Denis replied using a technique that he was to fashion and hone in his relations with the trade unions. He claimed that he had been attempting to take CBI advice and was very depressed at the reaction to his goodwill.

At a press conference afterwards, Sir Michael Clapham repeated the charge that the Budget was anti-industry and damaging to investment. I was the Treasury Minister present, at the suggestion of Harold Wilson who considered that I had a good profile with industry. The best I could do by way of response was to refer to the fact that the latest figures available at the time of the Budget, those for the third quarter of 1973, showed company liquidity at the historically very high level of about £9.5 billion, to claim that the CBI simply did not know how that figure had moved in the interim, and to promise that the matter could be reconsidered later in the year if the CBI fears were realized. What I did not know at the time was that there had been a sharp fall in company liquidity in the fourth quarter of 1973 caused by the first payment of VAT by manufacturing companies. And, during the first half of 1974, there was a further very sharp fall in liquidity for a number of reasons of which the three-day week was one. Another factor was that stock appreciation had become a major element in gross trading profits. The ratio of stock appreciation to gross trading profits, which in 1971 had been £881 million : £4,429 million, had risen by the first half of 1974 to £3,330 million : £2,930 million. Companies were paying tax on profits inflated by increases in the value of stocks which needed to be replaced in the course of business.[22] Nor were the banks prepared to relieve the severe liquidity crisis which industry faced. Although figures for company liquidity were not then available beyond the third quarter of 1973, the factors operating on company liquidity in the interim were sufficiently well known to have suggested a more cautious response to the CBI than this incoming Government in fact exhibited.[23]

The Department of Industry, at official level, proved itself more sensitive to the question than was the Treasury. The Government had inherited from its predecessor a Price Commission charged with responsibility for price control. The Department of Industry feared the effect of price control on company liquidity. It argued that industry should be permitted to put all wage increases through the Price Commission as an allowable cost in calculating prices. This implied the abolition of the so-called 'productivity deduction' under which, at the time, only 50 per cent of wage increases were allowed in the calculation of prices, subject to a profit floor. It was estimated that this change would give industry an extra £600 million. Tony Benn records that, as early as 11 April, his Permanent Secretary Sir Antony Part put to him a proposition along these lines. Benn refused to support the proposal and suggested that the argument should be put to the Treasury.[24] Shirley Williams's price control legislation had, however, been carried through all its legislative stages before the Easter adjournment on 11 April.[25] It would certainly have been politically impossible to reverse the Government's stance and to follow Part's advice at that stage.

I received a message that the Bank of England would want to talk to me privately. My diary says that the trouble with the Bank was that it seemed to think that I was some sort of socialist saviour of the City and industry to whom it could turn at all points, 'without realizing that really I have absolutely no influence in this Government'. The Bank also saw the relaxation of price control as an answer to the problem. I explained that, even if the proposal had been politically possible, the removal of price control could stimulate inflation because it would remove one pressure on employers to resist wage claims.

Healey and the Treasury

Given the uncertainties in making a Budget judgement and the controversy inevitably surrounding it, given also the uncertainties in forecasting, the Treasury keeps in its cupboard a store of justifications for use whatever the policy and whatever the out-turn of policy. In this case, the Treasury's store contained justifications whether the budget turned out to be deflationary, as was Healey's original intention; neutral, as he was compelled to make it by the politically unacceptable tax implications of a deflationary budget; or reflationary, as Treasury forecasting errors arranged for it to be.

Despite the availability of such justifications, Healey's first Budget had not enhanced his confidence in Treasury advice. On a number of important issues he felt he had been badly advised. On nothing had he received the strong advice that a new Chancellor might expect from experienced officials. The Labour Government had come into office with illusions which there was no chance of making real. No doubt Treasury officials did not consider it any part of their duty to instruct an incoming government to tear up its manifesto. That, however, did not excuse the lame service that Healey received and which neither I, nor my colleagues, had expected from a Department as highly regarded as the Treasury.

Notes

1. 14 Mar. 1974, Castle 42.
2. HC Debs., 26 Mar.1974, col. 278.
3. This distinction was discussed in *NIER* (May 1974), 43.
4. HC Debs., 26 Mar. 1974, col. 292.
5. HC Debs., 26 Mar. 1974, col. 286.
6. HC Debs., 26 Mar. 1974, col. 294.
7. HC Debs., 26 Mar. 1974, col. 278.
8. Additional expenditures included pensions at £860m. in 1974/5 and £1,200m. in the 12 months from 22 July, the date of implementation; £500m. on food subsidies; and £350m. on housing. There were to be savings on defence etc. and by raising nationalized industry prices. HC Debs., 26 Mar. 1974, cols. 295–304.
9. HC Debs., 26 Mar. 1974, cols. 326–7.
10. HC Debs., 15 April. 1975, col. 279.
11. In his November 1974 Budget, when the second 1974 general election had been and gone, Healey announced some of the reasons for the increase in the PSBR to that date. £340m. was attributable to his July measures. £1,000m. was the net effect of wage increases. Subsidies were responsible for nearly £1,100m. All this increased the estimate of the PSBR by about £2.75b. to about £5.5b. To this had to be added the £800m. which his November measures added to the PSBR making a total of £6.3b. HC Debs., 12 Nov. 1974, cols. 250–1. A further £300m. was due to the rescue of Burmah Oil and the Crown Agents, and to Channel Tunnel compensation.
12. Healey 380–1. He says £4 billion but it was nearer £5 billion.
13. Benn 127.
14. Castle 51.
15. Barnett 25.
16. HC Debs., 26 Mar. 1974, 284.
17. HC Debs., 26 Mar. 1974, col. 279.
18. Donoghue 81–2.
19. From 1 April 1974, companies, when they paid their advance corporation tax on distributions, were to be required to make an additional payment of half that sum. That payment would then be set off against their corporation tax liability for their accounting years ending in 1974/5. HC Debs., 26 Mar. 1974, col. 319.
20. MacDougall 212.
21. Benn 130.
22. Thirlwall 254.
23. See 'Department of Industry survey of company liquidity', in *Economic Trends* (Nov. 1974), esp. p. vii.
24. Benn 138–9.
25. Wilson (1976), 44–5.

F·I·V·E

The Triumph of Politics

Government without authority

Harold Wilson later wrote that when he became Prime Minister in March 1974: 'Britain was facing an unparalleled economic crisis, the worse in that we were confronted by fourfold oil-price increases and by balance-of-payments problems unprecedented in our history.'[1] Worldwide inflation, far-reaching monetary disturbance, and the balance of payments deficit were mentioned in the Queen's Speech. But there was little sense of 'unparalleled economic crisis' in the policies recommended by Labour to the electorate at the general election or in the new Prime Minister's presentation to the House. The programme with which his Government met Parliament was conceived as part of the coming general election campaign, as was indeed the Opposition's reaction to it.[2] The new Government showed as a whole no more awareness of the critical economic outlook than the characters in Jane Austen's novels did of the Napoleonic Wars.

The Government had its excuses for its lavish approach to its responsibilities. It was fulfilling its manifesto commitments. It was discharging its obligations to the TUC under the Social Contract. It was facing competition from the Tory Party at an election that could not be long delayed. The new Government was receiving advice from respected economists that reflation was the right policy and that the instrument of reflation should be even greater borrowing. Few governments, perhaps, could have resisted the temptation of following advice so consistent with political priorities and commitments. Indeed, did a conjuncture that could be handled so comfortably even deserve the name of crisis?

The history of the Short Parliament is of the triumph of politics. It was a symptom of a deeper crisis at the heart of British politics. The February election showed that neither of the major parties enjoyed good standing with the electorate. At one point during the election, so low was the confidence of the electorate in either of them that they appeared threatened by a massive Liberal revival. As recently as 1970, Labour had been judged to have failed when previously in office. Its dependence on the trade unions had been emphasized by its retreat on *In Place of Strife*. The Conservatives had demonstrated their own lack of belief in the policies they had put before the electorate in 1970 as soon as they were confronted with high unemployment. They had then executed the most dramatic U-turn in recent political history. While still commanding a substantial majority in the Commons, they had declared a totally unnecessary general election, an election which called into question their claim to be the party of one nation. Neither party could have felt confident of commanding credibility in explaining the real extent of the crisis, even if they had themselves fully understood it.

The period of the Short Parliament was devoted to the purchase of votes and the elaboration of White Papers. The votes intended to be purchased were those of sections of the electorate who had a definable need that could be satisfied out of the proceeds of our redistributive taxation system. The White Papers, on the other hand, were drafted to comfort other sections of the electorate with the assurance that Labour's policies were not as frightening as they had sometimes appeared. Thus did the Government launch itself on a course of policy that was more moderate than the public postures of the Labour Party in opposition, but was, for all that, unsustainable.

The buying of votes, otherwise described as the discharge of manifesto commitments, began in the first few weeks in office and was taken further in the Budget. Action to discharge these commitments was urgent. Ministers could not foresee when the Government might be voted down in the Commons and forced into a general election. It had been more by accident than design that the electorate handed to Labour rather than to the Conservatives the opportunity to occupy the next six months buying whatever votes were available for purchase before the next general election. There is nothing in their history to suggest that the Conservatives would have acted differently. As it turned out, fewer votes were for sale than had been hoped.

The social wage

Apart from settling with the miners, the first obligations to be discharged were those under the Social Contract. Food subsidies were introduced. There was an immediate rent freeze, at the cost of a sharp rise in housing subsidies. On the social security front, in the words of the Public Expenditure White Paper of January 1975 (Cmnd. 5879), 'One of the first decisions of the new Government in March [1974] was to bring the 1974 general uprating of benefits forward from the autumn to July. The increase in the pension represented a real improvement of about 13.5 per cent over the rate established in October 1973.' The government also bound itself by legislation to uprate unemployment and other short-term benefits in line with prices and to uprate pensions in line with either prices or earnings, whichever proved to be the more favourable. Some optimistic souls believed that if the Government's social expenditure, now to be greatly enhanced by various benefits and subsidies, could be presented as a 'social wage', and as a supplement to the ordinary wage packet, the trade unions might take it into account in making their wage claims. Barbara Castle was one of the most insistent on the importance of bringing the 'social wage' into such calculations.

Pensions

Bringing forward from the autumn to July the date at which the announced pensions increase would be implemented did not take place without some flurry between the demands of politics and of administration. Clearly the date of payment must be, if at all possible, before a further general election. But the date of the general election was unknown and might be forced prematurely by a vote in the House. That meant that the administrative machine must be denied the months of preparation previously required before an increase could be paid. The spirit of these first few weeks is amply caught in Barbara Castle's diary.

She describes her battle in Cabinet to bring forward the date of the pensions uprating.

Mike was very helpful, saying he was briefed by his department to support me because an early date like July would be important for the Social Contract . . . But the best effort came from Bob Mellish, who said vigorously that this was the sort of point on which we had got to behave politically. There might be . . . an election at any time. Were we to go into it with the pensioners still not having their increase? . . . Harold [Wilson] clearly was on my side. He suggested that the needs of demand management might change: we might even be faced with an increase in unemployment before too long. There were three decisive factors: first, the effect on the TUC and the need to win support for the Social Contract: secondly, the possibility of an early election: thirdly, that we might need an autumn budget to expand demand . . . to my astonishment, Denis's opposition collapsed.[3]

Unlike her Prime Minister, Barbara Castle did have some sense that there were limits.

It is not my fault that so many of the Manifesto commitments are in my field, and I know that, if I am not careful, there will be nothing left for the health side. That is why I have been busy joining with Treasury in shooting down Harold [Wilson]'s series of suggestions for *ad hoc* (and vote-catching) concessions for pensioners, such as free TV licences and making concessionary fares mandatory. We are already landed with the Christmas bonus, thanks to the Tories, who, for all their sneers at Harold's 'gimmickry', have excelled at it themselves.[4]

Rumblings in Cabinet regarding the concessions made to the Unions

Relations with the trade unions were the keystone of the arch but there were already rumblings among Cabinet Ministers. Michael Foot was introducing a Bill to replace the Tory Industrial Relations Act. It was proposed as a safeguard that independent review should be provided of any case where a worker had been dismissed because of 'unreasonable' expulsion or exclusion by a trade union. On 25 April 1974 the clause intended to provide machinery for this purpose was discussed in Cabinet. As this clause was opposed by the TUC, Michael Foot wanted to postpone it to a later Bill, probably in the next Parliament when, no doubt, it would be opposed by the TUC again. Crosland complained: 'We are putting a great many goodies on the table for the trade unions and it is becoming urgent that we should see what is coming from the other side.' In this rebellion he was at once opposed by Healey: 'I support Michael . . . We fought and won the election on the basis of co-operation rather than confrontation. We are engaged in an experiment. We must trust Michael to get the best he can.'[5] As always, Bob Mellish made the point most brutally: 'As long as we were committed to wage control by voluntary agreement we had to take the trade unions with us'.

Barbara Castle, whose love and admiration for Michael Foot could not expunge her resentment at his role in the defeat of *In Place of Strife*, records a conversation she had with an old friend from her own days at Employment, Conrad Heron, now Foot's Permanent Secretary. 'I asked Conrad how he got on with Michael Foot. "Oh, what a charming man," he exclaimed, but I detected something less than idolatry. "How does he get on with the administrative side?" I asked. "Ah, well, his only policy is to find out what the unions want," he replied'.[6]

Rents and mortgages

The Heath Government had announced council house rent increases to come into effect on 1 April. One of the first actions of the new Government was to freeze the rents of 2.5 million council houses and of a further 3.55 million privately owned units of rented accommodation.[7] Mortgage rates had already risen very severely during the previous year, and were now at 11 per cent. Owing to lack of funds flowing into the building societies, there was considerable danger that the mortgage rate would have to be raised further to about 13 per cent. The fear was that if a Labour government having frozen rents was then seen to have done nothing about mortgages, it would look as though it intended to discriminate against owner occupiers. Harold Wilson, sitting on the front bench, said to John Gilbert that the problem was very simple: either we prevented the mortgage rate going up and we would win the election, or we allowed it to go up and we would lose the election.

The Treasury had a scheme under which help could be given to recent house owners who had taken out mortgages in the last two or three years and who, therefore, might be expected to be suffering harshly from the increased rate of interest. Harold Lever took the view that it was necessary to keep mortgage interest down because anything else would be inflationary. Although Denis Healey fought for the Treasury view, the Cabinet decided, unanimously except for Healey, that negotiations should be entered into with the building societies to find some way of preventing an increase in mortgage rates. Harold Lever had a scheme to borrow the necessary funds from abroad. 'Harold would never have the Government spend its own money if it could borrow someone else's.'[8] He was requested, though under the nominal control of Tony Crosland, to negotiate a deal with the building societies.[9] I had to go along, representing the Treasury, to try to ensure that the whole Exchequer was not emptied to achieve this objective.

The Department of the Environment had said that it would be impossible to persuade the building societies to co-operate with any such project.[10] But Harold Lever worked his charm on them. Never has anyone exuded more charm in persuading a reluctant borrower to take his money. The building societies went away with an offer of £500 million of government money at subsidized rates of interest on condition that there was no change in the mortgage rate of 11 per cent.[11] By the end of June this offer of £500 million had already been used to the extent of the first three tranches, that is £300 million.

When the money would be repaid would depend on the uncertain fluctuation of interest rates. The movement of interest rates could be influenced by the Government, for example by the release by the Bank of England of special deposits. Nevertheless, interest rates were not entirely within the control of the British Government. Interest rates could not fall far in the UK because of the increases that were taking place in the United States. The building societies were sceptical about Lever's assurances that a scheme such as he was proposing could be temporary because interest rates would fall.[12] In fact it initially proved possible to bring down interest rates a little and by June this was encouraging a flow of money into the building societies.

The Lever triumph in lending money to the building societies at subsidized rates was not the end of the matter. Subsidy was not enough. A guarantee of reserves had to be offered. On 27 June 1974, 'Tony [Crosland] . . . told us that . . . the building societies are threatening to raise the lending rate by a half per cent and the Ministerial Committee had agreed to try to persuade them to run down their reserves instead, against a Government guarantee'.[13] Again they needed some persuading. But the building societies have a preference for being on good terms with the government of the day, and there is no one in the world with whom it is easier to be on good terms than Harold Lever in his unendingly generous moods. On 11 July 1974,

At Cabinet Harold Lever reported another victory over the building societies. He had offered them a Government guarantee of their reserves to enable them to maintain the mortgage rate at 11 per cent till the end of the year. They didn't like this at all . . . but had agreed to hold the rate for another three months.[14]

Three months would serve the purpose just as the rent freeze would serve its purpose. But on 1 April 1975, Crosland told the Cabinet rents would rise by more than would have happened under the Tories' Housing Finance Act.[15]

The money for the Lever project came from the Exchequer.[16] There was no direct foreign borrowing for this purpose. Lever would presumably claim that his project, by helping to keep inflation down, would reinforce foreign confidence in the UK economy and thus encourage foreign lending. In my own view this was another example of the Government's fruitless attempts to control inflation by subsidizing prices. I would not have ruled out the subsidization of prices as a matter of principle. But I did not consider it to be an appropriate risk in the current situation of the UK with inflation mounting in an alarming way. Such arguments about economic policy did not, however, carry much weight. The Government was determined to keep mortgage rates down until after the election and Lever pulled off the required coup.

Voluntary aided schools

It would have demonstrated an extraordinary degree of self-denial for any interest group to ignore their exceptional opportunity. On 24 June I went to a meeting at No. 10 with the Prime Minister, Ted Short, Reg Prentice, Willie Ross, and John Morris to discuss assistance to voluntary aided schools. Reg Prentice as Secretary of State for Education argued that the 80 per cent capital grant which voluntary aided schools were then receiving was enough. To go higher would bring their voluntary aided status into question. If more came from the public purse, the public might as well take them over. The Prime Minister replied that he had heard that argument used again and again ever since the figure had been about 50 per cent in the 1950s. It became rapidly obvious that for electoral reasons he wanted the 80 per cent to go up to 85 per cent. He said that he had, in April, talked to Archbishop Beck, the archbishop of Liverpool. Wilson kept on insisting, 'Remember we have an election to win.' Ted Short referred to various statements he had made during the election which, although not committing the Government to an increase in the percentage grant, implied such an increase. The Prime Minister was ready to overrule any Treasury objections. 'After all I too am a Treasury Minister.'

Benn exploits the prevailing cynicism

Tony Benn was provoked by the cynicism of it, though prepared to exploit the opportunity to support his own idealism. He wanted to continue sustenance for the Merseyside workers' co-operative IPD. He went to the Industrial Development Committee of the Cabinet on 10 September 1974 to plead for more money so that the Receiver could keep it going until November. Harold Wilson said that it had been in his last election address so 'We'll have to do something until the Election is over'. [17] Benn comments: 'Utterly cynical. Frankly if that little discussion had been recorded, it would have destroyed the credibility of the Party completely.'[18]

Concorde

Benn was capable of equal cynicism. He saw the unions as his principal support against the right wing in the Government, and Wilson, with his eye on the forthcoming election, allowed him to get away with it. Denis Healey made up his mind that Concorde must be cancelled.[19] When, on 23 May 1974, Benn rallied the TUC and the Confederation of Shipbuilding and Engineering Unions against the cancellation, Healey complained: 'If we allow the unions not merely to decide our social priorities but what we spend our money on for economic reasons, it will be the death of the whole idea of public participation in industry. Public participation must not be made to seem a device for spending money on white elephants.'[20]

The Cabinet instructed Benn to secure agreement from the French to the discontinuance of the Concorde programme. It had also, however, been decided that if the French insisted on producing the sixteen copies to which both governments were committed, their view should be accepted. Before the second 1974 general election, Benn prompted Sir George Edwards, Chairman of the British Aircraft Corporation, to persuade the French to insist on the production of the sixteen Concordes. That he felt guilty about this is confirmed by the furtive manner in which, contrary to his usual openness, it was done. He persuaded himself that he acted in this way because 'there is a complete collapse of morale in the top leadership of this country'.[21] Unfriendly observers might note that he had a constituency interest in the production of Concorde, that his seat in Bristol was marginal, and that he was going behind the backs of his colleagues in first betraying

Cabinet secrecy and then turning the betrayal to constituency advantage. This is not, of course, to suggest that the French view was changed by any intervention from the Chairman of BAC. Concorde's survival was only the first of Denis's defeats at the hands of Tony Benn.

Devolution

Commitment to devolution for Scotland and Wales was the greatest capitulation to the demands of electoral victory. Wilson was ruthless in pushing devolution through the Cabinet. In charge of the issue was Ted Short, deputy leader of the Labour Party. Although Short was unclear on the substance of the matter and often seemed to have sent his own papers, unread, to Cabinet and Cabinet Committees, yet he had no doubt about the political imperatives.

On 24 July 1974, there was a meeting at No. 10. Wilson started the meeting by cornering Willie Ross, Secretary of State for Scotland. He discussed with him the divergent attitudes of the Scottish Trade Union Congress and of the Labour Party in Scotland. The Scottish Labour Party was deeply split. Its Executive Committee had passed a motion against devolution by a majority of six to five. Only a minority of those present had voted. The Scottish TUC, on the other hand, which was dominated by Alex Kitson and the Transport and General Workers' Union, was in favour of legislative devolution. Clearly an early task was to reverse that vote in the Executive Committee.

Willie Ross was in great distress. He had a record of stern opposition to the nationalists. He claimed that, owing to the terrible handling of the subject by the Labour Government, we had now been driven into an impossible situation. We should have stood up and fought. Every time Wilson asked him: 'All right, what do you think?', he veered off and lamented the way we had been manœuvred into this position. Again Wilson insisted: 'Tell me what you think'. At last Ross conceded that a modified scheme of legislative devolution had become inevitable. Wilson then turned to John Morris, Secretary of State for Wales. Morris said that Labour MPs in Wales had long been committed to executive devolution in Wales, that there was no need at all for Wales to have exactly the same as Scotland. Whether or not Scotland had anything, Wales had to have this scheme. Willie Ross interjected that if Wales was given something it would indeed be intolerable if Scotland did not get some form of devolution too.

Ted Short was convinced that something was desirable and in any case was electorally essential. At this point Roy Jenkins, who had been straining at the leash, said he was horrified at the way in which this question was being considered, as an issue concerned with winning a few seats in an election. It was not the way in which to deal with a decision which could affect the history of the United Kingdom and even its unity for 100 years to come. At this Ted Short started expostulating once more about electoral necessity. Roy Jenkins interrupted: 'You cannot break up the United Kingdom in order to win a few seats in an election.'

I then spoke and said that I too was horrified at the way the matter was being treated, as an electoral issue. John Morris had quoted the election programme, issued in Wales during the general election, which apparently had said that Wales would not lose by the arrangement. I asked why Wales should have a guarantee from England against loss. The issue in Scotland was related primarily to the prospects from North Sea oil and I argued that a minimal scheme of devolution which my colleagues seemed to think would suffice would in no way satisfy the demand arising from North Sea oil. The best thing to do was to stand up and fight. Ted Short turned away in obvious disgust. Others who spoke all supported the devolution cause. It could not be stopped then, or at further meetings when others such as Tony Crosland spoke against it. The conclusion was inescapable. The winning of a few seats in Scotland, not the future of the United Kingdom, was the issue.

Labour's devolution legislation was eventually passed but never implemented. It broke in Wales on the opposition of the majority of Welsh Labour MPs and of the overwhelming majority of the Welsh population. It broke in Scotland due to lack of enthusiasm among the Scottish electorate at a time when the Callaghan Government was profoundly unpopular. This was fortunate. The policy was adopted without the preliminary precaution of ensuring that the proposals were practical, or likely to be acceptable to an English electorate which had, for long, accepted the cost of special help to these two other nations of the United Kingdom. The frivolity with which the question of devolution in the United Kingdom was treated by the Wilson Government reduced hardened civil servants to despair. No credible plans for implementing 'devolution' had been developed despite years of work. That, however, was not enough to impede its adoption as Labour policy at a time of dire electoral need.

'We are a much more political government this time'

This was Jim Callaghan's assessment early in the life of the Government. As the Treasury Minister present when many of these decisions were taken, it was my function to argue economic merit in face of what was regarded by colleagues as political necessity. Occasionally Wilson would say to me, 'Think politically.' It appeared to me that there were enough people around the table thinking politically and that a few contributions arguing merit, however brushed aside with contempt, did serve some purpose. But beyond that, I was by no means sure of the political necessity or, in the case of devolution, of the desirability of succumbing to political necessity if the likely consequence was the break-up of the United Kingdom. In my diary I questioned whether 'all this clever calculation of what will or will not influence votes' would even be 'significantly successful'. Whether it was successful must remain a matter of judgement. Wilson would probably claim that it was because, in the October general election, Labour barely won its overall majority. It had therefore been worthwhile to buy any group of votes however small. I preferred to think that an attempt to place before the electorate the realities of our economic plight would have won more credit and, indeed, more votes. But what I preferred to think may have had little relation to the truth. Certainly it would have needed a leader with more credibility than had Harold Wilson in 1974.

Notes

1. Wilson (1979), 13. See also p. 16.
2. For the Queen's Speech and Wilson's subsequent challenge to Heath to defeat the new Government, see Wilson (1979), 15–16. See also HC Debs., 12 Mar. 1974.
3. 15 Mar. 1974, Castle 43. Michael Foot was Secretary of State for Employment.
4. 23 July 1974, Castle 150–1.
5. Castle 90–1.
6. Castle 159.
7. Wilson (1979), 12.
8. Healey 389.
9. For an account of the discussion in Cabinet on 4 April 1974, see Castle 69.
10. See Crosland 267–8.
11. They had accepted a loan of £100m. for Apr. at 10.5% with another £400m. to follow at the rate of £100m. a month on terms to be agreed. This involved a small element of subsidy.
12. The building societies had had a £15m. subsidy from the previous government the year before, a subsidy given them on the promise that interest rates would fall. They did not.

13. 27 June 1974, Castle 124.
14. 11 July 1974, Castle 143.
15. Benn 240.
16. For further details, see Cmnd. 5879 and Cmnd. 6393.
17. Harold Wilson was Member for a Merseyside constituency.
18. Benn 222–3.
19. Tony Benn gives his account of how he saved Concorde in Benn *passim*.
20. Castle 106.
21. Benn 169. See also pp. 159–60. On p. 172 he tells Barbara Castle that cancellation of Concorde would involve sacking 21,000 people in his constituency.

S·I·X

Debates on Economic Policy

An economic strategy?

Life in the Treasury was often frustrating but it was not dull. In addition to the massive problem with the UK balance of payments, inflation was high and rising. Abroad, economic growth and international trade growth were both slowing. Denmark and Italy had restricted imports. The non-oil developing countries were also finding further restriction of imports an unavoidable necessity. Already visible were the destabilizing effects of large capital flows moving in response to interest rate differentials and speculation about exchange rates. There was little sign of the international co-operation on which some of my colleagues were relying.

Economic policy was discussed in the Treasury but it was very little discussed elsewhere in government. Bernard Donoughue, head of the Prime Minister's Policy Unit, writes:

> To me as a newcomer to central government, the most striking feature of the first twelve months of Harold Wilson's third and fourth administrations was the infrequency of collective Cabinet discussions on economic policy. Indeed, I cannot recall a single sustained discussion in Cabinet or Cabinet Committee, of central economic policy ... until December 1974.[1]

This abstention from sustained collective discussion of economic policy occurred during the deepest crisis the UK had had to face in the post-war world. Apparently economic policy was little discussed even between the Prime Minister and the Chancellor of the Exchequer. Donoughue speaks of Healey making a 'rare report' to Wilson in late May during which he was 'characteristically buoyant'.[2] But the official Treasury at least realized it had the responsibility to alert Ministers to the fragility of our economy even if it did not have the will or the conviction actually to press policies upon them.

The costs and attractions of theory

The oil price hike was inflationary so far as the overall price level was concerned but it exercised a strong contractionary effect on output and employment. Keynesian economists wished to meet the contractionary impact by expansionary measures. International co-operation, they thought, demanded such a response. The UK should show the way. Even where expansionary measures were not specifically advocated, there was no sense of urgency about the reduction in the balance of payments deficit. Further deflationary action was to be avoided because it might lead to an unacceptable level of unemployment. Government should stand ready to increase demand if threatened with unacceptable increases in unemployment. Any attack on the balance of payments deficit should be limited to the underlying deficit before the oil price increase and even that attack should not be too strenuous. If the required improvement in the deficit proved impossible without deflation, that would not be a matter primarily for the UK Government but for international discussion.[3] Thus the responsibility of the UK Government for the UK economy was to be placed on the agenda of international discussions.

Towards the end of 1973 Sir Donald MacDougall left the Treasury, where he had been Chief Economic Adviser, to join the CBI with the same title. At the CBI Council just before Christmas 1973, after the Barber measures, he

> argued that it would be a wrong response to the oil producers' action if the UK and other industrial countries took further deflationary measures; these would do little to reduce their enormous external deficits on current account resulting from the jump in oil prices and would largely result in a pointless, beggar-my-neighbour cutting of imports from each other.[4]

This was the received Keynesian wisdom of the time. MacDougall's advice to the CBI expressed the views of many he had left behind him in the Treasury.

Thus, in his supposedly neutral Budget, Healey had acted, by the standards of this guidance, with commendable caution. He would not lack intellectual justification for expansionary policies in the coming months. All he would need to show was that the current posture of the

UK economy was too deflationary, that it would lead to increased unemployment, and would damage trading partners by cutting imports. One of the costs of theory, particularly of a theory that seems to have served successfully for a long period, is that it may delay accommodation to new facts. Adherents strive to squeeze the new facts into the old theory. It may require strong external pressure and there may be much waste of time before they realize that it cannot be done. Unfortunately the time lacked a Keynes to adapt Keynesianism to the circumstances faced by the UK in 1974.

The IMF provides an alibi

In a speech to the World Banking Conference in London in January 1974, the IMF's Managing Director Johannes Witteveen considered the effects of the oil price hike on the world economy. His views were endorsed in a statement issued on 18 January 1974 by the IMF's Committee of Twenty after a meeting at which Witteveen was present. The Committee had been set up to consider the reform of the international monetary system. It concluded:

In these difficult circumstances the Committee agreed that in managing their international payments, countries must not adopt policies which would merely aggravate the problems of other countries. Accordingly, they stressed the importance of avoiding competitive depreciation and the escalation of restrictions on trade and payments. They further resolved to pursue policies that would sustain appropriate levels of economic activity and employment, while minimizing inflation.[5]

IMF statements carried great authority. The IMF had the reputation of forcing tough fiscal and monetary policies on its clients as a condition of assistance. Anything it said that appeared to condone UK policies would certainly be called in aid. On numerous occasions over the next difficult years, this statement was summoned from the files by Ministers and officials to defend the posture of the British Government. The UK, they claimed, had acted like a good world citizen in the spirit of the IMF's own recommendations, and was not therefore to be blamed for getting into trouble.

This statement by the IMF's Committee of Twenty, the predecessor of the IMF's Interim Committee, was made about two months before Healey became Chancellor. Experience was to prove that little weight could be placed upon it. Healey comments:

Britain and Italy were the only countries to fulfil this undertaking. The United States, Japan and West Germany did the opposite; they deflated their economies so as to reduce their deficits at our expense; within twelve months the industrialized countries had turned their collective deficit of $10 billion into a surplus of $19 billion. Because, within the whole, Britain and Italy still had big deficits, their currencies were vulnerable to pressure, though sterling was still buoyed up by the presence of surplus funds from the Arab countries in OPEC.[6]

Healey, subsequently, acknowledged his mistake. '[M]y first budget made Britain's balance of payments worse; we exported less than we expected because world trade was shrinking. It is not possible for a country like Britain to grow alone when the rest of the world is contracting.'[7]

The UK's convenient interpretation of the IMF guidance was, from the beginning, misguided. Witteveen was one of the more innovative managing directors of the IMF. He was creative in his approach to the problem of avoiding a total breakdown in international economic relations. He was not, however, given to inventing alibis for the UK. The Interim Committee of the IMF repeatedly made clear that advice to avoid deflationary policies was directed to those countries with a strong balance of payments and which had made progress in reducing inflation. Such criteria were certainly not met by the UK for some years to come.[8] Healey was a member of the Interim Committee. He could not possibly have misunderstood its message. The most that the UK Government was entitled to conclude from these statements of international high principle was that the UK's position was made more difficult by the failure of the stronger economies to respect them.

The role of Harold Lever

It is a nice judgement how far UK policy was fashioned by Keynesian economics, and IMF calls for international solidarity, and how far by the compulsions of domestic politics. Certainly it was helpful that Keynesian advice ran so much in tune with domestic political compulsions. One Cabinet Minister who was promoting comfortable advice was Harold Lever who sought 'a prosperous disequilibrium', another term for extensive borrowing. 'Everyone has now come to see that there is no choice but to be in current account disequilibrium of a major character.'[9]

Harold Lever retrospectively defended his advocacy in an article in the *Sunday Times* of 5 March 1978:

> If deficit countries will respond to the receipt of the surplus country investment by organising the restoration of demand lost as the deficit is created, they will strengthen their economies, help to revive world trade, and they, too, will in turn become surplus countries. Of course, deficit countries have to combat inflation as they seek to end the deficit. All their policies, including the exchange rate, should relate to this. This is where the temptation to deflate has arisen. It has been seen as a way of avoiding inflation and correcting the deficit. But deflation for the sake of short-term gains on the balance of payments is self-defeating because it injures future long term competitiveness.

This was Harold Lever's rationalization of his borrowing strategy. This Keynesian consensus, to which Lever was giving expression, ignored critical aspects of the UK's position. It underestimated the weakness of the UK economy which left it exceptionally exposed to adverse swings in confidence. A country already forced to make major borrowings to fund its existing deficit was not the most obvious candidate to lead in expansionary policies which, in the absence of international co-operation, could only take it further into debt. It ignored the high and rising inflation. It ignored the fact that, with Lever's encouragement, the UK was not simply avoiding deflation but positively reflating by a vast expansion of public expenditure. It ignored the risks involved in a policy of reflation which would tend to accumulate debt. It ignored the confidence effects of policies which appeared to the market, and with much justification, to sacrifice elementary economic prudence to political convenience and to trade union demands. It ignored therefore the possibility that the UK might run out of credit and be unable to borrow, other than conditionally from the IMF.

A further failure was to mistake the probable response of other industrialized countries. The probability always was that their response would be more concerned with limiting exposure to confidence factors than with international solidarity. Response to the crisis would be determined by the different circumstances of each country and by judgements made by their governments as to what risks were acceptable. Some countries might avoid further deflation. They might indeed act cautiously to restore demand as in fact many of them did. OECD production did, quite rapidly, recover. But what was possible for some other OECD countries was not possible for the UK.

Neither Germany nor Japan have ever regarded international economic relations as an essay in collaborative self-sacrifice. Germany did not fall into deficit at all and Japan speedily eliminated its deficit on oil account and achieved a rapidly increasing external surplus. In fact Germany and Japan, then and subsequently, acted with consummate skill to free themselves from the worst consequences of the crisis and to restore their domestic demand safely. Those countries that are strong enough to be secure, make themselves secure. Security is a strong current account. The UK, with a much poorer economic performance, was unlikely to be able to match Germany and Japan and restore current account balance rapidly. It would therefore certainly be compelled to borrow. But that fact should not have led it to make a fetish of borrowing.

Harold Lever was not ignorant of the differences between the policy of the British Government and those being followed by other governments. When, in July 1974, Denis Healey took reflationary measures, Harold Lever announced: 'When I look at what other countries are doing, I have to congratulate the Chancellor on his courage.'[10] What Lever said was what the British Cabinet and the British Prime Minister wanted to hear. Anything that freed them from the constraints under which otherwise they would have had to operate was music to their ears. Harold Wilson writes of the economic crisis which the Government faced when it came into office in March 1974:

[T]he leading financial powers reacted in the wrong way. Few saw this at the time: an exception was Harold Lever . . . He would have sought, by borrowing, to raise our reserves to a level high enough to cover any losses due to our payments deficit and at the same time to repel any speculative attacks on sterling, while working for international action to spread reserves. But the forces of Treasury orthodoxy all over the world were too strong.[11]

Whatever Healey himself thought about such arguments, he could not ignore their influence on Cabinet. Lever had more support in the Treasury than Wilson perhaps realized. Yet the mere statement of the Lever approach should have been enough to generate scepticism as to its practicality, at least in a Prime Minister. Wilson and the Cabinet unfortunately neglected to appreciate that even if the policy had theoretical attractions, which it did not, then their responsibility for managing the *British* economy should have led them to take greater account of the precise fact that this was not the way the managers of other, and more powerful and successful, economies were operating.[12]

The idea that, in these circumstances, the British economy could be managed differently was ludicrous.[13]

Unfortunately Lever's charm and persuasiveness were more influential on a Cabinet that wanted to be persuaded than on central bankers and Ministries of Finance overseas who could hardly believe their ears when such arguments were deployed before them. It was this policy that led, inevitably and foreseeably, to the IMF crisis of the autumn of 1976. It was unlikely, at that stage, that the IMF would impose less harsh conditions because it was told by British Ministers that they had only been acting in accordance with its prescription.

The strength of sterling

Lever was permitted to present arguments that in other circumstances could not have been taken seriously, by one aspect of the economic conjuncture that for the moment concealed the extent of Britain's peril. The temporary strength of sterling made more plausible Lever's advocacy of an almost indefinite British power to borrow.[14] Healey has described the situation thus:

> [w]e had enormous problems on the foreign exchange markets. These were masked the first year because the Arab OPEC countries, which suddenly found themselves with enormous unspendable surpluses, chose to keep them in London. They kept sterling afloat until Easter 1975. But as they became more used to the opportunities available all over the world, they started putting money into other countries, and we had a major sterling crisis in 1976.[15]

Sterling, indeed, for a time held at a level quite inconsistent with what, these days, are sometimes called 'the fundamentals'. But the world was becoming sceptical. On Monday 5 August 1974 I went to lunch at No. 10 where the Prime Minister was entertaining the Ruler of Qatar. The Ruler's son was Minister of Finance. He was obviously considering where he should put his surplus revenues, and addressed me very aggressively about the future of the pound sterling. He said: 'You are always devaluing the £'. Then he searched round for when we had last devalued. 'You devalued in 1966, didn't you?' I said: 'No, 1967'. He said: 'Yes, then there was something else wasn't there?' I said that in 1972 we had floated and that had brought about a further devaluation. In my diary I noted: 'These boys are understandably uppity now they have got some money.'

A different approach

My own approach was derived from considerations very different from anything in the Lever canon. It derived from no sophisticated economic theory but rather from a few crude economic and political judgements. These judgements seemed to me relevant whatever the range of forecasts emanating from the Treasury and other experts. First, in the light of the oil price hike it seemed to me inescapable that increases in public expenditure would be inflationary in an already dangerously inflationary situation. I was aware that, in the circumstances, transfers of resources into the balance of payments would also exert inflationary pressure. Therefore a judgement had to be made between the need to improve the current account and the inflationary pressure that would thereby be exerted. I was sure that more should be done than Harold Lever was prepared to concede.

Secondly, I was sceptical of the prospects for international collaboration at a time of manifest crisis in international economic relationships. Thirdly, to the degree that collaboration would be available, I did not believe that the UK could expect it in pursuit of a policy so different from those followed by its trading partners. Fourthly, I was sure that as we had large deficits to fund rather than surpluses to invest, we had better behave in a way which would reassure lenders that they would be repaid. That implied, fifthly, a policy which, after two years of large deficits, with more likely to come, would give confidence that our accounts were moving towards balance. As Healey, in a lecture to the Council for Foreign Affairs in Washington in October 1979, acknowledged: 'A government takes risks when it flies in the face of market opinion . . . however misguided that opinion may be.' He was, in the period between 1974 and 1979, to have many occasions for confirming that the British economy is not one easily steered on the edge of a breakdown in international financial confidence.

Sixthly, I was concerned by the threat of Scottish nationalism. Scottish colleagues were telling me that the United Kingdom would not exist in ten years' time. I hoped that this was unduly alarmist but clearly there was reason for alarm. The implication for economic policy of these fears of Scottish separatism was that the UK could not afford experiments which might end in crises more serious even than that with which we were currently confronted. The UK needed sound policies which carried with them, after a necessary period of adjustment, the prospect of sustained, if slow, growth, not a whirligig of stop–go. In my view, these considerations pointed to the need for vigorous action to transfer resources into the balance of payments, and a reduction in the PSBR preferably by strict control over public expenditure.

Such a stance would certainly call into question the Government's relationship with the trade unions. I believed that there would, in the end, be no choice but to face the problems implicit in the Social Contract. The Social Contract implied increases in expenditure which would prove unsustainable. There was the question what to do about the inflation. In May/June of 1974, when the post-Budget economic debates were beginning, there was still no choice, politically, other than to rely on the Social Contract. But the sooner the ground could be prepared for a switch in policy, the better. The truth would have to be told, however unpopular with our closest supporters.

Healey in his listening mode

On 7 June 1974 there was a meeting in Denis Healey's office based on the latest medium-term forecast. Present, apart from Treasury Ministers, were senior Treasury and Bank of England officials. Harold Lever was also present. Denis Healey was in a listening mode. He wanted advice. He did not that day intend to make any decisions. Decisions would be taken later on the basis of the short-term forecast. The discussion that day could have a delightful academic freedom.

Normally Treasury papers at this time were monolithic. There was one point of view. Later Denis took steps to change this. He wanted to know all the arguments as well as the conclusion. This led to a change in the presentation of Treasury papers. The official paper, prepared for discussion at the 7 June meeting was untypical at the time in presenting two options entitled Cases 1 and 2. The disagreements within the Treasury were thus made clear. No preference was stated as between these two options.

Case 1 proposed a very slow progress towards balance in our overseas payments and only a very slight diversion of resources into the balance of payments. Case 2 represented what those officials who supported it no doubt thought was the most strenuous course which Ministers were likely to accept. It proposed a rather larger diversion of resources into the balance of payments and therefore rather faster progress. Case 1 would involve transferring £100 million p.a. into the balance of payments, that is about 5 per cent of the expected annual growth. Case 2 would mean transferring 20 per cent of annual growth into the balance of payments, that is four times as much. The Case 1 projection meant that something like 2.5 per cent annual growth would be available for distribution in one form or another within the country. Case 2 would leave about 2 per cent.

Not too much attention could, or should, have been devoted to such calculations. They suggested a spurious accuracy in forecasting in a conjuncture even more difficult than usual to analyse. For example, few realized at the time how poor would be the UK's rate of growth over the period covered by the forecast.[16] The best that could be said of the two Cases is that they suggested paths of policy believed within the Treasury to represent politically and economically credible alternatives.

The economic models which generate estimates as to the consequences of particular policies are themselves suspect and at the time were highly controversial. The New Cambridge School, represented in the Treasury by Nicholas Kaldor and, occasionally, by Wynne Godley, had discovered a relationship between the budget deficit and the balance of payments which left the Government totally responsible for any balance of payments deficit that arose. But their analyses were not accepted by the predominant school of thought in the Treasury or by others who modelled on a more conventional basis such as those at NIESR.[17] Monetarists had much to say about the relationship of the money supply to the level of inflation and about the risk of government expenditure 'crowding out' private activity with consequent ill effects on the balance of payments. But these arguments too were controversial, appeared too simplistic as an analysis of a complex economy, and would not have been permitted to take the full burden of responsibility for forecasts on which government policy was to depend.[18]

The discussion at the meeting developed into a battle between Harold Lever and me. Lever supported Case 1. This was consistent with his view that the rate of reduction in the balance of payments deficit should be very slow. He did not expect there to be any serious problems in financing the deficits that would accrue over the years before North Sea oil came to our rescue. To divert much in the way of resources into the balance of payments would cause political difficulties, and might imperil the Social Contract and put further pressure behind inflation. He pointed to the disaster, as he saw it, of Roy Jenkins's policies: 1968 and 1969 had been in part responsible for subsequent inflation. Harold

Lever saw the Social Contract as the Labour Government's answer to inflation. To sustain the Social Contract was a major element in his thinking.

Against this I argued that it was right to make rather more rapid progress at bringing the country back into balance. The balance of payments outlook for 1974 was deeply worrying. Such a current account deficit exposed the country to grave risks. Funding it would depend on movements of confidence that we could neither forecast nor control. The risks were intensified by the increasing volatility of currency movements in an increasingly open and interdependent world. Political realism told me I could not hope for more than Case 2, once the official Treasury had put it forward as the tougher option. Case 2 did have the political merit that it showed the choice to be a great deal less stark than Lever made it out to be. I claimed that, if the estimates made in the medium-term forecast had any validity, we were not required to make politically unacceptable transfers into the balance of payments in order to achieve a rather more satisfactory result. Undoubtedly there were political pressures. We needed to stand firm against them. If we started by recognizing all the political difficulties and therefore adopted a very accommodating policy we would be pushed even further off course and that could take us to the brink of disaster. If we started with a fairly hard line and were pushed a bit, we could still be making reasonable progress towards balance.

Among Treasury officials it was the international side that took the tougher line. They knew better what to make of the illusion entertained by so many economists that there was a solution to the world economic crisis based on international co-operation and that therefore the UK should not lead the way to deflation. But they too were not tough enough. They themselves seemed to have been influenced to some extent by their Keynesian colleagues. They should not have been happy with Case 2. I would have preferred Case 2 to be presented as the minimum option and that officials should then challenge Ministers to take a firmer line.

I could hardly complain that Treasury officials had presented Case 1. It represented the favoured option of influential, Keynesian, elements in the official Treasury. But if Case 1 had to be presented, the international side should have insisted on presenting a Case 3. The international side should not have made weakness respectable as a policy. They should have known that weak governments incline to weak policies, that weak governments are easily pushed. They made weakness too easy. They were making a political judgement as to what Ministers would tolerate. A fuller range of options should have been brought forward.[19]

Tony Benn records a conversation he had had on 3 February 1974 with Francis Cripps of the New Cambridge School. After the election, Francis Cripps was to become an adviser to Benn.

He prophesied that when the next Labour Government came to power, the Treasury would get hold of Denis within five minutes and tell him the situation was critical: the international monetary community would insist on this and that, and we would have absolutely massive measures announced within twenty-four hours.[20]

This prophecy corresponded with the Treasury's reputation and with the thesis that Labour Chancellors always succumb to mandarin pressure. But here we were, already two months after the election, and so far from the Treasury bringing pressure on Denis, officials were presenting weak options, and could not make up their own minds which to recommend to the Chancellor. I wished that Treasury reputation corresponded with Treasury performance.

The debate continued, primarily between Harold Lever and myself, with Joel Barnett cheering on Harold, and Bank officials cheering me on. Denis Healey maintained an impartial chairmanship. When Harold was making his points Denis Healey would swing to my side. When I was making my points, Denis Healey swung to Harold's side. It was all good fun. I was optimistic enough to believe that Denis would come down on my side in the end. He claimed to want to achieve export-led growth. He could hardly regard Case 1 as consistent with that objective. But the influence of Harold Lever was certainly a worry.

After Denis's meeting I went to lunch with Lever. We reverted to the discussion that we had had at the meeting. He said: 'Of course I realize the reason Joel Barnett was supporting me was that he thinks that my attitude leads to an easier position on public expenditure. But that is the point at which he and I are going to fall out.' I said: 'Harold, the trouble with your policy is that it is unacceptable as a political tactic. We will be pushed and if we are pushed from your position the situation will be far worse than if we are pushed from mine.' He replied: 'I accept that is the real criticism of my position. And that is the reason at the end of the meeting I made some statement'—I could not remember his making any such statement—anyhow he said he made some statement which indicated he was aware of all the political risks and perhaps when it came down to actually making decisions, he and I would be agreed. It appeared suddenly that the disagreements of the morning were evaporating and that as a matter of political tactics he would support my view.

As it happened, Harold Lever did not give me the satisfaction of falling out with Joel Barnett on public expenditure. As Barnett says, writing in retrospect, 'In my early days as Chief Secretary I was not involved in major expenditure-cutting exercises. Indeed it might be said that the first months of the new Government were characterized by our spending money which in the event we did not have.' In those first few months grave damage was done to the economy. Barnett adds that the lack of control over public expenditure in the early months 'meant that because there was virtually no growth in the economy between 1974 and 1977, we had to preside over very substantial increases in taxation to avoid even larger borrowing'. He attributes this lack of control to the fact that

> the Chancellor had made the fundamental decision to react to the oil crisis in a different way from the Germans and Japanese, and indeed from many other developed countries. Instead of cutting expenditure to take account of the massive oil price increases of 1973, which in our case cut living standards at a stroke by some 5 per cent, the Chancellor decided to maintain our expenditure plans and borrow to meet the deficit. This may have made life easier at the time, but it had some dramatic consequences both for me personally and the country in general.[21]

Whatever the reasons for the lack of control, the consequences for public expenditure were dramatic. In the fiscal year 1974/5, public spending rose by no less than 35 per cent in cash terms, or nearly 13.5 per cent in real terms.[22]

The problem of unemployment

The Keynesian argument exaggerated the control a British government could exercise over the level of unemployment. Contrariwise, there was in my argument an assumption difficult for any Labour government to accept. This assumption was that a rise in unemployment was inescapable. The effect of the Healey policies in 1974, combined with the stimuli earlier provided by Chancellor Anthony Barber, was to delay the onset of higher unemployment. By mid-1975 unemployment had risen by a considerably lower percentage in the UK than in France, Germany,

Japan, or the United States.[23] Under the policies I was recommending it would rise more than under the easier option presented in the official Treasury paper. Unemployment was bound to rise as a result of any additional attempt to divert resources into the balance of payments. My response could only be that, if the easier option proved in the event not to be credible, it would probably in the end cause more damage not less. This in fact occurred. UK unemployment continued to rise rapidly at a time when, in these other countries, it appeared to have stabilized.[24] But however inescapable an increase in unemployment, critics within the Labour movement would see my policy as the deliberate planning of that increase. It was not surprising that Denis Healey should find such a position unacceptable, especially pending a further general election, though we did not have to wait long to be reminded, by unofficial forecasts, of the direction which the unemployment statistics were likely to take even on the present highly accommodating policies.[25]

XYZ

On 19 June, at the monthly XYZ dinner, the speaker was Wynne Godley.[26] He estimated that by November prices would be up by at least 17 per cent as compared with the year before. Thus there would be eleven triggers by November. This would produce great distortions in income relationships which it would be difficult to sort out by means of an incomes policy. As a result of the oil price increase there would be a negative demand effect. This had been underestimated, and could produce a very severe recession in the UK with unemployment up to 1,500,000. This problem could not be dealt with by increasing public expenditure which in this case would be inflationary. It should be dealt with by reductions in indirect taxation in July. However, the medium-term policy could not be expansionary if we were ever to get back into balance of payments, and as to incomes policy, he said he did not really know what to do, or how the crisis due to these eleven triggers could be avoided.

In discussion Kaldor surprised me by saying that 1.5 million unemployed for a winter or so, perhaps even for two winters, would not in his judgement be unacceptable provided that over the lifetime of the Government it was again reduced by export-oriented growth. After that, there was a very untypical love scene between Wynne Godley of the New Cambridge School and David Worswick of NIESR. David

Worswick did not see things in colours quite as black as did Wynne Godley. But they were substantially agreed on the trend. This was not a meeting to improve the morale of those in government responsible for economic policy. On the other hand nothing in it dissuaded me from the course of policy I was recommending to the Chancellor.

The official Treasury tries to make up its mind

A further strategy document now appeared. Treasury officials had decided that they ought to make a recommendation. The recommendation was Case 2. However, I was told in private discussion that the official Treasury was far from united behind the recommendation.

This paper was discussed on 21 June. Denis Healey opened by saying that he had decided on Case 1 because Case 2 would require some early movement down in the exchange rate. Case 1 produced in 1975 a slightly better balance of payments outcome than Case 2 because of the operation of the J-curve, and by 1976 North Sea oil would be on stream.[27] Case 1 involved less cost to distributable resources, and would thus enable a slightly greater increase in the standard of living than would be possible under Case 2. Therefore it was better from the point of view of social strain and anti-inflationary policy. Harold Lever and Joel Barnett agreed.

Throughout his Chancellorship, Healey was disinclined to policies involving the depreciation of sterling because of the inflationary consequences. This did not prevent his exploiting any depreciation that occurred against his will by arguing that he was thereby doing British industry a service by increasing its competitiveness. But he disliked tinkering with the exchange rate and in this instance that inclination supported an intention to make the more comfortable choice.

I attacked Healey's view strongly. I said that he was overestimating the significance of the figures in the medium term forecast. I was not arguing in favour of depreciation. The key question was how far policy was to be directed to moving resources into the balance of payments. On what basis were we going to formulate policy? Was it to be in anticipation of almost indefinite borrowings, or on a rather harder intention to get the balance of payments more rapidly into an acceptable condition. I argued that it was misguided to look at North Sea oil as the panacea. With support from some Treasury officials, I asserted that there had been a very large deterioration in our position over recent years. We could end up with so much debt, and so high a continuing balance of payments deficit, that even North Sea oil, possibly by that time commanding lower prices, would not be enough to keep us creditworthy. In fact we could end up with North Sea oil *and* a balance of payments deficit.

It was quite clear that Denis Healey was strongly influenced by short term considerations. Nor was it difficult to discern what these were. In my view there was very great danger that these same short-term considerations would land us in trouble either twelve or eighteen months hence, or in a shorter period if things did not go even as well in that period as the medium term forecast currently suggested.

Most surprising at this meeting was the failure of officials to defend their recommendation. They had told the Chancellor in writing that they favoured Case 2. Yet they let it go by default. I was rather angry. Earlier that morning, I had by chance met one senior official in the corridor. He had said how important it was that we should not be rushed into premature reflationary policies, as the newspapers now seemed to suggest we were likely to be. Despite this warning, to me unnecessary, nothing was said at the meeting with the Chancellor of the Exchequer to defend the official Treasury recommendation.

Perhaps this collapse of the official Treasury arose from the strength of the disagreements in their own ranks. Some of them thought that Healey was making the correct choice. Or perhaps those officials who did prefer Case 2 thought that as there were no immediate decisions to be made, the battle could be deferred. Action would be based on the short-term forecast rather than on the medium-term forecast. Nevertheless Healey's preference for Case 1 showed what would be the drift of policy when decisions did come to be made. There was no reason to believe they would have more stomach for battle on any later occasion.

As I was leaving Healey's office after the meeting, one official positioned himself in the doorway. He said: 'Paymaster, I would like to say how much I agree with you. We have been running before the wind too long.' I acknowledged this and walked off to my office. Where shortly arrived another senior official who had remained virtually silent throughout the meeting. He apologized for not having come to my support but said it would not have done any good. 'He had obviously made up his mind.'

North Sea oil

In addition to the political factors militating against firm decisions, North Sea oil encouraged delay and prevarication. In the distance, but nevertheless only just beyond the horizon, was the reality of this vital and expensive raw material, gurgling out of the sea to save us from the consequence of our follies. As Harold Wilson put it subsequently, 'For years . . . Government and Opposition had played a macabre game of musical chairs, in the hope of being in possession of the chair when the oil began to flow in quantity.'[28] Undoubtedly the prospective availability of North Sea oil offered the Government a powerful excuse for drift.

Healey, who was inclined to derive excessive comfort from the coming of North Sea oil, has since argued, 'we had a net cost in developing North Sea oil while we were getting no benefits from it. We only got the first oil out of the North Sea when I was about halfway through my period as chancellor.'[29] Two points need to be made in qualification of this statement. Much of the development work on North Sea oil was funded by an inflow of capital from overseas, so the net cost to UK resources was probably not large. Secondly, the oil began to flow at the end of 1975 and was making a significant contribution to the balance of payments in 1976. The problem was not the cost of developing North Sea oil. It was the overestimate too readily made of the benefits of North Sea oil to the UK economy.

'One must select one's time'

On 28 June, I went to have drinks with senior members of the Treasury on the occasion of Sir Douglas Allen's departure as Permanent Secretary. A senior official said to me that evidently I wanted a small economic crisis. I asked him what he meant. He replied that he took it to be my view that it would take a small economic crisis to bring the Government to its senses. A few days after this, the same official and I were walking together down the stairs at No. 11. I was saying that I just could not understand how lightly our economic situation was being taken. He replied: 'We don't take it lightly. But one must select one's time. I assure you one must select one's time.'

Delay had become a conscious element in policy, or an excuse for acquiescence, both at political and official level. Donoughue observes:

Debates on Economic Policy

[Wilson had] shrewdly learned from long and painful previous experience that if a major economic crisis is looming it is politically better to wait until the seriousness of the situation is unmistakably apparent to one's ministerial colleagues . . . That was certainly also the Treasury officials' view in late 1974 and the early summer of 1975, when they were still biding their time . . . and waiting for the crisis to erupt.[30]

This cynical and accommodating attitude would have been defensible only if nothing could have been done to avert the coming crisis. As it was, inflation was accelerating and decisions were being made, for example in the realm of public expenditure, that could only exacerbate an already perilous situation. It is this kind of 'wisdom' that has helped to undermine the British economy and has exposed the UK to frequent humiliations in face of world opinion.

Buying out inflation: the Lever and DPCP versions

The idea of subsidizing the cost of living in order to defeat inflation was being seriously advocated. To some degree that policy was already being implemented. In 1974, the UK spent over £500 million on food subsidies and that was estimated to have produced a saving of about 1.5 points on the retail prices index. This example stimulated Ministers and officials to look to ever greater subsidies as a remedy. That there was an immense problem could not be doubted. Inflation was escalating, apparently out of control. But that did not mean that the subsidy solution was sensible, and it would not have become more sensible by being taken to the further lengths now proposed.

Barbara Castle records a meeting of the Ministerial Committee on Economic Strategy on 17 June to which she had been invited. Harold Wilson

> expounded Harold Lever's 'new macro-economics'; borrow abroad . . . Threshold payments must affect prices, so we should subsidize the cost of living on a massive scale. Roy [Jenkins] surprised me by saying there was a sense in which Lever was right, because if you have massive price rises and hold back wage increases you create a slump. We were in a new situation—on the edge of hyper-inflation—and therefore needed a new approach.[31]

On 1 July I had an opportunity to discuss with Lever what, in my diary, I describe as 'his crazy economic strategy'. The discussion confirmed my worst fears. His strategy appeared to consist very largely of importing a higher standard of living by borrowing even more oil money than we would be compelled to borrow in any case. He was very enthusiastic for this idea although what it would do to our total borrowings even he could not guess. The total effect of it all was to be a reduction in the RPI over a year by about 4 or 5 per cent. He himself said: 'Let's start with that level and then we can go on and reduce it even further.'

I searched around for some argument that might move him away from these absurdities. I said that none of this would do any good unless there was an understanding in the trade union movement that they must not use their power in an inflationary way. The strong unions would have to abdicate their power to fight for wage settlements which would only generate further inflation. Harold Lever seemed greatly struck by this idea. He said: 'Yes, we must put it to the trade union movement. They must accept responsibility for not putting each other out of work. I am sure that if I say to the coal miners that if they make absurd wage demands they will simply be putting other trade unionists out of work, they won't do it that way.' He started thanking me effusively for putting this idea into his head. In future this was the way he was going to present his idea. He was going to make an offer to the trade unions but it would be in the context of an agreement that they would not use their power in a way which would lead to unemployment for other working people.

At dinner on 9 July 1974 at the Charing Cross Hotel, Michael Foot explained to Barbara Castle what was going on in the Ministerial Committee on Economic Strategy:

'Denis and Harold Lever are in favour of borrowing like hell,' he said. And he added, 'I must say I am a Haroldite.' We should borrow what we can, reduce inflation as much as we can. 'The worst part of the programme is to keep public expenditure down. I hope we will reflate a bit.'[32]

On the afternoon of 9 July I went out for a walk in St James's Park and met an old friend who was a senior official in Shirley Williams's Department of Prices and Consumer Protection. He asked whether I had five minutes and we sat down together. He complained about the papers that Denis Healey had put in to the Economic Strategy Committee. They concealed information. Indeed they were positively dishonest in suggesting that inflation could be kept down simply on the basis of the TUC's guidance. As a result of the failure of the Treasury and Treasury Ministers to provide adequate information, other Ministers were prevented from taking a rational part in the discussions at the Economic

Strategy Committee. He said he had a strategy for a 10 per cent reduction in the RPI paid for not by borrowing but by tax increases. This was an idea that persisted in Shirley Williams's Department for some time thereafter. It illustrates nothing else than the desperation in government at the rising inflation.[33]

I told him exactly what I thought. I said that Harold Lever's way of dealing with the retail prices index was impossible. We could not borrow the additional money abroad to finance it without very grave risk, if at all. I then said that his scheme for reducing the RPI by 10 per cent was also impossible, and that the only basis on which I would even begin to consider any such idea would be if we had a very much more cut-and-dried and enforceable agreement with the TUC. He thought such an agreement might be possible on the basis of action to reduce the RPI by 10 per cent. I disagreed. And, as I pointed out, the whole scheme could be defeated either by demand inflation or by a fall in the exchange rate due to lack of confidence abroad. I said to him that one trick or another, a bit of reflation here or a bit of RPI cutting there, did not go to the root of the issue.

We talked for half an hour rather than five minutes. Then we parted. I had rejected his ideas out of hand because they were not practical, and if practical were not likely to be helpful. I had given him no comfort in his unhappy job of briefing Shirley Williams. He must have thought I had gone native in the Treasury but, in truth, the Treasury had become part of the problem.

Notes

1. Donoughue 51.
2. Donoughue 56.
3. *NIER* (Feb. 1974), 5.
4. MacDougall 208.
5. Garritsen de Vries (1985), 199.
6. Healey 422–3.
7. Healey 393.
8. A typical statement was that issued by the Interim Committee on 31 August 1975; 'The Committee felt that industrial countries which have slack domestic demand conditions and relatively strong balance of payments positions and which have made progress in reducing inflation, should lead in the promotion of a satisfactory rate of expansion in world trade activity.' Garritsen de Vries (1985), 222. Similar statements were made by the Interim Committee on 16 January 1975 and 8 January 1976, see pp. 218, 226.

9. 'A modern monetary system has to be one which organizes a prosperous disequilibrium, not one which seeks a strait-jacket of accounting equilibrium on the affairs between nations.' HC Debs., 1 Apr. 1974, col. 901.
10. Castle 150.
11. Wilson (1979), 22–3.
12. 'Background developments in the world economy have not been encouraged as governments attempt to deal with both inflation and balance of payments problems by increasingly restrictive monetary and fiscal policies . . . This tendency is apparent, so far, even in countries like the United States and West Germany which have little or no balance of payments problems and inflation rates well below those of Japan and some other industrial countries.' NIER (Aug. 1974), 4.
13. 'The United Kingdom, like other European countries, responded inappropriately to the challenge of rising oil prices. Attempts were made to avoid recessionary tendencies by excessive increases in public spending, which were ultimately followed by the worst of both worlds, record inflation as well as rising unemployment.' Ball 43.
14. 'In 1973 the unprecedented current deficit and capital surplus combined to give the smallest movement in official financing since 1963. This type of balance has almost never occurred since the war although current surpluses with capital deficits have been common; the only other examples of the 1973 pattern were in 1947 and 1960. There is thus no precedent for financing a current deficit with autonomous capital movements for over two years, as is now anticipated.' NIER (May 1974), 22.
15. *Institutional Investor* (June 1987), 68.
16. Pliatzky recalls: '[T]he prevailing economic advice in the Treasury was that, though there would be no growth at all for one year, over the medium term the trend growth rate of something like 3 per cent would be achieved . . . The economic projections in the January 1975 White Paper took a 3 per cent growth rate from 1973 to 1979 as the central case, with 2.5 per cent and 3.5 per cent as, respectively, a more cautious and a more optimistic variant. But by then some at least of the Treasury people had come to a private belief that 2.5 per cent would have been a better choice as central case . . . this possibility was reflected in the text of the White Paper though not in the tables.' Pliatzky (1982), 128.
17. Thirlwall 251.
18. For a contemporary discussion of the economics of the New Cambridge School and of monetarism, see J. A. Bispham in *NIER* (Nov. 1975).
19. Pliatzky has commented on the occasional official unreadiness to give to Ministers advice that they may find distasteful: 'If there is sometimes a disposition for officials to refrain from giving what they believe to be sound advice but which ministers would not like, that tendency . . . has always been more to be found than resistance by officials to ministerial policies.' Pliatzky (1989), 164.
20. Benn 102–3.
21. These quotations come from Barnett 23.
22. Smith 61.
23. *NIER* (Feb. 1976), 81.
24. *NIER* (Feb. 1976), 81.

25. On 10 June, *NIER* published a forecast which included the possibility, on unchanged policies, of a significant rise in unemployment and a very much flatter growth rate than that looked for in the Financial Statement and Budget Review. *NIER* (May 1974).
26. XYZ was a private dining club including Labour MPs, economists, and City personalities which met at the House of Commons.
27. *NIER* (May 1974), 43, forecast that, on unchanged policies, the 'non-oil' deficit of £1.5b which was being forecast for 1974 would be more than eliminated in 1975. In August, this forecast was revised. 'The balance of payments outlook has worsened: on current account we expect the deficit to be nearly £4 billion this year and £2.75 billion in 1975. Of these the "oil-deficit" . . . accounts for £2.4 billion and £2 billion respectively . . . The forecast . . . shows the nation living beyond its means this year to the extent of about 6 per cent of GDP. There is no justification for this in the long term, but the same problem is shared by a number of countries and its solution should not be sought in measures which would do further harm to others.' *NIER* (Aug. 1974), 4, 5, and 15–17.
28. Wilson (1979), 16.
29. *Institutional Investor* (June 1987), 68.
30. Donoughue 60.
31. Castle 116–17.
32. Castle 141.
33. See e.g. Benn 394.

S·E·V·E·N

The July Measures

Electioneering economics

As the summer of 1974 wore on Denis Healey became increasingly optimistic about the economy. At a meeting of the Liaison Committee between the Government and the TUC on 24 June, he reported that he had just returned from Washington and had found that confidence in the British economy was far greater abroad than it was at home. He thought the OECD forecast of a £4 billion deficit was excessive, though he had always known it would be about £3.5 billion. The central problem was inflation. It would be 20 per cent by the end of the year. Wages, he said, had not played a major part in 1974. There were, however, signs that commodity prices were falling, so that the key to inflation in 1975 would be the level of wage claims. Healey was interested therefore in how far the TUC was prepared to introduce monitoring machinery. He got a dusty answer from the TUC leaders present, Alf Allen, David Basnett, Jack Jones, and Len Murray.[1]

Healey let it be known through press leaks that he was preparing a reflationary and anti-inflationary package. This intention had some justification in the advice to which he was listening. But he would not have forgotten the coming general election. No Minister is to be dissuaded from doing right simply because it might also be electorally advantageous. A package directed at inflation would be attractive to overseas opinion and, if it had some reflationary element, it would go some way to conciliating back-bench opinion concerned at forecasts of mounting unemployment. To me, it seemed unwise to leak to the press that there was going to be a package before its contents and justification

The July Measures

were clear. In practice, by July, Healey had effectively shut off all his options.

Yet, by now, even some of those who had optimistically spoken in terms of international co-operation in facing the OPEC surpluses had begun to have some doubts. *NIER* said in August:

> Our earlier hopes that the rest of the advanced world might be persuaded to adopt moderate expansionary policies to counter the contractionary effects of higher oil prices have so far come to nothing—in fact the reverse. The inhibition which this places on the use of domestic demand management to prevent a rise in unemployment is now, we think, compounded by the worsened outlook for domestically generated inflation, and indeed emphasizes this as the single most important problem.[2]

On 5 July, I was unavoidably absent from a meeting at which Healey, I was subsequently told, had taken various decisions about the content of a mini-Budget. For example, he had seemed attached to a 5 per cent cut in VAT, to me a quite ludicrous proposal. I sent him a minute arguing strongly against doing anything; certainly against doing anything as large as the package which, I had heard, he was then contemplating. The minute is reproduced in full in the Appendix to this chapter.

On 8 July, I had a private meeting with Denis at No. 11. I told him that he would be seen to have repudiated the balance of payments and PSBR objectives which he had announced in his Budget statement the previous March and that the measures were likely to be ineffective as regards inflation. I said that I would prefer to continue on the present course.[3] From my conversation with him it appeared that he was not yet committed to its detailed contents or to the size of the package, but nevertheless he was obviously intending to introduce a mini-Budget of some kind. The size would be the decisive point for overseas confidence. He was greatly taken with a proposal that Regional Employment Premium (REP) should be multiplied four times and that something relatively small should be done on VAT. He told me that, at his meeting, officials had taken a rather more optimistic view of the effect of the package on overseas confidence than had the Bank of England. They now thought that a clearly anti-inflationary package might indeed buoy up overseas confidence. The Bank, on the other hand, was very much more sceptical. I emphasized the need for the Government to put itself in a position of some strength opposite the trade unions and not just give in at every turn. He clearly thought that the present relationship with the trade unions was the most hopeful way of dealing with inflation. If it failed, the only thing left would be an indexed freeze.

On 10 July, I went to a meeting with Denis Healey and senior Treasury officials to discuss the July package. It appeared that Denis had come off the idea of a £1,500 million package, particularly I imagine because he had come to realize that this would have a very unfavourable impact internationally and might be dangerous from an electoral point of view by bringing about a run on sterling just before an election. We discussed the idea that had emerged in the Treasury that some reflation could be undertaken through the medium of an increase in REP together with some domestic rate relief. If Ministers persist in pursuing damaging policies, officials are bound to help them by suggesting the least damaging ways of accomplishing their ends. But I suspected that this idea had emerged within the Treasury voluntarily rather than under the compulsion of Ministers seeking for solutions. Denis asked me what I thought about the idea of an increase in REP. I said: 'As you know, I would prefer to do nothing. But if you have to do something, and you've really made it politically impossible not to do something by all this talk there's been about a July package, then I prefer an increase in REP to any of the other ideas.'

He replied: 'All right. But don't be so lugubrious about it.' I did not at once reply. The discussion continued and it was quite clear that the package was shrinking as compared with the previous Friday. After some further discussion, Denis said: 'I suppose that this might be called fine-tuning, and we are supposed to be against fine-tuning, aren't we?' At this I broke out laughing, and he turned to me and said: 'You are just too cynical.' At this I told him rather firmly that this whole package was the acme of cynicism. Denis said: 'I'm very glad to see you're getting angry now.' We exchanged some rather vigorous words to the obvious embarrassment of officials. The whole incident might be described as a flaming row. At the end of the meeting I said to Denis that I hoped he understood that I did not want to be at the Treasury for one moment longer than he found it useful. He said: 'I do find it useful.'

On 16 July, I had a further discussion about the package with Denis. I said to him again that this was not my idea of economic management. I explained to him my assessment of the economic position from which he very strongly dissented. I argued that we were having to run larger and larger budget deficits in order to achieve anything like full employment. But he would not accept this on the ground that the higher rates of unemployment we then had as compared with some years earlier, when 350,000 rather than 550,000 was typical, could be explained away in terms of redundancy payment schemes and earnings-related unemployment benefits. The discussion was rather more friendly though it was quite clear that we were not going to have any meeting of minds.

Keynes and Keynesianism

As a result I was not included in all the meetings which were preparing the package. But I was kept informed. On 18 July I had a private discussion with officials about the package which, evidently, had grown again. There had been a meeting at the Commons the previous evening to which I had not been invited, and at which it was put in a final form. It was now worth something in the order of £900 million. Concern was being expressed about this both in the Treasury and at the Bank of England. There was agreement that all this was really totally unnecessary, especially as the Tories had given the Chancellor a perfect excuse for cutting his package by adding to the PSBR through amendments to the Finance Bill they had passed the previous Tuesday. From here my meeting moved to a general economic discussion, and about the harm Keynesians had done to economic policy in this country. I denounced the Keynesians for putting in the hands of governments this weapon of demand management which they had so inadequately understood. I was told that within the last twenty-four hours, Nicky Kaldor had expressed similar views. My diary comment was, 'So we are all anti-Keynesians now'.

Eventually Healey was to come to similar conclusions. He writes:

I abandoned Keynesianism in 1975 . . . his theories had two important weaknesses when applied in postwar Britain. They ignored the economic impact of social institutions, particularly the trade unions; in fact Keynesian policies were unlikely to work in Britain without strict control of incomes, a point of which the Treasury was already well aware. And they ignored the outside world.[4]

My own objections were not to Keynes whom I regarded as a supreme pragmatist, who would certainly have moulded his recommendations to the new facts, but to the Keynesians who, it appeared to me, did ignore the unavoidable impact on Britain of an increasingly interdependent world.

The Budget statement and Tory cowardice

On Monday 22 July came Denis's long-awaited statement. He said: 'The first and main objective . . . is to attack inflation at its source'. Retail prices had risen 16 to 17 per cent in the previous year. The threshold had already been triggered six times. He was relatively optimistic about the trade position.

Apart from the extra cost of oil, our trade deficit was running in the second quarter of this year at a rate 40 per cent lower than in the last quarter of 1973 . . . we can look for further improvement . . . So far we have been able to finance our remaining deficit without having to maintain large interest rate differentials so as to attract funds to London.

He had not had to draw on the $2,500 million loan negotiated at the time of the Budget. Now agreement had been reached with the Imperial Iranian Government which had offered to provide the UK with a line of credit of $1200 million to be drawn down in the form of three separate loans by public sector bodies within three years.

Against this background he was reducing VAT from 10 per cent to 8 per cent, introducing rate relief for domestic ratepayers whose rates were going up by more than 20 per cent that year, and releasing £50 million not so far committed out of the £500 million provided for food subsidies in the March Budget. He estimated that all this would have a direct impact on retail prices of 1.5 per cent within the following three months with more to come as the rest of the food subsidies provision was allocated. This would avoid one threshold payment, and possibly two, by the end of October. 'The eventual effect . . . should reduce the retail price index by about 2.5 per cent.' In addition he was doubling REP. The total economic effect of all these measures would be to add under £200 million to demand by the end of 1974 and 'a relatively small amount', some £340 million, to the PSBR. Above all, these measures would strengthen the Social Contract.[5]

The statement passed without any very great controversy. It was rapidly assessed to be a collection of electioneering trivia. It was hardly surprising that the non-oil deficit was down in view of the contractionary effect of the oil price increase. The principal question remained how long the UK would be able to meet its liabilities from unconditional flows on the basis of current policies. Robert Carr did question the suitability of reflationary action in a country in the UK's position.[6] This made the Tories' feeble reaction to the July measures, their acceptance of some of them, their failure to vote against others which in their speeches they criticized, the more pitiable. Their apprehensive conduct in Opposition certainly denied them the right to any complaint at the use Healey and others made of the short-term effects of the July measures in the election campaign that followed.

No one used the electioneering potential of the July measures to more questionable purposes than Healey himself. Basing his claim on the estimated reduction in the rate of inflation consequent on these measures he permitted himself to inform the electorate that the three-month rate of inflation was down to 8.4 per cent on an annualized basis. Labour, evidently, had won a great victory over inflation.[7] In more serious public presentation, Healey represented himself as having navigated the wide path between the monetarists, or deflationists, on the one hand, and the reflationists on the other. He was faced by a wide spread of advice coming from the different schools of economic thought. The spread entitled him to his swipes at the 'science' of economics which could offer such contrary advice. '[T]o suggest . . . that I should feed £2,000 million of extra demand into the domestic economy immediately, at a time when both inflation and the balance of payments deficit were running at record levels, would be no less a recipe for catastrophe than to follow the deflationist school.'[8] He was proceeding, he argued, with statesmanlike caution. Indeed, 'I must frankly tell the House that in my judgement if I made a mistake yesterday [in his July measures announced the previous day] it was once again on the side of caution.'[9]

The Left still dissatisfied

For all his reflationary zeal, Healey failed to satisfy his left-wing critics in Cabinet. On 17 July, there had been a Husbands and Wives Dinner, the regular gathering of the Cabinet and near-Cabinet Left. Barbara tells us:

I was trying to stir Mike, Peter *et al* into supporting my attempt to ensure that any reflationary measures [Denis] takes shall be directed through the public expenditure field. It remains a continuing contradiction to proper social and economic planning that expenditure decisions are strictly controlled by Treasury, while the rest of us have no control over taxation policy, which is equally vital to demand management.[10]

Then at the mini-Budget Cabinet on the day of the July statement, Barbara said:

I was sorry he had chosen to reduce VAT rather than increase family allowances . . . None the less I appreciated why he was driven to adopt an anti-inflationary strategy. But I flatly denounced his proposal to tackle unemployment by doubling Regional Employment Premium, which was indiscriminate, rather than through investment in construction in development areas through an expansion of public expenditure on housing and hospitals. Wedgie and Mike supported me on this.[11]

The criticism had no immediate effect. The Cabinet had received their usual last-minute briefing when it was too late to change. Nevertheless, Healey could not be uninfluenced by this continual Cabinet pressure and discontent.

Healey was under great pressure in Cabinet to reflate. He might have done worse and more. The forecasts of the level of unemployment on existing policies showed it rising seriously. When, on 26 July, he tried to get agreement on limiting the growth of public expenditure to 2.75 per cent per annum, he was told that the success of the Social Contract depended on keeping unemployment down and, according to Barbara Castle, 'we should never make a success of the Social Contract unless we succeeded in converting trade unionists to the importance to them of the social wage'. Michael Foot felt that the constraints were so great that some other way had to be found, for example stimulating productivity through the extension of industrial democracy. The remedies were becoming desperate.[12]

The problem of company liquidity threatens to become urgent

At a meeting in Denis Healey's office on 6 August we discussed papers, written by the Treasury, which argued that the financial position of companies might become serious in 1975, or at the end of 1974. We went through the various options that were available to deal with the problem and, at the end of the meeting, the Bank of England was asked to produce a further paper on prospects for company finance. During the course of the meeting Denis Healey asked a very pointed question. Why until recently had the Treasury been briefing Treasury Ministers to the effect that the CBI was grossly exaggerating the problem of company finance?[13]

Treasury officials and economists were shaken by this demand that they account for their evident change of view. They reminded the Chancellor that they had told him at the time of the Budget that the company financial sector would be in deficit in 1974. They insisted that the situation was not yet serious but they agreed that it might become serious. Their main defence was that, as a result of the ACT surcharge, the financial position of companies, though depressed in 1974, would be improved in 1975 because they would already have paid about £300 million of their corporation tax liability. Moreover officials were able to take comfort from the July mini-Budget, which had benefited companies' financial position by about £300 million in a full year. Nevertheless they could not escape the accusation that they had advised the ACT surcharge and, by August, they were obviously rather doubtful as to whether the advice had been sensible.

The problem of company liquidity could well become urgent. But to solve it would have a reflationary effect and reflation, especially after Healey's July measures, was likely to be damaging. Treasury officials were divided about where the balance of advantage lay. As one of them put it at the meeting: 'I don't want you to assume that I am recommending you to reflate further.' Healey replied in his usual bantering way that he would have to make up his own mind on that, getting the response: 'Well, I'm not saying I would be against it. I'm just not asking you to think that I'm for it at the moment.' But if Treasury officials had not yet made up their minds about the desirability of reflation, Healey was already busily committing himself to yet further reflation in the autumn.

Preparing the November measures

On 18 September the election was declared for 10 October. On 19 September, assuming our survival, there was a meeting on the interim Budget judgement for the November Budget. Healey had announced, at the time of his July measures, his intention to introduce an autumn budget. It was quite clear that, in November, he would want to reduce taxation by something in the order of £1,000 million even though, according to the estimates with which we were presented, this would have an estimated cost on the balance of payments of about £500 million and would relieve the growing unemployment by the winter of 1975/6 only by about 30,000. It can take a long time for reflationary measures to bring about a significant reduction in unemployment.

Treasury officials were still divided. Some pointed to the dangers of reflationary policies. Others, and notably the economists, argued that on the contrary there was plenty of room for expansion of exports without further unemployment, that it would be very well worth while to reflate to that extent, and that the additional £500 million on the balance of payments could be covered by borrowing, which they were sure would be available.

On 20 September there was a meeting at the Treasury with most of the senior Treasury and Bank people present, to discuss exchange rate policy. It had been in debate the previous August because of the thought that international competitiveness could be improved, and economic activity in the UK raised, by action on the stubbornly high sterling exchange rate. It was still holding up at a depreciation of about 17 per cent as compared with Smithsonian. One Treasury paper argued against the use of the exchange rate as a convenient instrument of policy. Among the dangers was a loss of confidence if we were seen to be deliberately forcing the rate down. On the other hand there was a contrary Treasury paper arguing that we should still keep exchange rate policy well to the fore, that we should not allow a loss of competitiveness through failure to compensate through the exchange rate. This was not a meeting for decisions but to go over the ground. Denis Healey's prejudice was clearly against taking action on the exchange rate, and that too was the view of the Bank. If exchange rates were to become an instrument of policy, the most suitable tool of all, it was agreed, was not the exchange equalization account but interest rates. A reduction in interest rates would not be seen as direct action on the exchange rate but rather as an attempt to assist the domestic economy. This argument seemed to me far fetched. If the effect was to lower the exchange rate then, whatever the publicly announced motivation of a reduction in interest rates, it could result in a very rapid swing of short-term money out of sterling.

Denis Healey was still relying on North Sea oil. He said: 'In 1977 North Sea oil will be supplying 50 per cent of our requirements. There will be great confidence in the United Kingdom economy. People will be delighted to lend us money'. Depreciation would have the short-term effect of increasing our balance of payments deficit. Why in 1975 should we increase our balance of payments deficit and thus cause concern, when by 1977 we would be 50 per cent self-sufficient in oil, which would give a boost to confidence and enable us to finance ourselves out of any trouble? I said that I thought this was a bit optimistic. The continuing decline in the competitiveness of UK industry could imply balance of payments deficits even when North Sea oil was fully on stream unless we had large amounts spare to export. That again would not prevent further declines in the competitiveness of British industry.

There was one interesting consequence of the Treasury's continuing inability to make up its mind. It made it easier to provide Ministers with papers arguing different cases and leading to different policy conclusions. After one of these pre-election meetings, one official remarked to me that in all his years at the Treasury this was the first time that the Treasury had not presented a monolithic face to Ministers. He said: 'If this is not yet open government, it is the beginning of government open to Ministers'. I would have been more ready to congratulate officials had I not suspected that, in a divided Treasury, officials were being allowed too easy a way out. Ministerial responsibility is the ark of the covenant; it should not excuse officials from their responsibility to give strong and, if necessary, unpopular advice, advice that Ministers may not want to hear. Their readiness to do so alone justifies the existence of a permanent Civil Service. But how could the Treasury give strong advice if it could not make up its own mind?

I end this chapter with Barbara Castle's account of lunch at the joint Cabinet/NEC meeting on 16 September 1974: 'As we grew mellow over stilton and burgundy, Denis said: "You must admit I am the most political Chancellor you have ever had." "I do," I replied, "and I appreciate it." '[14]

Appendix: Minute on the July measures: 6 July 1974

My views on the July measures were sent to the Chancellor by my Private Secretary John Beastall. I had been unavoidably absent from the Chancellor's meeting on the previous day, 5 July 1974. The minute was headed 'BUDGET—SECRET' and was copied to the Chief Secretary, the Financial Secretary, Douglas Wass, Sir Kenneth Berrill, and Sir Derek Mitchell. The minute read as follows:

REFLATIONARY MEASURES

The Paymaster General has the following comments on the proposals which emerged from the Chancellor's meeting on Friday afternoon.

I do not know that I have anything to say other than to re-iterate the considerable dangers which I see in this high-risk policy, dangers that the Chancellor will already have considered in coming to his decision. Nevertheless I draw attention to the following factors:—

1. There is already comment that Government policies are more directed to winning the next election than to the needs of the economic situation. It is inevitable that the proposed package will be interpreted in that way. The risks inherent in the package are therefore substantially greater even than they would be given a Government without short-term electoral pre-occupations. They are probably rather greater than they would be if the Government were not a Labour Government.

2. The Chancellor has several clear commitments arising from his Budget statement:

(a) to reduce the balance of payments deficit;
(b) substantially to reduce the borrowing requirement;
(c) to make a vigorous attack on inflation.

The proposed measures will be considered to be inconsistent with the first two of these objectives. I know that the forecast still shows, even given these measures, a £1000 million reduction in the deficit between 1974 and 1975. I do not know how far the forecast takes account of the possible effect on the exchange rate of the proposed measures. Such forecasts are in any event highly uncertain. The important short-term point is that we will be believed to have put the balance of payments objective at risk—and for political reasons.

Even on existing policies the PSBR is going to be substantially higher in 1974 than forecast in the Budget. This is already widely suspected. Given the proposed measures, it will be taken that the borrowing requirement objective has been totally abandoned—even if one can argue that the measures will have a delayed effect which will only be seen in full in 1975 rather than in 1974. The 1975 borrowing requirement will, I imagine, be well up into the Barber stratosphere. I do not think that the Chancellor can publicly abandon such a commitment without serious results.

3. I quite see the attractions of the proposed measures on the inflation front. It is a delicate matter of judgement in dealing with inflation to decide the balance of advantage between subsidy effects and demand effects. I am sure that there is a place for subsidies and controls. But as a country rises up the inflation league I suspect the balance of advantage changes. As a matter of personal reminiscence, I have seen too many Latin American Governments attempting to subsidise themselves out of inflation—to believe that there is much hope in this course of action at high rates of inflation. I can only hope that the Chancellor will be proved right and to have caught the disease in time. But the danger is that exchange rate effects will wipe out the subsidy effects and we will end up with both higher rates of inflation and a deteriorating balance of payments. I would not willingly take that risk for the sake of these possible benefits.

4. I particularly draw the Chancellor's attention to the risk of catastrophic failure. The risk is no doubt less than it would have been in similar circumstances in the sixties because we are floating. I do not think it can be

discounted. In a totally rational world we might be able to rely on fine statements about the oil deficit and on universal rejection of mutually destructive policies—although even then I wonder whether it would be widely accepted that we in the UK were entitled to conduct ourselves on the assumption that the rest of the world should indefinitely contribute £40 per annum to the standard of living of each one of us. I believe we have a duty to strengthen our international standing, not weaken it further. The risk I see is that catastrophic failure will force us into deflation and protectionism, to that siege economy that some colleagues advocate without perhaps understanding all the costs. I fear that then it will be neither the EEC nor the open seas but a highly protected stagnation of unforeseeable duration.

5. In short, I would much prefer for the time being to keep on the present course and I do not believe that the short-term forecast—with all its uncertainties—by any means rules out that alternative.'

J. S. BEASTALL
6 July 1974

Notes

1. Castle 120–1. The actual current account deficit in 1974 was £3.6b.
2. *NIER* (Aug. 1974), 5.
3. I did not yet know how far out of line the Budget forecast of the PSBR would prove to be though it was already clear that the forecast would be exceeded.
4. Healey 378–9.
5. HC Debs., 22 July 1974, cols. 1048–53.
6. HC Debs., 23 July 1974, cols. 1331–2.
7. Healey's calculation enabled Margaret Thatcher, a year later, to riposte, 'Inflation is now over 26 per cent at an annual rate, while the three-month rate, or the "Healey half-truth", is running at 48 per cent.' HC Debs., 21 July 1975, cols. 77 and 87.
8. HC Debs., 23 July 1974, col. 1315.
9. HC Debs., 23 July 1974, col. 1317.
10. Castle 148.
11. Castle 150.
12. Castle 155–6.
13. During the Budget debate Healey had given strong reassurance to the House on the company liquidity problem. HC Debs., 1 Apr. 1974, col. 1007.
14. Castle 181. Castle reports Healey repeating the claim at a meeting at Chequers on public expenditure on 4 Aug. 1975. Castle 485.

E·I·G·H·T

The Regeneration of British Industry?

The pros and cons of Tony Benn

I was glad that the Prime Minister had not offered me an appointment at the Department of Industry with Tony Benn, much as I liked him. I could not have accepted. In the 1960s I was, for over a year, a junior Minister to Tony Benn at the Ministry of Technology. Meetings with him were enjoyable and stimulating. He was able to infect with his enthusiasms even that eminent Treasury mandarin Sir Richard ('Otto') Clarke, who came to him as Permanent Secretary. There was no one in Cabinet or Cabinet Committee more enjoyable to listen to, even when he was talking nonsense, as in my view he often was. He did it with eloquence and *élan* and with humour. My principal quarrel with him at the Ministry of Technology was that he spent too much public money too indiscriminately. He called it injecting the public interest into the private sector. When he came back to office as Secretary of State for Industry in 1974, he discovered that government support to private industry was running at about £750 million a year. He used that fact as a weapon to throw industry on to the defensive. But he himself was by no means without responsibility for this disturbingly high level of support.[1]

In the months after the February 1974 general election, Benn and industrial policy became, in the public mind, synonymous. Industry felt threatened. The feeling of threat was particularly severe because of Benn's frequent victories over Denis Healey and the Treasury. His successes against the Treasury were the more disappointing in that one positive aspect of Labour's industrial policy, if the words could be believed, was a determination that public money should be directed to supporting what was hopeful, if risky, and not to the rescue of lame ducks. Instead, one of the most public aspects of industrial policy, as conducted by Benn over the recumbent body of the Treasury, was the creation of workers' co-operatives with little chance of survival without repeated injections of public money.

Benn and the Civil Service

Benn records in May 1974:

> Frances [Morrell] said this afternoon that she was convinced that the Department of Industry was sabotaging my industrial proposals. I feel the same ... I told [Sir Antony Part] that I was really very unhappy ... I had to rely on the Department to put forward proposals that I strongly believed in and I hoped that he would bend.[2]

Later he speculated on getting rid of Part if Labour was successful in the second 1974 general election.[3] The machinery of government depends upon trust and upon the ability of officials faithfully to reflect their Ministers' wishes. It is the duty of civil servants to service Ministers. But civil servants can only do this if Ministers want to be serviced. In the Department of Industry that essential relationship broke down. Given Benn's attitudes, it was unlikely it would be restored under any other Permanent Secretary. In any event, it is unlikely that Wilson would have gone so far as to replace Part at Benn's request. To have done so would have been a symbolic act conveying a highly damaging message to the private sector. Part thought he was doing his duty as Permanent Secretary in assisting Benn to develop his policies. He denies having received any guidance from Wilson about the line he should take with Benn. He established a strong team to help Benn. It was led by Alan Lord who had been Deputy Chairman of the Inland Revenue and was now Deputy Secretary at the Department of Industry. Ron Dearing was second in command, and Peter Gregson third.[4] But Benn's distrust was formidably persistent.

Planning agreements

So far as industrial policy was concerned, the two key questions were the NEB and the nature of planning agreements. Planning agreements were to be agreements of some undefined kind between a Labour government and major companies. Labour's adoption of the idea of planning agreements derived originally from a paper presented by Stuart Holland to the Industrial Policy Sub-Committee of the NEC while we were in Opposition. It was, supposedly, based on foreign experience. As so often with parties in Opposition, the most vigorous authors of papers, and the most articulate exponents of ideas, hold the initiative in the formulation of policy. Holland could produce a lengthy paper at the drop of a hat. Others less committed, or less certain that Labour would again have a chance to act on any of these ideas, were more backward in offering their services. Despite Holland's activity, no one in March 1974 had the least idea what should constitute a planning agreement. But partly because Tony Benn was made Secretary of State for Industry, the idea evoked great concern in the minds of industrialists who felt that they might be compelled by planning agreements, compulsorily imposed, to enter into unreasonable commitments against the interests of their shareholders and employees.

The Treasury and industrial policy

The disarray in the Department of Industry was an encouragement to Healey to initiate a Treasury industrial policy. He was enough of a supply-sider not to need much encouragement. He was also no doubt influenced by the widespread feeling that, in existing circumstances, industrial policy would be safer in Treasury hands. In this policy he had the support of Douglas Wass who, after a visit to Japan, was keen that the Treasury should play a part in managing industrial policy.[5] We had a series of meetings at the Treasury to discuss our reactions to Benn papers and also the nature of a Treasury industrial policy. Yet more important to the private sector would have been a reversal of the effects of the March Budget on company liquidity and a speedy reduction in the rate of inflation. Both were eventually to come but neither had that special character of 'selective' intervention then so attractive to Labour thinking.

An undelivered speech

I was becoming increasingly disturbed by the breakdown in relations between the Government and the private sector. I decided to use an opportunity given me by an invitation to address the Luton Chamber of

Commerce on 14 June. I prepared a speech which would, by implication, severely criticize the outpourings of Tony Benn on industrial policy. The speech argued against turning the relations between Government and industry into an ideological debate. It emphasized the essential contribution of the private sector to national economic success, a contribution that Government could not itself make or substitute. It supported the idea of an NEB but on pragmatic grounds, not in order to achieve 'vast extensions of public ownership into manufacturing industry'.

I hope that discussion about such an agency can be conducted on the merits of the argument without its being disfigured by ideological outrage on one side or indeed by pretensions on the other that the creation of such an agency can portend in short order vast changes in the structure, competitiveness or ownership of British industry.

The speech ended with a quotation from the Report of the Bolton Committee on Small Companies: 'There appears to be a tendency to mistrust initiatives of a Labour Government on principle and irrespective of their merits'; and with a plea from me that 'some attempt will be made to consider the issues that inevitably arise on their merits. That would be for the good of the country, of British industry and indeed of the present British Government.'

I sent my speech across to Harold Lever to see what he thought of it. Although Harold Lever and I were in strong disagreement on economic policy, we did share a philosophy of the relations between Government and the private sector. Sharing a philosophy did not always mean that we saw eye to eye on individual rescue operations. But this did not affect our joint wish to put an end to the antics of Benn. Lever expressed himself as delighted with the speech and was absolutely sure I should make it. It was an honourable and upright speech, well argued, and would get a good press. It was exactly what was wanted at the moment.

Treasury officials are often more sensitive politically than are their political masters. They were worried about my delivering the speech without consulting the Prime Minister. I came to the conclusion that it probably would look rather bad if I made it without letting the Prime Minister see it in advance. So I sent it across to No. 10. No. 10 reacted very quickly with a request that I should not make that speech but should make a speech on nationalized industry prices, a very sensitive issue at that moment. At this I was very angry. I decided to go to see the Prime Minister.

I went down to his office in the House. I told Wilson I objected to being stopped making this speech and I objected to what Tony Benn was doing. He said:

Yes, so does everyone else. So did the Cabinet at its meeting this morning. I am going to take charge of everything. I am going to take charge with a speech tomorrow night. But don't you do anything. If you do anything then Heffer will come in and there will be thirty speeches. It will look simply like an attack of a right wing pro-Marketeer.

I said to him if he took charge then good, I would not make the speech. Nevertheless he must understand the position. He must also understand there would be questions at my meeting and I had been warned that these questions would be primarily about Benn. I would have to give honest answers. He was rather worried about that and said: 'Look, you refer to the fact that I am going to make this speech tomorrow night if you are asked about it. That should take care of it.'[6]

Friday 14 June was the day we were both speaking, he in the evening and I at lunchtime. In the car I read a copy of the Prime Minister's speech. There had been a phone call from No. 10 to say that it was not the final draft. I was appalled by it. There were, indeed, a few phrases referring to collective responsibility and it said that he, the Prime Minister, supported everything that the Secretary of State for Industry had said in Parliament, thereby perhaps implying that he did not approve of everything that Benn had said outside Parliament. Still hoping that the draft I had seen was not the final draft and that Wilson would discharge the promise he had given me, I made a routine speech on the economic situation and then answered questions. Surprisingly, no one raised Benn at all. At 10 o'clock I listened to the news. It said that Harold Wilson had made a speech in support of Benn. So did the newspapers the following day. It was clear that the draft I had seen had not been significantly changed and that there had not been any briefing which would have alerted the media to any special significance in the speech. Wilson had simply ratted on me.[7]

The following Monday, I had a word with Denis Healey. I found that Harold Wilson had mentioned to him the incident of my speech. I said I would send Denis a copy. I added that Wilson's speech was totally useless and that nobody but a microscopist would have seen anything in it at all critical of Benn. Denis said that there was going to be a great confrontation later in the afternoon at which Harold Wilson would lay down the law to Tony Benn. This was something that I was no longer prepared to believe until it had actually happened. In fact the confrontation between Wilson and Benn did take place and is extensively reported in Benn's diaries. In the course of angry exchanges Wilson said to Benn: 'I had to restrain a senior Minister this weekend who was determined to make a speech attacking your policy.'[8]

So it appears that the fact that I had prepared the speech, and that Harold Wilson had seen it, and the fact that I had then been to see him, may have made some useful impact, even though I had not delivered it. The idea that it may have done a little good was confirmed later that day. I spoke to Harold Lever on the phone late in the afternoon and he said he wanted to talk to me. He was rather vague. He said: 'I want to tell you certain things you do know and certain things you do not know.' It seemed that all this mystery might relate to my *démarche* with the Prime Minister. We talked together two days later. Lever was in conversational mood. He was only too ready to reveal to me all his own discontents about the way the Government was going.

I said to him that it was about time the more sensible people in the Cabinet got together and made a *démarche* to Wilson. Wilson's continuance as Prime Minister depended on them far more than on Benn. The difficulty was that they all, except Harold Lever, wanted to be Prime Minister. At this Harold Lever started jumping up and down with excitement saying, yes, this was a very good idea, and he would immediately take action to bring it about. Not revealing my presence, he phoned Denis Healey. He gave his account of the previous Thursday's Cabinet meeting at which Denis had not been present because he was in Washington and at which he, Lever, had launched an attack on Benn. He said the subject was going to be renewed the following Thursday and he wanted Denis to take a very strong line. Denis said yes he would. He was fed up with Benn. Denis Healey then, without any prompting from Harold Lever, started talking about my speech and said what an excellent speech it was and what a pity it was that I had not been able to deliver it. Harold Lever revealed that he had seen it and agreed. For me it was rather uncomfortable because Denis did not know I was listening to this conversation.

Constituting the National Enterprise Board

In the division lobby on Thursday 20 June when voting on industrial policy, Michael Meacher came up and asked me: 'How does Edward Heath know your views about the NEB? I did not know you had expressed them so strongly.' Then Gwynoro Jones came up and also told me that Heath had quoted me. On examining Hansard I found that he had quoted from my *Observer* article of about a year previously. The words Heath had quoted were: 'My concern with the NEB suggestion is simply that it is a bad idea. It derives from a vision of a monopolistic society ruled by technocrats.'[9] I doubt, however, that it was the excellence of this analysis of an earlier NEB proposal that resulted in the two defeats the Government suffered in the Commons that evening on industrial policy. But, apparently I was not alone in my view of the Benn NEB. Many other Ministers were opposing the creation of an NEB on the Benn model.[10]

Barbara Castle reports on a memo on Benn's industrial policy circulated by Denis Healey. In it Healey declared himself to be strongly in favour of a substantial extension of public ownership and a more dynamic industrial policy. He supported the idea of the NEB and agreed the functions Benn had outlined for it. But he stressed that a further important objective was to ensure that the manufacturing sector which remained in private hands was able to operate vigorously and competitively. Therefore uncertainty must be removed as soon as possible. He did not oppose the nationalization of the aircraft industry and shipbuilding. But compensation to the owners would have implications for the Government's borrowing requirement and he could not sign a blank cheque. So programmes should be defined as closely and as soon as possible. On planning agreements he welcomed the intention to introduce these on a limited scale in the first place. He was sure the Government should not be thinking in terms of the biggest hundred firms, but rather in terms of the sectors most urgently requiring attention—e.g. engineering rather than food or tobacco. Co-operation should be the objective rather than sanctions. Barbara Castle comments: 'I must say I find all this common sense.'[11]

On Friday 28 June the Industrial Development Committee presided over by the Prime Minister met and Denis Healey's paper on industrial policy and Tony Benn's Green Paper on the NEB and planning agreements were discussed. Apart from Peter Shore and Willie Ross, no member of the Committee supported Benn. Healey was very happy about the outcome. Benn had been slaughtered both by him and by others and, he said, a great victory had been obtained. There seemed to be only one fly in the ointment and it was pointed out to me by a senior Treasury official who had spoken, after the meeting, to the Cabinet Office. The Prime Minister had left the slaughtering of Benn to his colleagues and had barely said a word himself. The suspicion in the Cabinet Office was that should Benn take his battle to the country, Wilson would be able to present himself as not having opposed Benn's wild schemes. No one, apparently, trusted Wilson.[12]

Wilson recalls:

It was not until late July that the Department of Industry's draft White Paper emerged. As I had feared, it proved to be a sloppy and half-baked document, polemical, indeed menacing in tone, redolent more of an NEC Home Policy Committee document than a Command Paper. One basic weakness was that it appeared to place more emphasis on the somewhat amorphous proposals for planning agreements than on the NEB.[13]

This curious summary of months of discussion on industrial policy can only be attributed to loss of memory. It is true that Benn had had to be prevented from making regional grants to large companies dependent on their entering into planning agreements. But Benn's proposals regarding the NEB caused much more difficulty than did planning agreements. The essential point was to ensure that the NEB had no powers of compulsory acquisition. In the end, as drafted, there was no question of the NEB having powers of compulsory purchase, or of its secretly acquiring shares in target companies.[14] Any compulsory acquisition would require an Act of Parliament.

Benn considered that, in these discussions, he had done 'far better than I expected'.[15] It is often the case that in fighting against the most objectionable characteristics in a draft, much is left that would have been better eliminated. When the drafting was mainly in the hands of Benn, too much of Benn would certainly in the end be left uncorrected, enough at least for Benn to claim that 'The NEB is an absolute dream.'[16] Yet the policy when it was eventually announced was perfectly compatible with the more moderate objectives for industrial policy and for the NEB that I had myself supported. Much would depend on whose hands wielded the powers to be taken but the most objectionable elements in the original draft had been eliminated.

Unfortunately Wilson was engaged in one of his complicated political calculations. The TUC and the Left must be persuaded that the Government had lost none of its industrial policy radicalism. Instead of himself launching the Industrial Policy White Paper, now called *The Regeneration of British Industry*,[17] he allowed Tony Benn to do so. Not surprisingly, in his public presentation of the White Paper, Benn claimed victory for his policies. Wilson contented himself with background briefing to the effect that it was the moderates that had won the internal battles. The consequence, in subsequent press reporting, was that a quite reasonable document served further to undermine confidence in the economic policies of the Labour Government.

No chance for Dell

In certain sections of the government machine, and indeed outside it, there was a gross overestimate of my ability to bring about modifications in the Government's policies. One day I was lunching with one very senior Bank official. We were talking about what seemed the inevitably approaching confrontation with industry, and he said to me: 'You could do something about this.' If he believed what he was saying, he grossly overrated my influence. Any power that I had to achieve consensus with industry was insignificant compared with that of Benn with his very large support on the left of the party and his intense dedication to his extraordinary theses, helped as he was by a quiescent Prime Minister.

There was not the least chance of my being appointed Secretary of State for Industry and any illusion that might have been circulated from No. 10, and reflected in the press, could only have been designed to postpone an explosion from industry. The political impossibility of it was confirmed to me by Denis Healey. He might himself have wished it but he knew there was no chance of it, as indeed did I. Early in August, he and I were discussing how the White Paper on industrial policy was coming along. In general the position was satisfactory. The main problem, however, was Benn. Denis Healey said to me again as he had in the past, as Harold Wilson himself had said to me, that there was some suspicion that Tony Benn was riding a course which could lead to resignation. Denis Healey remarked: 'The best thing would be if you were appointed Secretary of State for Industry. You would like that, wouldn't you?' I said: 'Yes'. He said: 'Well, the Prime Minister has no such intention.'

How to handle commitments made in Opposition

The discussions on industrial policy were symptomatic of a fundamental problem within the Government. In Opposition the Labour Party had agreed to an industrial policy that was quite impractical, certainly in that economic climate. If attempts had been made seriously to implement it, the result would have been major damage to the British economy. Yet it was very difficult to argue that what Benn was proposing was inconsistent with previously agreed policy. There were many elements in the policy adopted in Opposition that had only carried Wilson's reluctant acquiescence. But, reluctantly or not, he had acquiesced. Benn tells how during final discussions in Cabinet Committee on the industrial strategy White Paper, he suggested that words should be added that 'The NEB will act also as a means to a further substantial expansion of public ownership through its power to take a controlling interest in relevant companies in profitable manufacturing industry'. The Prime Minister objected and Benn pointed out that these words were taken from a speech made by Wilson himself at the Labour Party Conference.[18] Callaghan's comment on the situation was, 'You can't write a Manifesto for the Party in opposition and expect it to have any relationship to what the Party does in Government. We're now entirely free to do what we like.'[19]

Wilson and Benn

Wilson had not needed to make Benn Secretary of State for Industry. Wilson had fond memories of the Ministry of Technology and he may have thought that Benn would respond to the responsibilities of ministerial office. Even when he had lost hope of responsible behaviour, Wilson, whether through cowardice, or through concern for the prospects of the party on the eve of an election, would not sack Benn. He would merely talk about sacking him. There were strong party arguments for keeping him though under firm Prime Ministerial discipline. Nor would that have been impossible. The last thing Benn intended was to resign or to be sacked. He enjoyed ministerial life too much and Cabinet office was then, probably, the only route to the leadership of the party. There were also arguments for sacking him if it was proved that he would not submit to firm Prime Ministerial discipline. But there was no argument at all for threatening it and not doing it. It led to an increasing impression of feeble leadership.

Donoughue writes:

Mr Wilson decided in the summer of 1974 that he would try to provoke Benn to resign—and anyway would ultimately move him from the Industry post to some less important department (again hoping that this final humiliation would lead to his resignation). I never shared the Prime Minister's optimism on this point. It seemed transparently clear to a detached observer that there was no humiliation which Tony Benn would not swallow in order to stay in the Cabinet.[20]

It must be extremely doubtful whether Wilson wished to provoke Benn into resignation. He resented Benn. He liked to contemplate the day when he would be able to bring himself to sack Benn. Meanwhile he had an election to win and he did not want to provoke public dissension within the party.[21]

Three weeks before the publication of the White Paper I had been treated, from the horse's mouth, to Wilson's views on Benn. Shirley Williams and I had gone to see Harold Wilson to make a *démarche* on the subject of Europe. Benn was the problem on Europe just as he was the problem on industrial policy. But we were not there to attack him but to make clear our concern about the course the party appeared to be taking on Europe. It was Wilson who introduced the subject of Tony Benn. Sucking his pipe, he enjoyed himself contemplating the prospect, at an appropriate time, of getting rid of Tony Benn. He said: 'The only crime in the Labour Party is a procedural crime.' He was just waiting for Tony Benn to make a procedural mistake. He did not want to sack him, at least until the White Paper on industrial policy was out. But if he broke ranks, and if there were further breaches of collective responsibility once the White Paper was out of the way, Benn would be at his mercy. No one would forgive Benn if he did breach some procedural rule like collective responsibility. It did not appear to matter that he had done it already several times.

Wilson speculated whether Benn was just developing an excuse for resignation. He referred to the way he had on one occasion rebuked Benn in Cabinet. Benn had protested that the party was expected to die whenever Labour was in office. He thought it was very possible that Benn was planning a resignation before the election for which, said Wilson, the party would never forgive him. He said: 'Even if he does not resign, or if I do not get rid of him before the election, one thing that happens after every election is that all portfolios are automatically handed in.' He seemed to suggest that when all the portfolios were automatically handed in, Benn might be sacrificed.

In my diary I commented:

It was really remarkable that he should go on and on like this about prospects of getting rid of Benn. He was obviously quite willing to talk to us, trusting to our keeping his confidence, about one of his own Cabinet Ministers whom he was not prepared to sack there and then but against whom he was prepared to entertain conspiratorial thoughts . . .

We left at this point . . . I went into Shirley's office and we had a chuckle and discussed whether it was possible to believe a word Wilson said. Shirley said to me that if Roy Jenkins, she and I resigned, he could not take it . . . However she said: 'If you are ever thinking of resigning, for God's sake come and discuss it with us first.' She was obviously thinking of the time in 1971 when I resigned without discussing it with them.

But I was never part of the Jenkins clan and I had no obligation to discuss resignation with anyone. If I concluded that the time had come to resign, I would resign.

The Stock Exchange in August

As the Minister in charge of the Treasury during the absences of the Chancellor of the Exchequer, I had my moments. If not moments of fulfilment, at least I could try my fingers for size as compared with the various holes appearing in the dyke.

On 19 August 1974, I was sitting in the garden at home when the phone rang. It was John Beastall from the Treasury. He told me that Harold Lever who was in Deauville had become very alarmed about the slide in the stock market. He wanted a statement from a Treasury Minister which would say the Government regretted this fall in share values, and that it saw no objective reason for it. Harold had also consulted the Prime Minister who was in the Scilly Isles. Wilson's view was that a statement would be counter-productive. His alternative idea was that perhaps we could extract a letter from some back-bencher to which I could then reply in a way which might give some confidence to the stock market. I was opposed to both proposals. First, if anything was going to be said it had to be said by the Prime Minister or the Chancellor of the Exchequer. Secondly, I disagreed with Harold Lever that there was no objective reason for the fall in the stock market.

There were many objective reasons for the fall. The economic environment was threatening, the Government was paying more attention to the electorate than to the economy, company liquidity was being squeezed, and, last but not least, Benn had been allowed to present the industry White Paper as a triumph for his policies. I was in no position to change the economic policies of the Government in the absence of the Chancellor and the Cabinet. There were, however, two proposals that might help if only marginally. The first was to relax the Price Code. The second was to persuade the Prime Minister to make a helpful statement on the industry White Paper. On the telephone to Deauville, I secured Harold Lever's agreement to support me on these two points.

I then phoned the Prime Minister in the Scilly Isles. Evidently he was out somewhere and I had to talk to him by telephone part of the way and by short-wave radio part of the way. Our conversation was punctuated by such words as 'roger' and 'over', until we both got fed up and just talked naturally. I said that there were two ideas that I could put to him, both on my own behalf and that of Harold Lever. One idea was action on the Price Code, although I would have to consult Michael Foot and Shirley Williams, and I had discovered that although Michael Foot was in London, Shirley Williams was in Tunis, which would be a problem. Secondly there could be from him a clarificatory statement on the industry White Paper. He reacted favourably to the prices point but very unfavourably to the idea of any further statement on the industry White Paper. He said that the reaction of the press had not really been that the NEB was malicious but that it was too open-ended. I replied that that was exactly the problem. However he was very strongly against a further statement and insisted that he would do no such thing.

Meanwhile the Stock Exchange was rising sharply, and therefore the need for action had declined. I received a message from the Prime Minister that he had discovered after speaking to me that the Stock Exchange had risen, and this inclined him to look with more favour at the idea of a letter from a back-bencher, but one to which he would reply, not one to which I would reply. I decided on a programme of action. I would see Michael Foot during the course of the afternoon, and talk to Shirley Williams later in the day or the following morning if she could be found. At the same time we were trying to locate Denis Healey.

The Regeneration of British Industry? 101

He was in Corsica. He had left telephone numbers behind but it had so far been impossible to contact him.

Both Michael Foot and Shirley Williams, when I found her, objected to any premature action on the Price Code. The effect on the TUC would be very bad and it would remove much of the influence remaining on employers not to concede inflationary settlements. All that was left by way of possible action was the letter which the Prime Minister might send to whatever back-bencher we could identify who could be persuaded to ask the Government's attitude to the fall in the Stock Exchange.

I phoned Harold Lever in Deauville. He was obviously very much calmer and agreed that action on the Price Code could be deferred for a fortnight in view of the opposition of Michael Foot and Shirley Williams and, if the Prime Minister would not come back from the Scilly Isles, he was not very much in favour of a letter. A letter date-lined Scilly Isles would be less effective than a letter date-lined London, to which Wilson could return by helicopter. Lever was not against the letter. It would not do any harm. It might do some good. But he was not terribly enthusiastic about it. He hoped he had not interfered with my holiday. He would have a meal with me when he got back to London.

A draft was prepared and also a covering letter from me to the Prime Minister. In it I said that I did not think very much of his letter idea though I would support urgent action to relax the Price Code. Thus ended one and a half days of futile activity. These events had demonstrated the undesirability of leaving any relaxation of the Price Code until November. This was the date at which we would arrive if the time-scale outlined for review of the Price Code was allowed to proceed at the originally intended pace. But the review continued on its previous somnambulant course to November and beyond.

My diary of these days comments particularly on Wilson's refusal to clarify the Industry Policy White Paper, and to correct Benn's presentation of it. The draft letter to the putative back-bench MP included a paragraph correcting that presentation. That was no doubt one of the reasons why it was not sent.

Notes

1. Benn 144.
2. Benn 152. See also p 159.
3. Benn 187.
4. Part 171, 172.

5. Pliatzky (1982), 125–7.
6. In April, Eric Heffer had made a speech criticizing the Government's policy regarding the return of certain warships to Chile and had been told by the Prime Minister that it was incompatible with his position as a Minister. Callaghan, on BBC1 o'clock news, said the speech was incompatible with collective responsibility. Benn 139–40. Hence, no doubt, Wilson's concern that any speech of mine would be replied to from the opposite point of view by Heffer. Heffer was not dismissed.
7. Tony Benn refers to Wilson's speech and to his subsequent discussion with Wilson in Benn 176–7.
8. Benn 177–9.
9. HC Debs., 20 June 1974, col. 699.
10. See e.g. Benn 184.
11. 15 July 1974, Castle 145–6.
12. Benn 187–9 and my diary.
13. Wilson (1979), 33. See also Wilson (1976), 66–7.
14. The decisive meetings on the industrial strategy White Paper, on 31 July (Cabinet Committee) and 2 August (Cabinet), are described in Benn 209–10 and 212–14. Barbara Castle also gives accounts of the final discussion in Cabinet Committee and Cabinet of the industrial policy White Paper. Castle 162 and 167. Both accounts show that Benn was fighting hard until the last for some of the ideas that had been stripped out of the White Paper.
15. Benn 214.
16. Benn 215.
17. Cmnd. 5710, 15 Aug. 1974.
18. Benn 209.
19. Benn 194.
20. Donoghue 54.
21. In recounting the switch of Varley and Benn after the European referendum, Wilson notes that, rather than accept the Department of Energy, it at first appeared that Benn would retire to the back benches, 'the last place where I wanted to see him'. Wilson (1979), 144.

N·I·N·E

A Disorderly Growth of Incomes

The policies of the Heath Government had added to the inflationary pressures already present when it took office. Then with the oil price hike, and rising commodity prices, real GNP had suffered a significant decline, adding still further to the inflationary pressures. There was an illusion that the decline in real GNP could be compensated for by high wage increases. Indeed, for some, this was true. If they had the power to force a redistribution in their favour of the reduced national resources, there might be compensation. But that could only be achieved, if at all, at the expense of other members of the community. It was a time when a statutory incomes policy might have helped.

No statutory policy

But the new Government had a history. The Wilson Government of the 1960s had operated a statutory prices and incomes policy. It had generated deep resentment among trade union activists. It had fractured relations between the Government and the trade union movement. The Government's exasperation with the trade unions had led to *In Place of Strife* and *In Place of Strife* had led to the humiliation of the Government. Now, if the new Government was committed to anything, it was committed against a statutory incomes policy. This was a commitment that Wilson was determined to respect. There would be no incomes policy, only the orderly growth of incomes, the cant term employed to acknowledge the need for an incomes policy of some kind while calling it by another name.

No determination against wage claims

The Government had committed itself to the abolition of the Pay Board and Pay Code. The question was how the transition from the statutory system of incomes control inherited from Heath could be managed in an atmosphere of accelerating inflation. Despite the Social Contract the Government was faced with inflationary wage demands. How determined would it be, contemplating an early election, in confronting the unions? That it would settle with the miners rapidly, expensively, and outside Phase 3 was expected, and in the circumstances was forgivable. The miners did not, however, prove to be the hoped for exception. Other unions crowded in behind. Civil servants rapidly gained the impression that their political masters were averse to any confrontation with any major union, and they even began to brief in that sense. A permissive incomes policy combined with a permissive fiscal policy brought the nation to the brink in the summer of 1975.

Michael Foot, as Secretary of State for Employment, started with a statutory policy in place in the form of Phase 3. At first it appeared that he had come to appreciate the advantages of continuing, as long as he could, with Phase 3, preferably until he had been able to work out with the TUC an orderly transition to whatever future policy was to be put in place. The abolition of the Pay Board required legislation. Foot told the House on 18 March 1974 that 'The Government intend shortly to introduce legislation to give them power to abolish the Pay Board and the associated statutory pay controls.' But the intention was to exercise the power only 'after discussions with the TUC, the CBI . . . about methods to secure . . . the orderly growth of incomes on a voluntary basis'. Meanwhile the Pay Board would have a continuing statutory duty to enforce the Pay Code, subject only to the power of the Secretary of State to grant consents, in truly exceptional circumstances, to settlements outside the Code.[1]

In order to discuss what consents should be given on particularly urgent wage claims, the Pay Sub-Committee of the Economic Policy Committee (ECP) was constituted. Michael normally presided. Eric Heffer, who was present as a Minister of State at the Department of Industry, decided that the very existence of ECP was contrary to the Social Contract. He said that consent should be given automatically because an incomes policy was intolerable. My interventions in which I argued that it was necessary to maintain some sort of control were popular neither with Heffer nor with Foot. Heffer left and thereafter absented himself permanently from ECP.

Eric need not have been too frightened because gradually the Phase 3 policy was eroded by the many consents that were given. The idea that consents were to be given only in truly exceptional cases was replaced by the politically more convenient idea of 'flexibility'.[2] These flexible consents followed what Foot described as 'sensible agreement after sensible negotiations' between unions and employers.[3] Healey, too, could be on the side of the flexible angels. Barbara Castle reports a discussion on 17 July 1974: 'But it was Denis who once again showed what a shrewd realist he is. "We are embarked," he said, "on a new experiment. Sometimes it is cheaper to the economy to settle." '[4] It was that realism that was leading in the direction of 30 per cent inflation or above. Even when ECP took its courage in both hands, and decided against union demands for increases in pay, an appeal to Cabinet undid what we had done. For the Cabinet, in a continuing pre-election period, flexibility was always the better part of valour.

Michael Foot

I was closely involved with Michael Foot in the management of incomes policy. I was the Treasury hawk sent to stiffen the backbone of the Department of Employment dove. Dove though he was, Foot was too statesmanlike for some of his supporters. He was very annoyed with the Engineers. Their funds had been sequestrated by the National Industrial Relations Court. They had refused to put in an appearance, and had called a national strike instead of awaiting the passage of the Trade Union and Industrial Relations Bill which was to abolish the Court. Denis Skinner came and sat beside Foot on the front bench. Skinner urged Foot not to say anything against this action. The conversation ended with Foot saying to Skinner: 'Yes, Denis, I know that you'll stab me in the back at the first opportunity.' To which Skinner replied: 'Well, Michael, we have to keep you on the straight and narrow.'

Foot's assignment to Employment was seen by many on the left, including Barbara Castle, as a Wilson master stroke. Yet it became a liability. He combined an inability to stand up to the unions, even on minor matters, with an inability to communicate across the class demarcation line of 1970s Britain. It was important to keep both the unions and management in line. But he was unable to resist the first or communicate with the second. He always spoke as to a public meeting, a characteristic shared by another great orator, Gladstone. This was particularly marked where he was forced to attempt communication with the CBI. On 17 June, I joined him at the Department of Employment for a meeting with the CBI. Campbell Adamson and Richard O'Brien represented the CBI. I knew both well. Both had been industrial advisers at the Department of Economic Affairs in my time there. They listed the inflationary dangers which the country faced. They pointed out that Plessey was expecting to have to increase its wages bill by about 21 per cent immediately the Pay Code was abolished. By the time they had met their threshold commitments, it might be 31 per cent.

Foot appeared to regard them as just another Commons audience. Every point had to be taken up and debated. Adamson evidently thought it necessary to impress upon him the seriousness of the position. He interrupted the Foot flow and said: 'We are in a serious position. I think the Government should talk about it, and make it clear repeatedly, not just be contented with an occasional statement.' Foot reacted as though it was an intervention from the Opposition benches. 'Well, it's not as serious as it was during the three day week.' To which Campbell not inappropriately responded that it was perhaps a little infelicitous to compare our present situation with a time when half the country was not working. Foot was obviously about to go off on another debating point. So I intervened quietly: 'I do not think the CBI need think the Government does not regard the situation as serious.' Michael launched into another speech, very defensive in character, saying how much the Government had done. He went on for about ten minutes. Then, to avoid anything else starting, the CBI team quietly withdrew. After they withdrew, Foot turned to me resentfully: 'Well, have you got any further instructions for me?' To which I responded: 'When we pass a rate of inflation of 30%, you can expect some instructions.'

Guidance to the public sector

At a meeting of the main Economic Committee on 16 July with Denis Healey in the chair, the principal business was a draft paper from Foot containing guidance to the public sector on wage claims. The intention was that the public sector should keep in line with the TUC guide-lines under the Social Contract, that is that wage increases should be limited to the amounts necessary to compensate for price increases in the previous year. That the Government had given such guidance to the public sector was to be kept secret. It would offend the TUC if they knew that the Government was basing its guidance to the public sector on the TUC guide-lines. It would be thought to be a first step towards a new incomes policy. I expressed doubt about the wisdom of secrecy. It would be expected that the Government should give guidance to the public sector. There was danger of considerable embarrassment when the document leaked if we had pretended that we had not given such guidance. Denis Healey, in his summing up, said that we were still at the draft stage. At that stage there was no intention of handing the document over to the nationalized industries and other elements in the public sector. However, although the document was to be kept a secret for the time being, we would reconsider the question in the autumn.

Breakdown

On 18 July, in the Lobby, when we were voting on the abolition of the Pay Board, Shirley Williams came up to me and said that she had just been at a dissolution dinner with the Pay Board. She had asked them what they foresaw for the next six months. They had replied that they foresaw a rate of inflation of 26 per cent, and their resurrection, or the resurrection of some similar body.

Just before the House rose for the summer recess, Treasury officials sent me a paper which indicated extreme alarm about the size of claims and the already threatened breakdown in the Social Contract. The Pay Board had been abolished only about a week before. But observance of the TUC guide-lines was rapidly crumbling. There did not seem to be any major case in which a settlement within the TUC guide-lines was likely. Denis, however, had only just introduced his counter-inflationary July measures. That should see us through for the moment. The summer recess was upon us and a general election was certain to follow. However serious the situation, further action must wait.

Notes

1. HC Debs., 18 Mar. 1974, cols. 694–5.
2. HC Debs., 18 July 1974, col. 697.
3. HC Debs., 18 July 1974, col. 708.
4. Castle 147.

Part III

The Mandarins

T·E·N

A Problematic Victory

It is better to win general elections than to lose them, whatever the responsibilities that follow. In this case the responsibilities were rather heavy. Carrying them was not made easier by the narrowness of the victory. Labour with 319 seats now had a majority over all the other parties with 316. But a majority so small could be lost in just a few by-elections. That could spell defeat, and the premature end of its term, well before the constitutional limit on the life of the new Parliament. The Speaker, Selwyn Lloyd, reminded me: 'Do you remember your guess as to the number of seats the Labour Party would win in this Election?' I remembered guessing 320. He said: 'Yes, 320. You were not far out. I hope your conduct of the nation's economic affairs is as accurate.'

The November Budget

On 25 October an enormous assembly met in Denis's room at the Treasury to constitute our first Budget Committee meeting on the November Budget. The situation looked pretty unpleasant. We now faced the prospect of a PSBR so large as to deny us the right to make debating points out of Anthony Barber's profligacy. We were contemplating the grave danger that our own economic policies would generate further inflationary pressure and must eventually undermine confidence in sterling. Denis asked what would be the principal presentational problems of the Budget. I replied that the principal problem would be its inflationary consequences.

On 30 October we had another meeting of the Budget Committee. The situation seemed inescapably dreadful. Among those to express alarm was Nicky Kaldor. He was in favour of action to help the company sector. But the inevitable consequence for the PSBR implied for him serious problems with the balance of payments as well as higher inflation.[1] For once even Nicky had no answer. All this re-emphasized how ill advised had been the July measures. It would have been too much to expect Denis to admit this, and he might even have argued that the narrowness of the Government's overall majority proved that something had been necessary in July politically, even if it had been questionable economically.

The market was waiting to see what Healey would do because he had indicated a clear intention to reflate to some extent. Denis believed that what he was intending to do would leave him just on the right side of a confidence break. But it was a risky calculation. Some of the figures we were looking at, if published in the usual way at the time of the 12 November Budget, could have a damaging effect on confidence. For example, forecasts showed imports rising at the rate of 8 per cent and exports rising at the rate of 4 per cent. He would have to announce an increase in the estimate of the PSBR for 1974/5 from the £2.7 billion he had stated as his objective in March to £6.3 billion. But he was now facing an estimate that in 1975/6 the PSBR would be £8.5 billion and domestic credit expansion over £10 billion. It would be a public relations gift to the monetarists.

It was suggested that perhaps Healey could present the new figures in the context of a four-year strategy which would get the economy into better balance. But any such presentation would be cynically received when the first of the four years was moving dramatically in the wrong direction. The alternative was to leave that piece of bad news until April when the estimates might be firmer than they could be in November. Meanwhile he would say to the House:

What matters is that a public sector deficit should not be allowed to become so large that its very existence causes a pressure on resources, a further deterioration in our balance of payments and a disproportionate increase in the money supply. I see no reason why the public sector deficit this year should involve any of these consequences.[2]

It was decided to cut the published forecast off at mid-1975, the date to which it would have reached if we had provided a normal forward forecast the previous March. This decision eliminated the line in one table which showed those worrying figures of export and import growth. As published, the figures displayed a better balance between the growth of exports and imports. Apart from the political arguments for concealment, there was an argument of substance. If the publication of bad figures causes the crisis that policy is trying to avoid, there may be justification in concealment. This would be especially true if, as in 1974, the world had been turned upside down and the basis of forecasts was even more questionable than usual. However such justifications, if available at all, are so only if policy is in fact directed to curing the ills foreseen. They are not available if policy is simply based on the hope that the ills will not occur.

The large PSBR had contradictory social effects. It had to be funded and that involved giving favours to top rate taxpayers. I held a meeting to discuss how to replace the 1965–75 3 per cent savings bond issue which was maturing. The Bank of England pressed strongly that there should be a new Treasury 3 per cent or thereabouts issue at a low price, attractive to high taxpayers. They pointed to the very large 1975/6 borrowing requirement, and insisted that this tax incentive was necessary if we were to have any hope of holding the money invested in the maturing savings bond. An Inland Revenue official complained that this amounted to legalized tax avoidance. He challenged me: 'How can you condemn tax avoidance when the Government itself is launching stocks which make this possible?' I listened sadly and agreed that we should go ahead.

My relations with Denis continued difficult. In private discussion, or with ministerial colleagues, he would portray himself as the great activist extending the scope of economic policy, and me as the great inactivist, a devotee of orthodoxy, or what would have been orthodoxy in any Treasury but this. I would reply that it did not seem to me that activity in itself was very useful when it was along lines that had already failed. But he did listen. On 7 November there occurred one of our regular Treasury Ministers' lunches. I argued that, even at this late stage in preparing his November Budget, he should put up excise duties and that he should increase income tax from April. Healey reacted by condemning my approach to economic policy. It was, he said, the approach of the right wing Tories. It would cause very heavy unemployment. I responded that the way we were going was bringing higher and higher unemployment.

He demanded: 'What is the evidence that the balance of the economy, the movement of resources into exports, would be assisted by your method?' I said I had no evidence but it nevertheless seemed to me probable that it would, and that the course that he was following was intolerably risky. Apart from the effect of what I was proposing on employment, he did not want to do anything that he did not have to do that would force up the price level. Against this, I argued that it was far more sensible to be realistic about the tax implications of the level of public expenditure. There was no comfort in the illusion that we had done little, by government action, to push up the price level. After all he himself had decided to bring realism to nationalized industry pricing, and the nationalized industries were going to be in surplus again. Eventually he did agree to look into the possibility of increasing excise duties but he then discovered that it was already too late for this Budget. The action I had recommended followed in April.

Company liquidity and the Price Code

Treasury Ministers now had to solve the problem of corporate liquidity which we had mishandled in the March 1974 Budget. The CBI was warning urgently that depleted company liquidity would result in cuts in investment, in unemployment, and in bankruptcies. One possibility, long discussed, was to relax the Price Code. Another, recommended by Nicky Kaldor, was through the tax system. We should help the liquidity of the corporate sector by reducing the tax levy on stock appreciation in excess of a certain percentage of trading profits. He had calculated that if the threshold was put at 10 per cent, the relief would amount in 1975/6 to £1.2 billion.[3] The difficulty was that this was bound to add substantially to the public sector financial deficit unless there were drastic and, for the moment, politically impossible cuts in public expenditure. This was the central dilemma and there seemed no way out of it.

The Price Code was, in the view of the Treasury, a major cause of industry's liquidity problems because the so-called 'productivity deduction' produced a very severe and rapid erosion of profits. The productivity deduction stood at 50 per cent which meant that only half of any wage increase could be passed on in prices, subject to a profit floor. The theory was that the balance of the 50 per cent should be absorbed in increased productivity. But, in that era of severe inflation and slow productivity growth, that was a forlorn hope. The productivity deduction had been introduced at the level of 50 per cent at a time when the rate of inflation was very much lower and the growth of the economy was very much faster. It had been calculated that a 10 per cent productivity deduction would, at the end of 1974, achieve the same impact as a 50 per cent productivity deduction had in 1972. Consideration of the Price Code absorbed enormous amounts of ministerial time in meeting after meeting. The tedium of managing a prices and incomes policy is a strong deterrent to embarking on one.

It was claimed that the Price Code encouraged employers to withstand wage claims. For this reason Shirley Williams was reluctant to abolish it altogether though willing to consider a relaxation of the restraint exercised by the productivity deduction. Denis Healey himself felt that it would be a mistake to reduce the productivity deduction to less than 20 per cent. This would mean that 80 per cent of wage increases could be passed on in prices but at least some control of prices would remain in being. Michael Foot considered that the TUC would be highly incensed by the abolition of the productivity deduction. It would appear too much like abolishing price control altogether. It would therefore be damaging to the Social Contract which was all the Government had by way of a counter-inflationary policy. That did not mean that the TUC was prepared to do anything effective to encourage productivity, such as the abandonment of restrictive practices. The TUC took the view it did even though a very drastic erosion of company profits was likely to lead to a severe fall in investment and employment, and the TUC was supposedly concerned about unemployment and about the lack of investment.

Decision was complicated by conflicting academic arguments that variously confirmed or denied that the Price Code was having the damaging effect attributed to it. Indeed, the information as to the actual impact of the Price Code was very uncertain. Nobody knew exactly what was its impact on firms, or what additional money would come to them if the productivity deduction was reduced, or how it was affecting one firm as against another, except that it had a bigger impact on labour-intensive firms than on capital-intensive firms. Nobody really knew whether competition would keep prices down even if the productivity deduction was relaxed.

There was then the question how much assistance the Chancellor should give to companies by means of Price Code relaxations, and how much by tax allowances on stock appreciation. My own view was to do more by way of Price Code relaxation and less by way of stock appreciation. Stock appreciation added to the Public Sector Borrowing

Requirement which was already high. Although Price Code relaxation affected the RPI, I was against allowing budgetary and economic policy to be totally determined by that fact. I also observed that price increases would have a negative demand effect which was not unimportant. Official advice to Healey was that he should do relatively less by way of Price Code relaxation in order to avoid too much of an increase in the RPI and relatively more in the form of stock appreciation despite the resulting increase in the PSBR. In the end Denis proposed in his November Budget to improve company profitability by £800 million through Price Code relaxations, and company liquidity by £800 million by means of the stock appreciation scheme.

Oil borrowing

On 21 October Tommy Balogh came to me on a mysterious errand the purpose of which he had refused to state in advance. He said that he had received notification that some people in Saudi Arabia, though not necessarily the Government, were thinking in terms of a 15 million ton a year oil loan to the United Kingdom which would continue over a period of five years, or even six years, from the beginning of 1975 to the end of 1980. The idea was that the loan would in due course be repaid at interest in royalty oil from the North Sea.

Balogh said he had discussed this idea with Nicky Kaldor, and they had assessed the pros and cons. They had come to the conclusion that the rate of interest must not be more than 4 per cent. It also depended on three particular considerations. First, what would happen to the price of oil? It would obviously be advantageous if the price of oil was going to fall because we would be repaying the Saudis in oil of a lower value than the oil we borrowed. The second consideration was the effect on our financial borrowing. Balogh said that he did not believe our borrowing capacity in Euro-dollars, or elsewhere in the world, was unlimited. It would be a major gain if the very considerable value of 15 million tons per annum of oil was taken off our national borrowing requirement. The third consideration, he said, was whether it would be easier to default on a money debt or an oil debt. He had come to the conclusion that it would if necessary be easier to default on oil debts.

There was a feeling among some of the more sophisticated members of the Government that, inevitably, the UK would be compelled to default on its borrowings. In putting forward this proposal, Balogh was influenced by his view that it would be easier to default in oil than in money. Without accepting the presumption of default, I agreed that the Treasury would consider this proposal which might well have more presentable attractions. I would then discuss it with Balogh with a view to making some report to Denis Healey. However, leaving aside the risks and the sophisticated financial calculations that would have to be made, it did seem to me undesirable to evince interest while there remained uncertainty on the question whether in fact Saudi Arabia was prepared to lend oil to the UK.

Treasury consideration of Balogh's oil borrowing scheme rapidly concluded that it was unlikely to be in the country's interests, even on the basis of assumptions more favourable to it than those posited in the papers prepared. A rate of interest of 6 per cent had been assumed and that had to be compared with what, at the time, was a negative rate of interest on money borrowing. The calculations were favourable only on the assumption of a low rate of oil interest. Even if a positive rate of interest was assumed on money borrowing, any attraction was doubtful. And there were wider considerations against it. First, it would be politically embarrassing in Scotland to make a direct pledge of North Sea oil against oil to be provided by Saudi Arabia in the period 1975–80. Secondly, it might endanger our whole borrowing programme if it was seen that certain lenders were getting specific pledges of North Sea oil. Lenders of money might begin themselves to ask for specific pledges of North Sea oil as collateral. We concluded that we did not want to put ourselves in the position of asking for such a loan.

In December, Healey visited Saudi Arabia. He wanted to hear about Balogh's oil borrowing scheme. Tommy returned to his theme that the most important question was to decide in what currency, oil or money, and indeed in what money, it would be better to default. He argued that a default on Euro-market borrowing would throw the whole system into chaos, whereas a default on a direct loan from an Arab government would not matter very much. He was absolutely sure that the day would come when the UK did default because of the enormous load of borrowing which was accumulating. We would not refuse to pay. We would reschedule our debts just like Chile and other countries, on agreed terms.

During Healey's visit to Saudi Arabia, the subject of oil borrowing was not raised. The UK Government did not borrow Saudi oil. Nor did it default.[4]

Competitiveness

In discussions at the end of October, there was concern about the deteriorating competitiveness of the UK economy at a time when the current account was heavily in deficit. There was a feeling that the exchange rate should be allowed to decline gently over the year. Harold Lever was opposed to fiddling around with exchange rates, an attitude with which in principle I had some sympathy though it seemed to me pointless equally to allow the British economy to become once more totally uncompetitive. I did, however, react when Harold Lever described depreciation as a soft option. I commented that I was entirely with him in opposing soft options but that the important soft options to avoid were the domestic soft options, and that he was the continuing advocate of domestic soft options. One senior official said: 'I would have warned more strongly but for the fact that I regard this depreciation as inevitable anyhow. The real question is whether it happens gradually as we want, or catastrophically as we do not want.' Prospects for sterling were, by December, being affected by a demand from Saudi Arabia that oil companies should pay their royalties in dollars.

Nicky Kaldor, who had once been the archpriest of devaluation, was now its strongest opponent. But never lacking a device, he had long advocated a wage subsidy. He discussed this proposal with Treasury officials, but they recommended against it. When, therefore, we came to consider a wage subsidy as an alternative to depreciation, Denis turned to Nicky and said: 'I suppose that you are against this recommendation?' And Nicky, with an angelic smile, replied that he did not intend to press the idea on Denis for this Budget or indeed for the spring Budget. He would, however, feel free to come back to it in due course. Apparently Nicky had been argued out of one of his panaceas.

Notes

1. See Chap. 11 for Kaldor's views on the relationship between the PSBR and the balance of payments.
2. HC Debs., 12 Nov. 1974, cols. 279–80.
3. Thirlwall 254.
4. An oil deal was agreed in 1973 between the shah of Iran and the Heath Government. It was a very different kind of deal from that proposed by Balogh but the fact that it had happened may have given additional interest to this further proposal. Part 165.

E·L·E·V·E·N

The Mandarins Revolt

By the end of 1974, events had impressed on the Co-ordinating Committee of Treasury Permanent Secretaries their responsibility to give firm advice to the Chancellor. A minute was prepared and sent to the Chancellor copied only to the Governor of the Bank of England. I discovered this outbreak of mandarin determination through what may be described as my usual channels. There had always been some senior officials in the Treasury who agreed with the views I had now, for nine months, been putting to the Chancellor. No doubt it would have been embarrassing to copy to me officially the memorandum conveying the Co-ordinating Committee's views. But I was aware of its existence almost at once and, within a few days, a copy was in my hands.

It was not before time. The UK was living 5–6 per cent above its earnings.[1] The PSBR had ballooned well nigh out of sight though some Keynesians were still providing convenient comfort by arguing that a high PSBR could be regarded as compensating in demand terms for the unusually high level of savings which followed, and paradoxically might have been caused by, the high level of inflation. During 1974 there had been a massive deficit in the current account of the balance of payments. There had been some shift of resources into the balance of payments. The volume of exports had risen by 7 per cent and the volume of imports only by 1 per cent. The net surplus on invisible account of £1.4 billion was £250 million above the 1973 level.[2] But these movements had been dwarfed by the unfavourable effects resulting from the more than fourfold increase in the price of oil. There had begun to be serious worries about whether the UK's 1975 balance of payments deficit could be financed.[3] This was a concern shared in private sector financial institutions which were warning that it might well not be possible for the

UK to borrow anything like as freely in 1975 as it had in 1974. The concern had been reinforced by the shock to international confidence constituted by the Burmah Oil débâcle at the beginning of 1975.[4]

The memorandum to the Chancellor said that current policies were unworkable. There was no longer any support for them at official level in the Treasury. A change was unavoidable. Officials were very sorry if that meant political difficulties for the Chancellor. To the memorandum there was attached a note which explained the position at rather greater length but unfortunately ended with a proposal from Sir Bryan Hopkin, the new Chief Economic Adviser, for a form of tax on inflation which, it suggested, should be further studied. I read the memorandum with modified satisfaction. I was, however, dismayed by the proposal that we study a tax on inflation. I was doubtful whether it would be workable. I feared it could prove a diversion from the main struggle to change the direction of policy.

The Downing Street Policy Unit under Bernard Donoughue was also made aware, if not of the memorandum itself, then at least of the *démarche* that was being made at the Treasury.

In January Robert Armstrong told me that the Head of the Treasury [Douglas Wass] and the Governor of the Bank of England [Gordon Richardson] had held talks about the looming crisis and concluded that a wage freeze was unavoidable. The Policy Unit at this time submitted a long and gloomy paper to the Prime Minister setting out the harsh realities and choices which faced his Government. We recommended a crisis package including public expenditure cuts to reduce the PSBR, some mixture of import controls or tariffs to help the balance of payments, and a much more vigorous effort to control wage inflation.[5]

I soon learnt Denis's reaction to the Treasury memorandum. He told officials that he would like specific proposals. But they must not constitute a typical deflationary Treasury package. He would only be prepared to follow advice if there were some purposive moves to deflect resources into the balance of payments. The oddity was that a typical Treasury deflationary package would not just be politically unacceptable to the Chancellor. It would also be politically unacceptable to some of the top layer of Treasury officials. The Treasury, they thought, had been weakened in its influence in government, and discredited in the opinion of the public, by its concentration on cutting public expenditure and the PSBR. Senior officials had come to think of this as bad for morale. They wanted to be participants in a more creative approach to economic policy, to win for themselves a brighter, more positive image, to cast aside their dry-as-dust reputation, and to look to the uplands of policy. This had been evident earlier but now re-emerged as a factor influencing policy recommendations. My view was that when Treasury officials begin to fear their traditional role as the defender of the arithmetic of resources, the nation is at risk.

Confronted with this official *démarche*, Denis Healey thought it wise to create the necessary atmosphere of apprehension within the Cabinet in the hope that what he appeared to threaten might turn out to be much worse than what he would eventually have to perform. He warned Cabinet, in my presence, that there might have to be a package, and anyone with any economic sophistication knew what that dreadful word 'package' might imply. I confess to having helped this process, not as a feint but in the hope that members of the Government would begin to appreciate the seriousness of our condition. For example, on 15 January 1975, Shirley asked me why there were all these rumours of impending action. I did not go into any details but I did confirm that action was necessary. She asked: 'Is anyone looking at it from a political point of view?' I replied that the Treasury was certainly thinking up ways of improving the presentation of the package so that it should not just be traditional Treasury deflation. But I gave her some indication how near we had been to action in December when the November trade figures were published, and how fortunate it was that the December figures had been better. I said we could not go on this way. The dangers of a run on sterling were too great.

Denis also warned Treasury Ministers on 23 January 1975 but without speaking of the memorandum that had now been in his possession for over three weeks. He indicated that we would have to have a tough Budget with increases in taxation. In my diary I noted 'the real question is how tough in the end he is going to be'. I found it rather disturbing that he was prepared only to tackle the problem from the angle of increased taxation. He was obviously very unwilling to confront his colleagues with proposals for cuts in public expenditure after they had fought so hard against earlier attempts to limit the increases.

My view was that we could not deal with the situation adequately simply by tax increases. When we first came into government we gave ourselves a target of 2.75 per cent increase in the demand effect of public expenditure per annum. In fact this target was considerably exceeded, we had been far too optimistic about growth, and left no room for any increase in privately financed private consumption. But Healey, who had confirmed the 2.75 per cent stance as recently as in his November Budget, was not willing to go back on it. But in the end he found himself forced to go for some public expenditure cuts to avoid unacceptable increases in taxation in his April Budget.

The deteriorating situation led to renewed discussion in the Treasury of what it would be wise to publish. On 28 January 1975 there was a meeting with Denis Healey and other Treasury Ministers and officials on whether we should publish our internal forecasts on key indicators such as the balance of payments, inflation, and unemployment. Joel Barnett and Bob Sheldon argued very strongly for publication. They showed considerable courage under the withering fire of Denis's assault but it was no good. Denis was not willing to listen to their arguments. He put down a barrage of questions, most of them unanswerable. 'Why should I stimulate people to criticize my policy? Will it not make it all the more difficult to carry through my policy if people know the assumptions on which it is based?' 'Why should I put weapons in my opponents' hands? Politics is a matter of exercising power, not arming your opponent.'

I had to agree with Denis that to publish these figures in our present political situation would make the task of rectifying it very much more difficult. It would lead to an immediate confrontation with a great body of Labour Party opinion. If people saw the estimates of future unemployment there would be a great clamour for a reversal of policy in precisely the wrong direction. Bad as the forecasts were for the current account, a forecast for what was called a 'full employment' current account would have shown it to be unsustainable. But the truth was that the trend of events was becoming so widely understood that there was little point in further concealment. If the Parliamentary Labour Party could not accept the realities, it must lead to the fall of the Government. It was probable that they would prefer to accept. Even *NIER* was at last facing up to this unhappy situation.

Normally, when faced with the prospect of rising unemployment on the scale which we envisage, the prescription would be to administer a fiscal stimulus to private consumption and/or public expenditure. As things stand this avenue is to a large extent blocked.

Nevertheless the *Review* did not go further than to advocate a neutral budget.[6]

A programme for incomes?

The first response from Treasury officials to Denis Healey's request for action proposals was a paper outlining a programme for incomes. The programme embodied varieties of statutory policy, but it was suggested that the objectives could be achieved by a voluntary norm. Forecasts of inflation were now accelerating to the 20–25 per cent range. There was little the UK could do to change the deteriorating world economic conjuncture. However, inflation was, in principle at least, within British control. Yet the Social Contract which had been intended to control inflationary wage demands was having the contrary effect. Settlements were anticipating inflation. Settlements of the order of 20 per cent and more were being justified as consistent with the Social Contract.

The Bank of England was pressing for a statutory incomes policy. In my private meetings with the Bank, I explained that I did not think a statutory incomes policy would be acceptable to the Government, other than perhaps in a position of absolute crisis. Therefore the main pressure must be for increases in taxation and reductions in public expenditure. Within the Bank there was some worry about this because of the implications for unemployment and because of uncertainty whether, without a statutory incomes policy, such a policy would in fact have any effect on inflation. It would be an exaggeration to suggest that within the Bank there was great enthusiasm for the idea of tax increases, particularly of the capital transfer tax type, though, to be fair, this was not just because of self-interest but because of their effect on confidence. At the same time I was briefing David Watt of the *Financial Times*. I told him that it might well be easier politically for the Government to follow a traditional deflationary policy sugared in one way or another than to do anything that implied a statutory incomes policy.[7] I continue the incomes policy story in Chapter 14.

The Treasury's alternative strategy

Treasury officials then provided a further instalment of advice. They were now recommending to the Chancellor a policy of deflation to bring the PSBR down from the expected figure of £10 billion to £8 billion in the next financial year, combined with an import surcharge/export subsidy scheme to alleviate the unemployment consequences. Such a scheme would also have less inflationary effect than an outright devaluation. Thus pressure for import controls was now coming from the official Treasury as well as from the Downing Street Policy Unit and, inevitably, from Nicky Kaldor. I watched all this with interest and apprehension. I agreed entirely with the necessity of bringing the PSBR down. It was the policy for which I had long been arguing. But the import surcharge/export subsidy scheme did not fill me with enthusiasm. Although I was not opposed in principle, it seemed to me a palliative whereas much more fundamental fiscal action was required. Moreover, it would be introduced in April and would probably result in a row with the European Community which would not be helpful shortly before the referendum. In my view, we needed, simply, a typical Treasury deflationary package.

Pressure from Tony Benn for the 'alternative strategy' was now building. At this stage it was known as Strategy B. This strategy had been worked out in the Department of Industry with the help of advisers including Francis Cripps. It was proposed as an alternative to 'Strategy A' which was a policy of heavy deflation. Strategy A was the strategy wrongly attributed by the Left to the Treasury. Strategy B opened up the different perspective of a more managed economy, including rationing and allocation of some imported raw materials. It combined selective import restrictions with a downward float of sterling. That it would have brought the UK into conflict with the European Community was not, for Benn, an objection. It might also, Benn conceded, strain international relations generally and lead to retaliatory measures. It was discussed in the Ministerial Committee on Economic Strategy on 25 February and nudged sideways by the Prime Minister into an official committee.[8]

Briefing Treasury Ministers

At last, on 6 March, Denis Healey brought his Treasury Ministers fully into the picture. He gave us a run-down on the discussions in progress since December, the discussions of which I had had private notice through a sight of the papers. He described the proposals currently before him. He started by asking my view. I said that I agreed with the necessity of reducing the PSBR. If we could not borrow to fund the current account deficit, it would have a devastating impact on the standard of living and would seriously heighten social tensions. That meant that we had to follow policies which would persuade the financial community that we were a good risk. On the other hand, I argued, there were strong arguments for deferring any decision about a surcharge/

subsidy scheme until later in the year, first because of its effect on the European decision, secondly because we certainly would not command international consent, and thirdly because we could not be sure at that stage what the balance of payments out-turn for the year was likely to be.

There was at that stage some uncertainty about the outlook for the current account. Though the estimate for the year was still very bad, we had had two months' good trade figures. It would be very difficult in a year like 1975 with flat or perhaps even falling world trade to impose an export subsidy. It would be vigorously opposed by all the countries whom we would need to persuade if we were to gain international assent. Without international assent, retaliation or the threat of retaliation might force us to withdraw the scheme prematurely. In other words, I supported the deflationary package but left a question mark against the surcharge/subsidy scheme. I followed up this discussion by minuting Denis that the right way of proceeding was to cut the PSBR plus as much as could be done on incomes.

In the afternoon, I happened to meet Denis Healey in the House. He asked me to go into his office and we had a further discussion on the economic situation. He was obviously in a very uncertain frame of mind, complaining as usual that he was not able to get an accurate picture from Treasury officials, that they were continually changing their minds, or changing the emphasis with which they advanced policies. He said that the Prime Minister, if given any choice, would always opt for the most comfortable policy. He referred to the political situation within the Cabinet and said that Harold Lever now thought he had discovered another way of borrowing large sums of money, this time from the American Government. Lever had been to the United States with Wilson. His visit had reinforced his confidence that further borrowing from the Americans was possible, at any rate in an emergency. Lever would therefore be an obstacle to the policies that Denis, tentatively, was prepared to contemplate. Denis did say that it was a great comfort to have Harold Lever available because he understood the City, but I began to think that he was beginning to understand that as an adviser on economic policy Lever's was a siren voice.

Nicky Kaldor

It was at this point that Nicky Kaldor decided that he might be able to persuade me to constitute myself a channel into Denis Healey's mind for his ideas on economic policy. At his request, he came to share a sandwich lunch with me on 16 January 1975. I had great respect for the Kaldor intellect. But our relations had not always been happy. I had first come to know him because my brother Sidney was a close friend and admirer. I had won Kaldor's approval, shortly after my election to Parliament in 1964, by being one of the few defenders of Callaghan's new corporation tax. My approval rating on the Kaldor index moved into a negative phase when, at the Board of Trade in 1969, I was, in his view, responsible for ending one of the regional employment subsidies he had earlier persuaded the Government to introduce.[9] We were still corresponding angrily about that even after the demise of that Wilson Government. He knew me to be, in the new Wilson Government, no friend of his equalizing tax proposals which appeared to me extreme and damaging to the economy.

But now we were concerned with greater issues. We both knew that we could not go on as we were, that there were likely to be problems in financing the current account deficit, and that the influence of Harold Lever on Harold Wilson and Denis Healey had proved disastrous. Nicky wanted our meetings to be private. He asked me particularly not to mention him in any minute I sent to Denis. The reason, no doubt, was that he was himself bombarding Denis with minutes and he did not want to appear as the ghost in my machine. The minutes with which he was bombarding Denis, and the message that he now brought to me, derived from a theory due to Kaldor.

Although Wynne Godley and Francis Cripps became the chief protagonists of the New Cambridge doctrine that the deficit on the balance of payments was the mirror image of the government's budget deficit, the idea seems to have emerged from Kaldor's brain. Later he himself became sceptical of the relationship, but at this stage he was still sufficiently convinced of it strongly to urge a cut in the budget deficit.[10] The problem was that a cut in the budget deficit would increase unemployment. He was opposed to a depreciation in the exchange rate. It would stimulate inflation. Therefore he wanted to deal with the unemployment consequences of a cut in the deficit by means of import controls.[11]

At that stage all that had emanated from Treasury officials by way of an answer to Denis's demand for a policy were their proposals about incomes. Kaldor began by saying that little could be achieved by incomes policy. The first necessity was to raise taxes and cut expenditure.[12] We could hope that, if the borrowing requirement was brought down, this would over time have an effect on inflation. What Kaldor had proposed regarding the PSBR was exactly my policy. Such a policy was regarded in some circles as 'monetarism'. It was not a good thing to be a Labour Minister and a monetarist. There was something unappetizing about both the idea and the word. The unpopularity of monetarism in the ranks of Labour did not actually cause me any spiritual difficulties. I was no more a monetarist than was Nicky Kaldor.[13] I have always been a sceptic about over-arching economic theories. Where Kaldor and I disagreed was on import controls and on the need for an effective incomes policy. But at least there was important agreement on what I saw as the first essential, a substantial cut in the PSBR.

We did not meet again privately for some weeks. In February the Cambridge Economic Policy Group associated with Wynne Godley and Nicky Kaldor published a report advocating import controls. The idea of import controls was also gaining wider academic support. The *NIER* was reminding the British public that there was a case 'for urging greater international acceptance of the principle of direct import control as part of a generally agreed balance of payments adjustment process'.[14] Similar ideas were emerging from Labour Party headquarters. Denis said that it was disturbing how close their analysis was to the Treasury analysis. At a meeting of the Council of Ministers on 17 February, following the publication of the CEPG report, I assured my European colleagues that the British Government had no intention of introducing import controls. This was perhaps forgivable as I had not at that time been officially informed of the Treasury's thinking on our economic dilemmas. In any case, it turned out that I was right.

My next private meeting with Kaldor took place after the whole Treasury plan for economic policy had been placed on the table. He had heard that the reception by Treasury Ministers for the Treasury package had been less than enthusiastic. He gave me a long lecture on the dangers of our situation, and on the necessity for taking action on the PSBR. He was opposed to devaluation because of its inflationary consequences. He then strongly recommended the subsidy/surcharge package although he said he himself would have preferred a dual exchange rate system which would achieve the same result.[15] It was obvious that he was the man behind the subsidy/surcharge scheme. Treasury officials had been searching for something with the necessary political appeal, and had found it in Nicky's idea of a dual exchange rate. But when the Bank of

England said that it could not operate a dual exchange rate, or it did not want to operate one, the alternative of a surcharge/subsidy scheme had been dragged forward.

I told Nicky that he was under some misapprehension. It was not I who had advocated devaluation. That proposal had come from Bob Sheldon, Joel Barnett, and John Gilbert. I was certainly not opposed to the deflationary package and the attack on the PSBR. On the contrary that was the case I had been arguing all the previous year. I had opposed the July measures, as indeed had he. The only question was whether it was sensible to introduce the surcharge/subsidy scheme now. I made to him the same points against it that I had put to Denis. But I said that if Denis said to me that the only circumstances in which he would be prepared to introduce an adequate deflationary package would be if accompanied by the surcharge/subsidy scheme, I would go along with it.

I seemed actually to shake Nicky Kaldor on the timing of his surcharge/subsidy proposal. He went so far as to confess that there might be advantages in deferring it. The attraction of introducing it at the time of the Budget was political. Denis would be able to demonstrate that he was not simply playing the old Treasury hand but was also doing something positive about the likely unemployment effects of the deflationary package. Actually the figures provided by officials as to the unemployment effect of the deflationary package were not worrying. Equally the figures showed that in the following eighteen months there was likely to be very little balance of payments effect either. In other words the effect over the period with which we were primarily concerned, that is the period up to the time in 1976 when it was expected world trade would begin to show an upturn, was small. True, there was reason for scepticism about these figures and Kaldor showed scepticism. But they did provide some support for the argument that one could reasonably wait to see whether in fact it would be necessary to implement such a scheme.

On 11 March, Nicky Kaldor came to my office for another chat before the meeting in the afternoon on economic strategy. He recounted discussions he had had with Joel Barnett, Bob Sheldon, and John Gilbert, who, he said, were not economists. He repeated how bad the devaluation option would be. He pressed me to make it clear to Denis that he had the choice now between being a great Chancellor and possible Prime Minister on the one hand, and being a complete flop and being driven out of office on the other. He insisted: 'I cannot say those things to Denis. You can say them so you say them.'

He had also been taken by the idea that the sensible approach would be to press for the deflationary package but delay the surcharge/subsidy package. He had been influenced not just by my arguments but by the opposition of the pro-Marketeers in the Cabinet, who apparently had heard some whisper of this idea, probably as a result of his lobbying. They saw that, if it came during the referendum campaign, the European Commission was bound to speak badly of it, and that might influence the result. Kaldor added that when Denis had spoken to the Prime Minister the previous Friday morning, Wilson had said that import surcharges were unthinkable. He was taking the same view of import surcharges as he had in his previous government about devaluation. So, for these reasons, Nicky was inclined to my idea of a deferment, at least until after the referendum.

But do they really mean it?

Thus, by mid-March 1975, Treasury mandarins had at last faced their responsibilities. With the help of Nicky Kaldor they had placed before the Chancellor their preferred options for policy. I watched and wondered. How firmly did the mandarins believe in what they had proposed? How hard would they fight for it? Would their package prove acceptable to the Chancellor and could he carry it politically in Cabinet? Was this the crunch or just a hiccup on the road to disaster?

Notes

1. According to Healey. Benn 325.
2. HC Debs., 17 Apr. 1975, col. 687.
3. Healey recognized this in his Budget speech. HC Debs., 15 Apr. 1975, col. 274.
4. The Burmah Oil Company was rescued by the Government to avoid a default by Burmah on its borrowings in the USA which could have seriously damaged sterling.
5. Donoughue 61.
6. *NIER* (Feb. 1975), 5, 7.
7. See the *Financial Times*, 3 Jan. 1975, article by David Watt.
8. Benn 324–6.
9. Selective employment additional payments in the development areas. See HC Debs., 25 June 1969, col. 1507.
10. The influence of the public sector deficit on the balance of payments is discussed in *NIER* (May 1973), 20–4. Reference is made to a leading article in *The Times* of 28 Feb. 1973, and a letter by Kaldor published 30 Mar. 1973.
11. Thirlwall 251.

12. 'Kaldor continually argued for increases in indirect taxes to reduce the size of the PSBR further and for the reintroduction of the selective employment tax.' Thirlwall 253.
13. In a speech to a Conference on Business Strategies for Inflation, 16 Apr. 1975, I argued: 'If, as I believe, the source of inflation is political, that it lies in competition for resources, it begs the question to proclaim control of the money supply as the answer. For to control the money supply effectively Government must have power to resist inflationary pressures demanding the relaxation of that control.'
14. *NIER* (Feb. 1975), 6.
15. Kaldor had various ideas for the control of imports. Some of them were put forward under the code name 'Delve Exercise'. They are listed in Thirlwall 252.

T·W·E·L·V·E

The Mandarins Retreat

During the last three weeks of March 1975 the Budget Committee seemed in almost permanent session, meeting for long hours to resolve problems which were politically intractable as well as economically controversial. My diary records seven full meetings in addition to which there were many smaller meetings, formal and informal. Despite all the problems, Denis was in tremendous form. Meetings at which no decisions were required but at which the ground was being cleared were conducted in his Socratic manner, asking questions then shooting down the answers. But good humour could turn sour when he felt he was not being well served. He was always very angry when estimates changed, particularly when the estimate of the PSBR changed. Ever since his March 1974 Budget he had been very alert to and critical of Treasury forecasting.

On 11 March our meeting on Budget strategy lasted nearly four hours. Denis began by saying that I had recommended to him deferment of the surcharge/subsidy scheme. He was greatly attracted to deferment. I wondered whether the reason was that the Prime Minister had told him he would not have an import surcharge at any price. Denis continued that he was worried about the inflationary effect of the package. The proposal was substantially to increase indirect taxation with an effect on the RPI of perhaps 4 or 5 per cent. This could bring the rate of inflation well nigh up to 30 per cent. Denis thought that, at that level, the economy would run totally out of control. For that reason, he felt that the forecast that thereafter the rate of inflation would fall fast lacked credibility. He accepted the idea that something had to be done about the PSBR for general confidence reasons, but he wanted a package which had less direct effect on the RPI. He asked for work to go forward on a

£1.5 or £1.6 billion package including a 2p increase in the rate of income tax, no valorization of allowances, and increases in indirect taxes with no more than a 3 per cent impact on the RPI.

Sir Bryan Hopkin, the Chief Economic Adviser, wanted a neutral Budget. He did not approve of the surcharge/subsidy scheme, and believed that an inflation tax might work if ingenuity could produce a scheme clever enough. He said that, if the surcharge/subsidy scheme was to be deferred, he hoped Denis would keep in mind the possibility of a package with smaller deflationary effect than the papers proposed. Hopkin's attitudes attracted strong criticism from Kaldor who felt that he was far too complacent about the size both of the PSBR and of the current account deficit.[1] But Denis replied that indeed he would bear in mind the possibility of a neutral budget particularly in view of the inflationary effect of any tax increases. After all, money was flowing into London and there had been a remission in the adverse news regarding the current account. He said: 'My impression is that all that is really expected from us is a neutral Budget. I see no reason to flay ourselves for its own sake.'

The next day, Wednesday 12 March, I provided lunch in my room at the Treasury for the other Treasury Ministers. Denis said that he was in a very strong position in the Cabinet because a threat of resignation would be enough to decide things in his favour. He thought the Prime Minister accepted that and would support anything he decided. He said that he had discussed the surcharge/subsidy scheme with Wilson. The Prime Minister had simply said that Denis should do what he thought right. This was directly contrary to the message that Nicky had conveyed. Nevertheless, Denis was not keen on the proposal. It was an enormous departure from the gospel he had been preaching around the world for the previous twelve months. When I put that point to him he said: 'Yes, but if we are going to change policy we might as well change policy.'

On 17 March, our meeting went on for three and a quarter hours. It was still accepted there would have to be a deflationary package. The main discussion concerned its size and what direct action should be taken, if any, on the current account. If there was to be direct action on the current account, the options were between a surcharge/subsidy scheme and a step devaluation of perhaps 20 per cent. I strongly advocated a heavy deflationary package but opposed both the step devaluation and the surcharge/subsidy proposal. Bob and Joel wanted a step devaluation. Nicky Kaldor preferred a two-tier exchange rate, but if that was to be denied, then he wanted the surcharge/subsidy scheme. The official Treasury followed Nicky close behind.

Towards the end of the meeting Denis went round the table and found that many Treasury officials below the top level, Deputy Secretaries and Under Secretaries, were in favour of postponing direct action on the balance of payments but supported deflationary action to reduce the PSBR. Everyone was influenced by the happier international environment and by an apparent improvement in the balance of payments during the first quarter of 1975. Germany had introduced its major reform in personal taxation. In the USA personal tax rebates had been designed to give a quick stimulus to demand. France and Japan had also taken moderately helpful action. During 1974 the UK had suffered a record current account deficit of about £3.6 billion, or more than 5 per cent of GNP. During the first quarter of 1975, the deficit was running at an annual rate of £1.25 billion. It was uncertain how far this improvement could be relied on owing to the erratic monthly figures and the effect of the London dock strike in March 1975. But an improvement is an improvement and the problem of the current account did seem less urgent whereas the problem of inflationary wage demands had become increasingly urgent.

By the end of the meeting Denis was ready to rule out the surcharge/subsidy scheme. But at the last minute he was told that if he ruled it out then, he would close the option for Budget Day. If he let the work continue he could keep the option open and still abort it at any time. On that ground, Denis agreed that preparation for the surcharge/subsidy scheme should continue.

It was already clear that the official Treasury had lost enthusiasm for the official Treasury strategy. The point was made explicitly by some senior Treasury officials that they had advanced the Kaldor scheme because they did not want the Treasury once more to be associated with a typical deflationary package. I commented that among all the political considerations that seemed relevant to these decisions, the defence of the Treasury's reputation was the least. The Treasury's reputation, it seemed to me, was more readily lost by weak leadership than by taking appropriate action to get the bloated PSBR under control.

On 24 March, we had a further meeting on the Budget. Denis decided to increase income tax by 2p. There was also a discussion on what increase there should be in indirect taxes. We had had a meeting on 24

January 1975 on whether we should introduce multiple rates for VAT. The previous November, a special rate of 25 per cent VAT on petrol had been introduced. The question now was whether a wider range of goods should be made subject to this higher rate of VAT. Joel and Bob had opposed and John Gilbert and I had supported provided it was done in a very limited way for products which were unquestionably luxuries. Denis Healey had come down on our side. So there was to be a new VAT rate for luxuries.

Officials now brought forward proposals for a 25 per cent rate on a narrow range of goods though extending well beyond luxuries. It was hoped that by keeping it to a narrow range the vast majority of shopkeepers would not have to deal with the higher rate. Bob Sheldon, who had taken over responsibility for Customs and Excise, attacked the idea of a multi-rate VAT. He argued for a single 10 per cent rate. He pointed out that the effect of returning the 8 per cent rate to 10 per cent would be, in RPI terms and in financial terms, not too dissimilar from the multi-rate VAT provisions that had been suggested. I supported him. Although I had earlier been prepared to have a multi-rate VAT, that had been on the assumption that, in addition, the intention would be to return the standard rate to 10 per cent. In other words the multi-rate VAT was to be part of a reasonably sized indirect taxes package. Denis was, understandably, against that because of the effect on the RPI. But he nevertheless wanted a multi-rate VAT. The TUC had been advocating a multi-rate VAT, although not at anything like the 25 per cent level, nor on so very narrow a range of goods. Denis always thought it politically worthwhile to be able to claim that he had been influenced by TUC ideas even where the influence was obscure.

I then went to dinner at No. 10 with the Prime Minister, the Governor of the Bank, and a bevy of worthies from the City and industry. We had a general discussion on economic policy. The Prime Minister responded with vast autobiographical sketches to every point put to him. He attacked the press. He took exception whenever anyone referred approvingly to speeches made, for example, by Denis Healey on the subject of inflation. He emphasized that he, too, had been making speeches on the subject of inflation. These, apparently, the press had not reported for some malevolent reason or other, such as that Reg Prentice had made a very bad speech on the same subject at the same time thus robbing the Prime Minister of his headlines. At 10 o'clock the Prime Minister and I drove to the House for the vote. As we were turning into

New Palace Yard he recalled the recent ruling of the Serjeant at Arms that Members of Parliament had precedence over journalists in queuing for taxis. This decision gained his hearty approval. He evidently wished me to have no doubt regarding his detestation of the press.

After this dinner Gordon Richardson and I had a long heart-to-heart chat. Gordon Richardson was in favour of a larger package of £2 billion, as indeed was I. He was also against a step depreciation which he said would not work, would be found intolerable by the main industrial countries, and would tend to break up the international financial system. He said: 'Everyone now admits that you are the best Government that we can hope to have at the moment. Why are you doing so many silly things?' He insisted: 'The NEB will do no good at all. The community land scheme is no good at all.' I commented on the odd behaviour of the Treasury. Proposals, such as the surcharge/subsidy scheme, were proposed with great enthusiasm. Yet, under consideration and cross-examination, the enthusiasm evaporated. We exchanged our various grievances until about half past midnight. Then off he went in his Rolls Royce, and off I went in my Wolseley, home.

On 25 March Nicky Kaldor and I had a long discussion. He was at last persuaded that the surcharge/subsidy scheme was not going to run in this Budget. It was not just my bad influence. Denis would not have it. We agreed that our principal joint objective should be a substantial deflationary package. When he left my office he said: 'There is not all that much difference between us.' Whether we would get what we wanted was a different matter. Denis was returning to the view that if there was nothing to be done by way of direct action on the balance of payments, he would not go too far in increases in taxation.

At 2.30 we began a further meeting of the Budget Committee at which all these options were once more discussed. There was a sharp exchange between Bob Sheldon and the Governor. Bob Sheldon advocated a 20 per cent step devaluation and the Governor said: '20% step devaluation is simply ruled out. It is impossible.' Bob Sheldon said: 'Why?' The Governor replied: 'Because everyone will immediately ask what those lunatics are going to do next.' However, there was serious consideration of whether there should be a 10 per cent step devaluation. Nicky Kaldor was one of the most articulate opponents of any such idea. For once there was a love match between the Governor and Kit McMahon of the Bank of England, on the one hand, and Nicky on the other. It was a delight to see the two central bankers chuntering their approval of

Nicky's highly articulate defence of the international financial system which, he argued, would be imperilled by any such move.

By about half past four Denis had definitely ruled out both the surcharge/subsidy scheme and the step devaluation. All the tons of paper produced over the previous three months on a dual exchange rate, a surcharge/subsidy scheme, a step devaluation, all were cast aside, put on the shelf, there to gather dust, perhaps for ever, perhaps just until after the referendum. We were back with a traditional Treasury deflationary package but Denis was rapidly nibbling away at that too because he could not deflect the expected hostility of his back-benchers by offering anything direct on the balance of payments. The brave initiative of Treasury officials the previous December had at last died. All we were now to do was to wait to see whether the trade figures, which for the previous three months had been, by our standards, reasonably good, would continue or whether there would be a deterioration which would force us into more stringent action.

On 26 March, there was a further meeting on the Budget. Denis wanted a bit of industrial policy by way of selective intervention to put in his Budget speech. We were told that the Department of Industry had proposals for spending money on the foundry industry. That seemed a better offer than a further increase in the industrial building allowance which had also been proposed. So we deferred any final decision until we had a sight of what the Department of Industry were actually proposing. I commented that it was indeed true that something needed to be done about the foundry industry. This had been true for the previous ten years. Various schemes had been introduced without any marked effect on its efficiency or the quality of its products. That intervention no doubt was written down as a further example of Dell cynicism. Neither scepticism nor cynicism undermined the attractions of the politics. In his Budget speech, Denis announced assistance for the foundry industry.[2]

The Budget statement

Tuesday 15 April was Budget Day. However desperate the situation, Chancellors of the Exchequer are seldom short of grounds for self-satisfaction. 'I have aimed to keep the rate of monetary expansion firmly under control . . . It is my intention that the growth of money supply should continue to be contained at a level which does not fuel inflation.'

Denis was now estimating the PSBR for 1974/5 at £7.6 billion. On the other hand the pre-Budget estimate for 1975/6 had been for a PSBR of over £10 billion. Expressed as a percentage of GNP, this estimate would represent an increase in the PSBR from 10 per cent in 1974/5 to 11 per cent in 1975/6. He, therefore, planned to reduce it in 1975/6 by well over £1 billion to £9 billion, or to 10 per cent of GDP as in the previous year. This compared with the £8 billion that he had been recommended by Treasury officials but he felt that, judged on a full employment basis, this PSBR could be contemplated 'without alarm'. In 1976/7 there would be a further reduction of about £3 billion. To achieve the reduction in the PSBR, there would be some cuts in public expenditure and, more importantly, tax increases. The tax increases included the 25 per cent VAT rate on a range of goods, increases in revenue duties, vehicle excise duty, and in income tax. The basic rate of income tax rose to 35 per cent, but Healey claimed to have achieved this in a way that would ensure that 9 million taxpayers, or 35 per cent of the whole, would pay less income tax.

He warned:

> my Budget measures will put up the RPI by about 2.75%. This means that for some months yet we must expect high figures for the RPI . . . By the middle of the year, once the increases I have mentioned have been digested, and the effects of lower food and commodity prices are feeding through, I would expect the rate of increase in the month-on-month index to begin to fall. In fact there are good prospects that between about June and December the cost of living will rise on average by not much more than 1% a month, implying an annual rate of the order of 12 to 16%. But . . . these figures will not be achieved if there is any acceleration in wage and salary increases.

He emphasized the need for a more rapid improvement in the current account of the balance of payments.

> We in Britain must keep control of our own policy . . . By relying unduly on borrowing we would run the risk of being forced to accept political and economic conditions imposed by the will of others. This would represent an absolute and unequivocal loss of sovereignty.

He forecast an improvement in the current account of at least £1 billion as compared with 1974. In other words the non-oil deficit would have turned into a substantial surplus.

> We argued continuously last year that the consuming countries should recognize that the size of the . . . petrodollar surplus would threaten a world

slump unless they were prepared to take compensating measures to increase demand. We ourselves did so in July and again in November to the extent which we felt we could afford, given the size of our external deficit and the rate of our domestic inflation. Others were much slower to react . . . The main reason why our rate of unemployment in Britain has risen so much less than that of nearly all our competitors is that we took action before the blow hit us.

The claim that unemployment in Britain had risen less than elsewhere was followed by the brave confession that unemployment would rise to one million, or 4 per cent, by the end of the year. But the Budget had been dictated by 'the harsh reality of the world we live in'. However, he said, referring to the action taken by the Germans and Americans, there were 'real grounds for confidence' about the world outlook in 1976.[3]

Thus, despite falling output and rising unemployment, Healey introduced a somewhat deflationary package. It was a clear break with Keynesian tradition. But Denis had not greatly exerted himself in a deflationary direction. He had done less than originally recommended by Treasury officials. The Budget was mildly contractionary but that was all. The policy of Chancellor Healey remained gently as you go, and the mandarins were swinging along behind him.

Notes

1. Thirlwall 253.
2. HC Debs., 15 Apr. 1975, col. 292.
3. Quotations are from Healey's Budget statement. HC Debs., 15 Apr. 1975.

T·H·I·R·T·E·E·N

Industrial Policy: The Excitement Fades

Benn survives

All ministerial portfolios are automatically handed in after a general election but Tony Benn, like the rest of us, found his handed back to him. Wilson's failure, despite many private threats, to act against Benn was taken as a sign that he was too powerful to be moved. As a result turmoil continued in the Department of Industry, with a total breakdown in confidence between the Secretary of State and his senior civil servants, resulting in the use on three occasions of that very rare procedure, an Accounting Officer's minute. Ministers must have their way subject to accountability to Parliament. But Permanent Secretaries in their role as Accounting Officers are accountable to the Public Accounts Committee before which they appear to defend their actions. They, therefore, have their rights and are entitled, in an extremity, to deny responsibility by means of an Accounting Officer's minute.[1] These incidents illustrated how impossible was the situation. It could have been relieved either by moving the civil servants, which would have been appropriate had Wilson considered them to be in the wrong, or by moving Benn. Wilson, evidently, did not believe the civil servants to be in the wrong, but equally he, apparently, continued to believe that Benn at Industry was a political necessity whatever the damage to relations between the Government and the private sector, and whatever the waste of public money.

The only remaining question was whether Benn was more exasperated by his civil servants, or by his ministerial colleagues. It was a close run thing. He recounts: 'I had to go to the Industrial Development Committee and it was one of the most unpleasant meetings I have ever attended. They are all unpleasant, but this was bloody awful.'[2] The Committee was discussing Meriden, one of his unsuccessful co-operatives, and he found himself opposed by Joel Barnett, Jim Callaghan, Harold Lever, Roy Jenkins, and Tony Crosland. Nevertheless, the Prime Minister summed up in his favour and allowed a further £4.95 million for Meriden and £8 million for export credits. So deeply was the Government embroiled in these projects that it was difficult to withdraw, whatever the wishes of the majority of Ministers.

The unpopularity of Tony Benn among industrialists in no way detracted from their preparedness to accept public money from his Department. When I met industrialists with their hands out for alms, I would raise the question whether there was any good reason why they should not rely simply on their own resources. I regularly took the chair at lunches to which Treasury Ministers, other than Denis, invited small groups of industrialists and, separately, trade unionists. Among those at lunch with us on 4 December 1974 was Arnold Weinstock, Managing Director of GEC. Weinstock took his opportunity to attack the Treasury: 'One thing I would say is that when the Department of Industry wants to give me £12 million to develop part of my electronic business the Treasury should not interfere and delay.' I replied that I, as yet, knew of no reason why he should receive £12 million or any other sum of public money. Why should not market forces be allowed to operate? Maurice Hodgson of ICI enquired, reasonably enough, what then was the purpose of planning agreements? That was a question that no one in the Government could yet answer. Even those Ministers most devoted to the idea had yet to decide what exactly planning agreements were meant to achieve.

The battle between the Department of Industry and the Treasury continued on a variety of issues such as the funding of British Leyland and the future of the HS 146 civil aircraft, with victory repeatedly going to Benn and with Denis waxing ever more furious. Benn recruited the trade unions to his side against any Cabinet decision he disliked.[3] Ever angrier letters passed between Denis Healey and Treasury officials on the one hand, and Tony Benn and Department of Industry officials on the other. There were also vigorous clashes at the Economic Committee where questions of industrial policy were discussed. Denis would get impatient and would interrupt Benn from the chair. Benn would retort as he always did when he could not think of any other response: 'Well, let me develop the argument.' Benn's self-justification was his interest in preserving jobs. He would not accept that other Ministers were also interested in preserving employment and feared that Benn's way would be destructive of jobs rather than the reverse.

British Leyland

A major subject of controversy was the future of the British Leyland Motor Company (BLMC). It became apparent in the autumn of 1974 that BLMC could not survive without government assistance. The Government felt compelled to give a guarantee to its creditors. We had to decide about its future and meanwhile to ensure that the existing management, protected by the government guarantee, did not enter into inflationary wage settlements and thus fuel inflation in the Midlands. It was decided that BLMC should come under the NEB. An enquiry chaired by Sir Don Ryder was established. There are always risks in bringing businessmen into government. There is grave danger of megalomania. Finding themselves, as they too frequently thought, with the resources of the nation at their disposal, they would exaggerate their ability to transform industrial performance. Labour Ministers, lacking much experience of industrial management, tended to be too impressed by industrial leaders who condescended to put their services at the disposal of the Government.

I was sceptical about Ryder. I was never certain that his long hours of work, which he publicized freely, should have been as great a source of comfort to the public as he evidently expected. However, there was no doubt that, as Chairman of Reed International, he was the head of a major enterprise and the Prime Minister was proud to have discovered him. We soon found that he was a man of grandiose ideas. I was horrified when the Government was presented by him with a bill for £500 million for investment by BLMC before he had even completed his enquiry. Against it was the catastrophic failure of the company itself and the lack of any persuasive evidence that it was a worthwhile recipient of resources on anything like that scale. A meeting of the Industrial Development Committee, on 22 January 1975, with the Prime Minister in the chair, had to consider a demand from Tony Benn for an additional £500 million for the NEB.

The Prime Minister was clucking happily about the list of names proposed by Benn for the first board of directors of the NEB. Toughies all of them, he said. Not the sort of men who would allow good money to be spent without good purpose. I was not prepared to rely on it. I had a brief skirmish with the Prime Minister as to whether Ryder's £500 million was simply an additional burden on the PSBR or whether it was also an additional burden on resources. In those days people who could talk knowingly about 'resources' earned for themselves a certain cachet. I therefore strove to become expert in the art. I contested the Prime Minister's argument that the £500 million would not be a demand on resources, only an addition to the PSBR. With help from this small intellectual victory, I managed to reduce Benn's bill by £200 million.

It was not a victory that could stick. When, in April, the Ryder report on BLMC was presented to the Government, it was as wondrous a proposal as I had feared. It could eventually involve £1.4 billion of public money.[4] Ryder seemed confident of the capacity of the firm to undertake this enormous investment commitment. He claimed that the quality of middle management at BLMC was sufficient for the purpose. It was always in middle management, he gave us to understand, that the real ability lay.

The Industry Bill

Benn had been allowed to present the White Paper *The Regeneration of British Industry* as a victory for his own conception of industrial policy and Wilson had resisted any invitation to correct the record. Although many of industry's fears had been soothed by seeing the Industry Bill itself, industrial leaders were entitled to be confused. According to Benn, the NEB and planning agreements were part of a programme for redistributing power to the working class. Yet, in other parts of government, the need for industry's voluntary co-operation in running a successful mixed economy was being emphasized. Who was to be believed? Wilson manœuvred desperately between Benn and the TUC on the one hand and the CBI on the other, trying to conciliate the CBI without falling out with the TUC. The CBI required a ritual meeting with the Prime Minister at which they could express their concern. Inevitably they laid out their concerns on the assumption that it was the Benn interpretation that was to be believed. Wilson assured them that legitimate concerns could lead to appropriate amendment.[5] For each

Industrial Policy: The Excitement Fades

meeting with the CBI there had to be at least one meeting with the TUC. For the TUC the industrial strategy was part of the Social Contract. They felt they were entitled to it however badly they were delivering on inflationary wage claims.

Two days were allotted for the Second Reading in the Commons. As it was his Bill, Tony Benn moved the Second Reading on the first day, 17 February 1975. In an attempt to bring peace of mind to embattled industrial leaders, I was put up to open the debate for the Government on the second day. I avoided showing my speech in advance to the Department of Industry so that they could not object to anything in it. Eric Heffer was very annoyed that he had not been able to get a sight of it before I made it. But I saw no harm in treating my colleagues at the Department of Industry in the way they so often treated the Treasury. My speaking in the debate could have caused some embarrassment due to my criticism, while in Opposition, of the earlier conceptions of the NEB. Well-briefed Tory Members were bound to be aware of my various public utterances. Indeed they were, and quotations from my articles and my book *Political Responsibility and Industry* are to be found dotted around the debate. I was not greatly worried because I could easily explain the difference between this Bill and what had been proposed in 1973. Certainly, in practice, the Industry Act was used far more in the spirit of my remarks on 18 February than in that of Benn's on 17 February.

Benn strikes oil

The referendum on 5 June 1975 confirmed British membership of the European Community. The result inspired Wilson with the resolution to exchange Tony Benn at Industry with Eric Varley at Energy. Wilson shrewdly provided the leaders of the Left with an excuse for abandoning Benn. He had assured Michael Foot that he would not exploit the referendum result to alter the left–right balance within the Government.[6] The Left concluded that the particular Cabinet portfolio held by Benn could not be a ground for resignation. The objections of the Left were further blunted by the fact that Varley had also been anti-market. To have replaced Benn by me as had been rumoured—probably as a result of briefing from No. 10—would have caused outrage.[7] It was not out of line with Wilson's techniques of political management to cause dismay at the thought of Dell, and then to compromise with the unobjectionable Varley.

The irony was that on any objective assessment of the two jobs, Energy was the more important and the more sensitive. The real victim of the exchange was Varley, not Benn. The Government was intervening vigorously in the development of North Sea oil. The Department of Industry, after the Industry Act, had little power to intervene against the objections of major industrial companies. To remain at Industry could have only been a source of intense frustration to a man of Benn's temperament. His arrival at Energy was tolerable only because I had already put the Petroleum Revenue Tax on the Statute Book and because Harold Lever and I were handling the participation discussions with the oil companies and had agreed between ourselves to manage them on the principle that there should be neither financial gain nor loss to the oil companies or to the Government as a result of participation. Although, eventually, Benn took over these negotiations, he was governed by the same principle, and I was still in the Government, whether at the Treasury or at the Department of Trade, to protect BP against the ambitions of BNOC. As Benn reveals, it needed protection.[8]

Notes

1. The incident is described in Benn 292–8, and by Part 175.
2. Benn 326.
3. Benn 247.
4. Benn 358 and 367.
5. Benn 315–17.
6. Benn 388.
7. Benn 377 and 382.
8. Benn 449.

F·O·U·R·T·E·E·N

The Social Contract on the Brink

Real national income

Speaking at the TUC Conference on 5 September 1974, Harold Wilson said:

[B]ecause of the crisis we face, including the oil surcharge, we cannot expect any significant increase in living standards over-all in the next year or two, indeed it will be a tremendous challenge to our statesmanship even to maintain average living standards'.[1]

My feeling when I read these words was that Wilson could never quite bring himself to speak the truth. Perhaps I was unjust. Perhaps these were not weasel words but, on the contrary, just before a general election, they showed unusual courage. But they did not spell out the whole truth. The truth was that, owing to the oil price hike and the increases in other commodity prices, there had been an actual reduction in real national income, estimated at about 5 per cent, which could not be compensated for by paying out more pounds sterling in wages without grave peril to the balance of payments.[2]

After the October election I tried, initially with some encouragement from the Prime Minister, to blurt out the grisly truth. A paper was prepared by Treasury officials under my supervision explaining the concept of real national income.[3] Denis Healey sent this paper to the Prime Minister and circulated it also to members of the Economic Strategy Committee. Wilson's response was enthusiastic. He wrote back that there ought to be a press conference about it. I prepared a speech for the Young Fabian Group on 14 January 1975. It was sent to No. 10 for clearance. It came back with all the paragraphs in which I drew the obvious implications crossed out and only the explanatory section left in. I wondered whether I should abandon the speech. I decided to deliver it because, even if I did not draw the implications, they were clear enough for any but the meagrest intelligence. It still contained the sentence: 'The major worsening in the terms of trade since 1972 now makes it essential that we attempt to measure changes in real national income so that public discussion of policy can take account of this change in our circumstances.'[4]

Wilson insisted that even if I consented to his cuts, the speech should go to Foot for his agreement. Fortunately Foot's agreement was forthcoming. Perhaps his liberal instincts were dominant. That the speech, even as cut, had been worth making was soon confirmed. On 28 January, I was at a meeting on an entirely different subject with the TUC. Len Murray said to me: 'Hello Edmund, you have been putting out some curious statistics recently.' I replied: 'They were prepared by the best statisticians in the game.' It was not unexpected that the TUC would find this particular piece of arithmetic distasteful. But it was not clear to me how a government could base its incomes policy on the voluntary co-operation of the TUC, if it was not frank in its communications with the TUC.

The Social Contract lives?

On 16 December 1974, there was a meeting of the Economic Committee. Officials had prepared a paper on ways of strengthening the Social Contract within a voluntary context. Barbara Castle asserted that nothing in the paper was worth a row of beans. 'There were dire warnings all around the table from Shirley, Edmund Dell and others.'[5] I argued that however admirable everything recommended might be, it was all quite inadequate to meet the actual inflationary situation.

By the beginning of 1975 the Social Contract was serving no purpose other than to provide Ministers with an excuse for inaction on the rising inflation. Wages nationally had risen 8–9 per cent faster during the previous year than prices in the shops. Retail prices were now rising by more than 20 per cent p.a., 'a faster peace-time increase than at any time in the previous 300 years'.[6] There was talk of pay settlements in the 40–50 per cent bracket. The UK could no longer blame rising prices of imported fuels and basic materials or excessive profit margins. Domestic cost increases were now the prime vehicle for inflation. Already our rate of inflation was twice that of almost all our main competitors. Britain was one of the few countries in which inflation continued to accelerate in 1975.[7] In the USA inflation rose to 11 per cent in 1974 but then fell back. In Germany, the inflation rate was held at 6–7 per cent. In Japan, 1974 was a year of very high inflation, 25 per cent, but the rate halved in 1975. Britain seemed threatened with Latin American levels of inflation. Nevertheless, Ministers were still publicly defending the Social Contract. What right had the Opposition, with a failed statutory policy in their record, to try to teach us? The Government was still relying on the co-operation of the TUC because that was the only policy it had. It was hardly encouraging that there was no better reason to rely on the Social Contract than that it had utterly failed.

At a meeting of the Liaison Committee with the TUC on 20 January, Healey explained the seriousness of the situation and the extent to which the country was spending more than it was earning. The consequence could be that further borrowing would become conditional on terms that a Labour government would find unacceptable. He ended with a plea to get wage settlements down. Michael Foot claimed that the guide-lines were 'not being followed. We should not argue about the guide-lines, but merely apply them as they stand'. He added that if the guide-lines were followed, the rate of inflation would be reduced.[8] But although Hugh Scanlon, in what was interpreted as a positive move, accepted the need to uphold the Social Contract, David Basnett emphasized: 'Any chance of renegotiating the Social Contract is just not there. Any attempt to reduce demand by reducing wage demands would increase unemployment'. Basnett was supported by Jack Jones.[9]

Healey's retrospective comment is that

Tony Barber's policies and the oil price increase had raised inflation to seventeen per cent by the time of my second budget in autumn 1974 and would have raised it higher in the following year. But if the unions had kept their promise, inflation would have been back to single figures by autumn 1975.[10]

However experience had revealed, even if it was not obvious before, that the Social Contract was acceptable to the TUC only as long as it *was* inflationary. Those still in employment were to be allowed to exploit their power at the expense of those already unemployed. Moreover rising unemployment gave the TUC an excuse to pursue its inflationary wage demands. The Chancellor was arguing that a reduction in wage settlements would improve the current account and make it possible to get unemployment down. The TUC did not see it that way. If the Chancellor would not reflate, the unions would do it for him.

On 5 February, there was a meeting of ECP. The principal paper reviewed progress on the Social Contract. I took the opportunity of attacking the Social Contract itself as well as its implementation. Within the Social Contract there could apparently be settlements of 10 per cent, or nearly 10 per cent, above the increase in the RPI. Under the Social Contract everyone was getting advances so much in excess of the increase in the RPI that they were enjoying an improved standard of living, funded by the oil sheikhs. The Social Contract was not an instrument of restraint but was itself seriously inflationary. It had taken no strain because even people who had settled in accordance with its provisions had improved their standard of living. Those people who had settled above it had done even better. Michael Foot replied gravely that while noting what I had said, he hoped that I did not say anything of the kind in public.

The situation raised questions which the Government could not escape if a rapid reduction in the rate of inflation remained a high priority. Even those who still argued that in due course the Social Contract would begin to slow the rise in money incomes had to concede that it was improbable that the process would be anything but gradual. Was a gradual approach still a realistic option given the need to borrow abroad to fund the balance of payments deficit? If, on the other hand, it was admitted that the Social Contract was no longer credible as a way of achieving a reduction in the rate of inflation, would the Government be compelled publicly to abandon its objective of full employment? The Government, while still defending the Social Contract, was in fact threatening that if it did not secure lower wage rises, unemployment would increase. But would yet higher unemployment have the required effect?[11] Was the Government facing, as its only realistic option, a return to statutory incomes control? There was also a longer-term question, whether completely unfettered free collective bargaining was compatible with the level of unemployment acceptable to 1970s political thinking.

Who cares for the 'social wage'?

Trade unionists and others, in fighting to maintain or increase the value of their personal expenditures, were voting against the concept of the 'social wage'. With typical determination, Barbara Castle fought to the end to have the 'social wage' better presented and better understood.[12] She strove to show the unions that 'if they go on pressing unreasonable wage demands they will only suffer a cut in the social wage'.[13] But did trade unionists want the Social Contract objectives enough to sacrifice the immediate satisfaction of wage increases? Barbara's expectation that unions could be deflected from wage claims by consideration of the 'social wage' proved unrealistic. The truth was that the Social Contract was only of interest to politically motivated trade union leaders and activists. For trade union members, the products of the social wage were free goods, irrelevant to the process of wage bargaining. Trade unionists generally were interested in wage increases, not in the Social Contract, and they took the social wage for granted. They were not prepared to sacrifice wage objectives for political objectives that had much lower, if any, priority.

In my speech in the Budget debate I touched on the question of what priority members of trade unions gave to the social wage. I remarked that the Social Contract had required increased social provision and an increased social wage. I added, tongue in cheek, that 'the suggestion cannot conceivably be that such increases in the social wage should not be paid for'. I went on to enquire, innocently, whether, 'the truth of the matter is that in asking for an increased social wage those who are doing so are not speaking for their members in giving [it] a higher priority than personal expenditure'. I expressed the hope that it was not true 'that the priorities have been got wrong'. I ended this passage by declaring: 'If higher and higher salaries and wages are conceded irrespective of movements in real national income, there will be continuing cuts in public expenditure, because it will be a sign that people are setting different priorities.'

No one did more than Denis Healey to instruct the TUC. Indeed, in order to secure TUC co-operation, disasters had to be described as achievements. At a meeting of the Liaison Committee with the TUC on 1 March Denis Healey insisted: 'The social wage has gone up by 10 per cent in the last year . . . But I am concerned as to whether . . . the spirit of the guide-lines is being followed. I hope the trade union movement will not be looking for ways round them, but for ways to carry them out.'[15] The TUC's reaction was not helpful. Jack Jones could only say: 'All we can do is to use what influence we can and I hope we shall not fall out on the basis that the unions are backsliding'.[16] That influence did not extend to preventing the use of a technique whereby the withdrawal of only a few hundred people could cause an employer considerable loss. It was a tactic which was being used increasingly in industrial disputes as a way of forcing through inflationary settlements. Reg Prentice accused the unions publicly of 'welching' on the Social Contract to which Michael Foot replied accusing Prentice of 'economic illiteracy'. This was unusual language between Cabinet colleagues in public. Barbara Castle's dry comment was that 'Economics anyway is a subject on which I would have thought Mike was slightly vulnerable'.[17]

It was estimated that the services provided by the Government, which it expected trade unionists to regard as their 'social wage', had a value of about £1,000 a year for every member of the working population. Healey records the failure of his attempt to educate the unions in his comment 'the unions defaulted on their part of the contract'.[18] In reality, it was the Government that needed the education. To add the costs of an increasing social wage to existing inflationary pressures, was not the least folly committed in the name of the Social Contract.

The impossible role of ECP

Ministers on ECP, who held executive responsibility for the incomes policy, were feeling increasingly helpless. Foot had submitted to Denis Healey a scheme to spend a further £2.5 billion in food subsidies in order to keep the RPI down. This additional subsidy was to be funded by an increase in tax. The scheme was nonsense but it did provide some evidence that Foot was becoming worried about the working of the Social Contract. Shirley Williams also was deeply worried. But she had her own impractical scheme. She was a devotee of an inflation tax. Departmental Ministers were compelled to spend an inordinate amount of time on questions of pay. Their proposals had to come for approval to ECP. They saw it as their function to protect those for whom they felt responsible from the effects of the rising inflation, rather than to join in the battle against it which the Treasury was still trying to conduct. First they told us how ineffectual we were in fighting inflation. Then they did their best to stimulate it further by their arguments in favour of their own departmental employees and those of the public agencies and nationalized industries sponsored by their Department.[19] Chairmen of nationalized industries saw little reason to co-operate. They were being asked to fight a battle which was clearly being lost. Why should they permit their industry to be devastated by strikes, when all around them others were giving way to pressure, and the Government itself did not seem to be very determined on implementing its own policy. Every inflationary settlement became a justification for the next.

The senior Civil Service had lost any confidence it had ever had in the Social Contract. They were, indeed, justified in their increasing despair and exasperation. Treasury officials, themselves ever more disillusioned, concluded that Ministers did not want a major battle on the incomes front. Wherever a public service was involved, the Government seemed unwilling to fight. On 11 March the principal item at ECP was the railways claim. The compromise package for which the Railways Board, supported by the Minister, wanted authorization was a clear breach of the guide-lines. To my surprise, I was briefed by Treasury officials to agree in order to get a settlement.

The Ministerial Committee on Economic Strategy had only just endorsed a paper from Denis Healey which insisted that henceforward we must be strict in ensuring that the guide-lines were followed in the spirit as well as in the letter, and in particular that people who had had a special settlement the previous year should have a strict guide-line settlement this year. I called in the responsible Deputy Secretary to discuss why his people had briefed me to support the Railways Board's 'compromise'. Why should we undermine this new and welcome determination emanating from Nos. 10 and 11 Downing Street? If we were going to fight anywhere, the railway dispute was something on which we could reasonably fight. The Deputy Secretary replied: 'All this briefing is drafted on the assumption that Ministers do not want a confrontation with any major union.' I said: 'All right, let us find out. We now have a policy, the policy approved by the Economic Strategy Committee. To go beyond the guide-lines in the railways case is a clear breach of that policy. If the Prime Minister and Denis Healey really want to breach the policy they have only just adopted, they must decide. We cannot decide that in ECP.' The response was immediate: 'Delighted to go along with that attitude, and actually force Ministers to face the facts of the situation.'

I then went to ECP. When we came to the railways issue I argued that what was intended was a breach of the guide-lines and inconsistent with the policy just adopted. If such a breach was to be permitted, it should be decided not by ECP but by the Economic Strategy Committee. Michael Foot and Eric Varley greeted with total disbelief the idea that we were going to keep to the guide-lines in this case. Eric Varley said: 'That may be what was decided in the Economic Strategy Committee but, when Ministers actually face the facts of this situation, they will say it is absurd to imagine we are going to get a guide-line settlement.' Michael Foot took the same line. So I said: 'Well, I must apologize for any naivety in believing that Ministers in the Economic Strategy Committee actually intended what they decided. But if they did not seriously intend it, they should be the people who come to that view, not we who are here merely concerned with implementing the policies which they have laid down'. It was agreed that the matter should go to the Economic Strategy Committee. Ministers would actually have their noses rubbed in their own decisions and we would see what conclusions they would then come to. The railways dispute became a factor in the eventual outbreak of ministerial determination.

There was one wage claim which we did fight and we felt very courageous. The previous November the board of Rolls Royce had capitulated to blackmail from their Glasgow work-force. It was therefore not surprising that when, in April 1975, Chairman Kenneth Keith told his employees at Glasgow that the firm had no money, the reply was simply: 'You give it to us and the Government will pay'. Keith and his colleagues were now willing to take a tough line. Keith told us that the firm could take an eight week strike. There were sufficient stocks of aero-engines around the world to keep the airlines supplied. On 10 April, ECP decided that the Government would not provide money for any settlement in the Rolls Royce case outside the Social Contract. Keith could make a small offer which the Government however would not fund. If there was a strike, the Government would stand by the company keeping it afloat until the strike was settled. The Government and the management won a victory at Rolls Royce. Sir William Nield, a director, gave me a lecture on the telephone on the virtues of standing firm. He said: 'Three Fs, firm, fair, and factual'. Give them the facts, tell them there is no money, tell them the Government will not give them any money, stand firm, be fair, and then everything will be all right. I did not ask him why he had capitulated the previous November.

The TUC still deaf to reason

The mounting feeling in many parts of the party and Government was that, after the first year's wage settlements had gone through, that is after July, there would have to be tougher guide-lines. Healey, in his

The Social Contract on the Brink

April Budget, had still been trying to bargain with the trade unions. '[S]ettlements so far beyond the increase in the cost of living are bound severely to restrict my room for manoeuvre in the Budget and to limit the pace at which the Government can carry out their remaining commitments under the Social Contract'.[20] But the TUC was not yet in a mood to listen. The TUC reaction to the Budget showed little concern about the increasing dangers of runaway inflation. The TUC thought that the Budget should have been reflationary. Hugh Scanlon said of the Budget that 'There can be no doubt that the overall position was an almost disdainful ignoring of the proposals of the TUC and an almost absolute compliance with the proposals of the CBI and the City'.[21] At a meeting of the Liaison Committee on 21 April, David Basnett 'harped on unemployment . . . This was the main issue, he said . . . We had got to get away from all this one-sided exhortation about wages. The Social Contract did not mean exhortation: it meant creating an atmosphere, and we had got to realize that the Budget hadn't helped'.[22] Basnett was supposed to be a 'moderate'. There was no sign yet of help from that source. The TUC's refusal to acknowledge Healey's problems while insisting on their right to influence his policies would have driven a weaker man to despair. Despite Healey's exhausting efforts at education the TUC did not realize that it was precisely the Government's failure to respond to rising unemployment by reflationary policies that demonstrated the seriousness of the situation.

By the end of April, time was clearly running out. The emotional Bob Mellish, Chief Whip and licensed spokesman for the non-political working classes, was becoming deeply worried. At ECP he was increasingly asking awkward questions. On 17 April, he even got himself to the edge of saying that there would have to be a statutory policy. He did not actually say it but it was obviously what he meant. Later that day, he and I had a chat about it. He could not see things being permitted to go on this way any longer. If Bob Mellish was turning, could other Ministers be far behind? Sometimes it appeared that even Michael Foot was getting fed up with the trade unions. After a meeting with TUC leaders, Crosland complimented Foot on how he had handled them. Michael Foot rejoined: 'Oh, don't compliment me on that. I have now, I assure you, very great practice in giving way to the TUC.' He recounted how the previous day he had spent two and a half hours going with them through the Employment Protection Bill, clause by clause. They had questioned point after point after point, mainly based on misunderstandings.

The battle for a statutory policy begins

On 5 May there was a meeting at the Treasury. I argued that whatever one could say about the lack of success for statutory policies under the last Labour government, there was a difference now with inflation at the present rate. Denis Healey by no means ruled out a statutory policy. He said that he would be having a word with Harold Wilson on the latter's return from Jamaica to see whether politically it would be on. Meanwhile further work should be done to elaborate both a statutory policy and the best voluntary policy one could hope to achieve.

I detected in the air the beginning of resolution.

Notes

1. Wilson (1979), 44.
2. Healey 379. GDP from 1974 continued to show small increases, but real national income suffered a significant fall.
3. Real national income is the measure of the nation's income adjusted for changes in the prices of those goods on which it spends the income. In particular, it measures the value of the nation's income after taking account of fluctuations in the terms of trade. See Treasury Press Notice of Payment General's speech to Young Fabian Group, 14 Jan. 1975.
4. Treasury Press Notice, 14 Jan. 1975.
5. Castle 252.
6. Gardner 55.
7. Smith 63.
8. Castle 286.
9. Castle 285.
10. Healey 394.
11. These questions were being asked in *NIER* (Feb. 1975), 6–7.
12. Castle 430 ff. *re* Liaison Committee with TUC on incomes policy, 23 June. See also p. 437.
13. Castle 293.
14. HC Debs., 17 Apr. 1975, cols. 680–1.
15. Castle 318.
16. Castle 319.
17. Castle 325–6.
18. Healey 394. In March 1975, DHSS calculated that the social wage was worth about £20 a week for every member of the working population. See Castle 319 n.
19. See e.g. Castle *passim*, for an account of her battles for the doctors.
20. HC Debs., 15 Apr. 1975, col. 281.
21. MacDougall 217.
22. Castle 372.

F·I·F·T·E·E·N

The Battle for a Statutory Incomes Policy

The need for direct action against inflation

The last defence that Ministers could find for the Social Contract was that, even if not successful in reducing inflation, at least it had brought social peace. But with inflation and unemployment exacerbating the tensions in society, it was far from certain that even that claim would have validity much longer. A more structured policy might impose some view of the national interest on wage bargaining. Rough and ready as that might be, the time had come when it would be better than the existing competitive battle for survival.

By May 1975, encouraged by my public demands for action against inflation, the press was forecasting a more structured incomes policy.[1] My views gained support mainly from commentators whose most natural instinct was not to support a Labour government. Kenneth Fleet commented on one speech: 'Mr Dell spelt out the realities of our economic situation with his customary clarity . . . it is a relief to find a member of the present Government defining the problems clearly.'[2] The *Financial Times* drew attention to my inference that, unless we acted against inflation, foreign funds would leave Britain.[3] But how wage inflation was to be tackled, and whether by statutory or voluntary action or by a combination of both, was inevitably as yet undiscussed publicly by anyone bound by collective responsibility even in the loose form that concept was operated in Wilson's last government.

On 21 May, the CBI Council, which had rejected pay restraint in November 1974, almost unanimously accepted proposals much more far-reaching than those rejected six months earlier. In addition to reiterating the need for tight fiscal and monetary policies, the CBI called on the Government to sponsor a pay policy in conjunction with both sides of industry. It proposed a three-year programme to reduce price inflation to 5 per cent or under, with price targets fixed each year and corresponding pay limits set.[4]

Nevertheless, interviewed by Robin Day on 23 May, Harold Wilson dismissed the strongly held belief that the Government was planning a counter-inflation package to be introduced after the referendum. 'If there were a package that would counter inflation, we would have introduced it already.' He ruled out statutory wage control: 'There are no circumstances short of war or something of that kind which would justify this.'[5] In an Open Letter, issued by Conservative Central Office on 8 June, the Shadow Chancellor Sir Geoffrey Howe said:

As Edmund Dell told the National Savings Assembly on 9th May: 'The 1974 level of borrowing cannot be allowed to continue, even if that were possible, because the eventual overhang of foreign indebtedness would be intolerably large' . . . The Government must, as Edmund Dell told the NUM on 20th May, 'Bring public expenditure under better control because it is at present making too great a demand on the total resources of the country.'

I continued my public pressure for action in a speech, on 11 June, to the Electronic Engineering Association. *The Times*, next day, reported my cry for a greater sense of urgency in this fight against inflation and that the Government would 'have to do very much better in controlling inflation over the next year than we were able to do during the last.' The *Financial Times* reported the industrial policy aspects of the 'remarkably conciliatory speech'. The inflationary situation, in my view, demanded consensus, not confrontation, between the Government and the private sector.

The date of the referendum on membership of the EEC was 5 June 1975. Thereby was removed one constraint on government action on the inflation front.

In June the latest figures for price inflation in the UK, those for May, were published. These showed the rate of price inflation running at 25 per cent, year-on-year. At that rate the retail prices index would virtually double every three years.[6] It was at last understood, even in the TUC, that something must be done. With Jack Jones in the lead, the Economic Committee of the TUC prepared a draft statement for the General

Council meeting on 25 June which contemplated the possibility of a norm and flat-rate increases.

The TUC resist responsibility for the past while contemplating more for the future

For Healey it was a major problem that neither Michael Foot nor the TUC were yet prepared to accept the extent to which wage increases were to blame for the inflation. The facts were just too unpleasant for TUC leaders, and particularly for their activist members, to face. As late as the middle of June, the figures being mentioned as the basis for an incomes policy norm, and even being seriously considered by some Ministers, were themselves grossly inflationary. They could only have been advanced by people who not merely said, but actually believed, that there were major factors other than the wage explosion to account for the inflation. The TUC, when they did begin to see danger in the mounting inflation, suggested £10 instead of the eventual £6 as well as a cut-off of £7,000. Even Joe Haines, the Prime Minister's Press Secretary, not the most sympathetic observer of Treasury caution, regarded these figures as 'absurd' though he goes on to add 'but negotiable'. Haines also comments that a £7,000 a year cut-off 'would have excluded many power engineers, the men more capable than anyone else of stopping British industry overnight'.[7] Barbara Castle records that, at her caucus meeting on 18 June, Michael Foot, while insisting that there was no alternative but to beaver away at a voluntary policy, 'had hopes of persuading the unions to adopt a 15% target of wages increases or a flat £9 across the board'.[8] Tony Benn, writing of the same occasion, says:

The real purpose of the dinner was to get support for Michael Foot's proposal—which had been put up by Jack Jones—for a flat rate 15 per cent increase, which is about £9 a week across the board, to be endorsed by the TUC and to replace the first mark of the Social Contract.'[9]

This proposal, so far from the requirements of the situation, shows the size of the problem faced by Denis Healey in achieving credible agreement with his colleagues, let alone with the TUC.

The dispute with the railwaymen had led to the threat of a strike. Joe Haines comments that:

The National Union of Railwaymen, under a new General Secretary, Sid Weighell, had rejected an arbitration award which gave them a wage increase of

27 per cent ... and were demanding increases of up to 35 per cent, claiming all the while that such increases were within the Social Contract, of which the NUR remained stout defenders, of course. The argument was humbug and everyone knew it. But so inordinate had the claims become—not least because of vast increases for senior civil servants and others covered by the Top Salaries Review Body—that a new leader of a union could hardly seek less.[10]

It was the threat of the railwaymen's strike that led Tony Crosland to intervene with a speech which angered Michael Foot. Crosland stated categorically that the present scale of pay and price rises meant that Britain was 'on a suicide course'. He ruled out a statutory wages policy because it had been shown not to work. To increase the level of unemployment would be a policy of despair. It probably would not work quickly enough, but the real objection was one of principle. Instead he proposed that the Social Contract should be tightened.

Principles of social justice should determine the distribution of our national wealth. But all governmental efforts to increase social justice are lost in the crazy haphazard lurches which characterize pay settlements under conditions of rapid inflation.[11]

Unfortunately this eloquent appeal to social justice has its place only in the library of lost causes along with Barbara Castle's social wage. Cabinet Ministers 'weakly approved an increase in pay for railway workers of 30 per cent'.[12]

Probably flat rate, not just voluntary, but how far statutory?

The Cabinet met at Chequers on 20 June. Healey stressed the urgency of the situation. There could be a run on sterling at any time. A crisis package would have to be announced by July as sterling would not hold much longer. £500 million had already been spent in its support. By September 1976, inflation had to be down to 10 per cent. That would require wage rises of no more than 10 per cent, or £5 per week if there was to be a flat rate. The Prime Minister summed up in support of the 10 per cent maximum and went so far as to say that, though the policy was still to be voluntary, there must be a tight timetable for a statutory policy if the voluntry approach failed.[13]

At the Chequers Cabinet it was clearly understood that there would have to be a pay policy. There had been a strong majority for a voluntary policy if that were obtainable. There was a feeling that it would be obtainable because the TUC realized that action was now essential. There was opposition to a statutory policy. But equally there was no doubt that a watershed had been reached. Donoughue, who was present, comments that this meeting represented 'a crucial step for the Prime Minister because the Labour Party's public stance was still apparently against the introduction of an incomes policy. However, Cabinet also decided to oppose a statutory policy.'[14] The word 'decided' oversimplifies what happened. The Cabinet was never likely to legislate against employees. A statutory policy directed against employers might not encounter comparable problems.

Discussions were also in progress between the TUC and the CBI. Sir Donald MacDougall has described the production of a joint CBI/TUC paper by himself and David Lea, the TUC's chief economist, which was discussed between the two bodies on 24 June. 'Thus by late June the TUC had agreed the essential features of the CBI policy.' He reports a discussion between Jack Jones and Ron Owen, for the CBI, on whether it should be £x a week or a percentage limit. 'Jack Jones won and we got a £6 a week limit for everyone except those earning over £8,500 a year who got nothing, for "Year 1" of the policy—between the summers of 1975 and 1976.' He comments 'This, together with the formula for "Year 2" which further squeezed differentials, helped to create serious anomalies and tensions that led to an upsurge in inflation later'. He believes that with a simple percentage the anomalies would have been considerably less serious, but concedes that Jack Jones's appreciation of the situation may have been right in that only a simple figure like £6, which could also be represented as helping the lower paid, would have been accepted and observed.[15] This account compresses the events of late June and early July but it does make clear that the CBI was prepared to reconcile itself to a flat rate policy if that was necessary to achieve the TUC's support.

The part played by Jack Jones in the summer of 1975 can hardly be overestimated. His motives, evidently, were mixed. They included suspicions about the intentions of some Ministers. He comments:

Whatever my misgivings, I was determined to back the Government 'warts and all'. Not least because Harold Wilson, Barbara Castle and others had told me that there were members of the Government who were looking for a break-up, and were ready to move towards a coalition.

And he quotes a speech he made at the July 1975 TGWU Conference in Blackpool: '[T]he betrayal of 1931 could happen again . . . The Macdonalds, the Snowdons, the Jimmy Thomases, are lurking around.'[16]

Jack Jones had been advocating a flat-rate policy for some time. 'At a union rally in Bournemouth early in May 1975, I called for a new approach to be made "to provide for wage increases to be on a flat-rate basis". The figure should be directly related to the cost of living. The one figure should then apply to all people at work—MPs, judges, civil servants and other workers.'[17] He carried the TUC General Council in favour of a flat rate at its meeting on 25 June. Jones recounts: '[O]verwhelming support was expressed for the idea, subject to agreement on a figure and the Government's adoption of a prices target . . . Only Hugh Scanlon put forward serious doubts: he said that the TUC could not deliver'.[18] Thus at the CBI on 24 June and at the General Council the next day, Jack Jones advocated a flat-rate policy.[19] If a flat rate was necessary to secure agreement, that in itself would be acceptable to the Government. The decisive question would be the size of the proposed flat-rate payment.

By this stage the debate within the Government was not whether there should be an incomes policy but how far it should have statutory elements. Denis Healey did not rule these out. On 26 June we had one of our Treasury Ministers' lunches. Healey said that he was pressing hard to be allowed to make a statement on incomes policy and public expenditure cuts. The Government could not afford his resignation and he was going to exploit that fact to the full. He considered his negotiating position within Cabinet to be still incomparably strong. In his view it was growing stronger as the economic situation deteriorated. The question as ever was how far he would in the event judge it politic to press his views in face of the opposition he was bound to meet.

The Policy Unit rides to the rescue

Donoughue is a principal source on what was happening at No. 10 during this period. But his account has regularly to be tested against both the probabilities and contrary evidence. In some respects his account of the events of June and July 1975, and indeed subsequently, is questionable. The No. 10 Policy Unit was among those invited to contribute to the confection of an effective incomes policy. According to

Donoughue, his Policy Unit it was that won a famous victory over the Treasury in favour of a voluntary policy. The Prime Minister, according to his account, had belatedly concluded that 'something must be done' and asked for suggestions from the Policy Unit which was joined, for this purpose, by Joe Haines. Donoughue dates this outbreak of Prime Ministerial determination as one week after the Chequers Cabinet. The Policy Unit had to work fast if it was to have any influence. It submitted to the Prime Minister a memorandum which

> suggested that the Government announce a radical economic package. It should contain a pay policy, but voluntary rather than statutory, in order not to conflict totally with previous election pledges. The policy should be based on a £6 per week increase for everybody, a suggestion that was made by Joe Haines (originally he proposed £5) who argued that to be acceptable an incomes policy should be simple.

Though voluntary, the policy would be backed by a 'battery of sanctions'. Any private employers breaking the policy would have tax penalties imposed, as well as being discriminated against in government contracts, regional subsidies, investment allowances, etc. There should also be a price code to ensure that prices as well as wages were held down. There was, of course, the usual problem. 'The heart of the policy's credibility was bound to depend on the support of the TUC.'[20] Donoughue attributes to Haines great insight in advocating a flat-rate policy. The insight might, of course, have been gained had Haines been reading the newspapers. A flat-rate policy was under public discussion well before Wilson involved the Policy Unit. Evidently Haines's ability to absorb the thoughts around him should not be underestimated but it did not make a decisive contribution to events.

Wilson, Donoughue reports, was attracted by the Policy Unit's proposals because they enabled him to have an effective incomes policy without breaching all past commitments to the electorate and to the Labour movement not to have a *statutory* policy. But, Donoughue says, the Treasury wanted a full statutory policy.

> Over the final two weeks in June there was a savage and very enjoyable Whitehall battle . . . I quickly learned from contacts in the Treasury that it had decided to try to get the voluntary proposals rejected and to 'bounce' a statutory policy through Ministers. I spoke to the Prime Minister about this and warned that, unless pressure was put on the Treasury, the voluntary approach would not be given a fair run in Whitehall. He . . . immediately despatched to the

Treasury what is the most commanding document ever sent in British government—a Prime Minister's minute. This [gave] blunt instructions not to proceed further with arguments for a statutory policy and to start analysing and constructing a voluntary policy . . . The Treasury ignored the Prime Minister's instructions. Instead it submitted to Cabinet at the end of June a paper on pay policy which, while acknowledging the suggestions for a voluntary policy, quickly dismissed them as impractical, and moved on to discuss and recommend only one approach—a full statutory policy.[21]

It is odd that Donoughue should place such emphasis on the 'commanding' nature of a Prime Minister's minute. Prime Ministers did not yet have the authority of the whole Cabinet and no Cabinet decisions had been taken. Even Donoughue and Haines were recommending a mixture of voluntary and statutory elements. It was only a convenient flexibility in ministerial consciences that permitted either their proposals or the policy eventually decided to be described as 'voluntary'. Haines, however, gives his account of what the Prime Minister said would be in his 'commanding' minute and it gives a rather different impression from that conveyed by Donoughue.

The Prime Minister told me that he intended to send a minute to the Chancellor of the Exchequer telling him not to let his officials waste their time on the two options which had been consistently rejected by the Government: a purely voluntary policy (which would be abdicating everything to the TUC) and a statutory policy which would, in the end, raise the probability that action would be taken in the courts against trade unions or their members.[22]

In other words the Prime Minister was rejecting a statutory policy of a kind that could end with action in the courts against trade unions and their members. This did not rule out all kinds of statutory policy and Wilson had not ruled out all kinds of statutory policy. The real significance of the Prime Minister's 'commanding' minute was his abandonment of the purely voluntary action against inflation which had been the policy of the party and Government hitherto. It indicated a change of position by the Prime Minister but there had still been no Cabinet decision.

On 30 June, the Governor of the Bank of England arrived to see the Prime Minister together with the Chancellor. Other Cabinet Ministers were also assembling at the time in No. 10 for a meeting to discuss pay policy. They were kept waiting for nearly half an hour while the Prime Minister listened to the Governor and the Chancellor. Donoughue tells us what was happening.

The Governor revealed . . . that sterling was indeed collapsing. Apparently £0.5 billion had been lost from the official reserves in the last few days. Against that background, the Prime Minister was urged to support the Chancellor in his proposals for a statutory pay policy. The famous Treasury 'bounce' technique had been launched, with the Bank of England as a powerful ally.[23]

Of course the real bounce was coming not from the Treasury nor from the Bank but from the markets. A statement in the House was necessary because sterling was under severe pressure. Joe Haines confirms that the Prime Minister had been severely shaken by threats that substantial sterling deposits would be taken out of London, for example by Kuwait and Saudi Arabia, if nothing sufficient was done to stabilize the value of sterling at about $2.20.[24] These threats were not the invention of the Treasury.

The Prime Minister and the Chancellor went into the Cabinet Room for the pay policy meeting. Healey, according to Donoughue, made his plea for a statutory policy. He asked approval for two White Papers: one to be published the very next day would propose a statutory incomes policy with a 10 per cent pay norm. The other, to be produced the following week, would list massive public expenditure cuts and price controls. He wanted to give Parliament advance warning of these cuts the following day at the same time as publishing the statutory pay policy. For both steps he needed Cabinet approval. Donoughue does not make clear that what Healey was asking for was agreement that it would be illegal for employers to grant pay increases of more than 10 per cent. He was not asking for statutory action against workers. That this was the distinction already in Wilson's mind is confirmed by Healey.

Harold Wilson had told me earlier in the year that he would support me on anything I wanted—except a statutory incomes policy . . . On Monday June 30 . . . he said he would after all support a statutory pay policy, providing the legal sanctions were directed only against employers who conceded too much, and not against workers who demanded too much.[25]

From this account it is clear that Healey was asking for statutory powers *against employers* who broke the proposed guide-lines. There is, thus, a conflict of evidence between Healey and Donoughue. Judging on the probabilities, and taking account of the over-excitement characteristic of his narrative, the reasonable conclusion is that Donoughue is wrong.

The assembled Ministers did not explicitly support the Chancellor's proposals. Most just listened solemnly. 'However, sitting in the Cabinet

Room', Donoughue comments, 'it was ominously clear to me that Mr Wilson was taking a less robust view'.[26] Haines reports a conversation that he and Donoughue had with the Prime Minister outside the Cabinet Room just after the conclusion of this meeting with Ministers. Haines argued that a compulsory policy would not work, that bringing in legislation would split the Government, and that he did not see how Harold Wilson could remain in office if he brought in a compulsory pay policy. The Prime Minister's response was that he had not yet agreed to a compulsory policy.[27] Haines also comments that there was, in any case, no chance of getting a compulsory policy through the Commons, 'a fact stated very forcibly to his colleagues earlier in the month by Bob Mellish, the Government's Chief Whip'.[28]
Donoughue continues

the same evening ... the inevitable Treasury memorandum 'bounced' into No. 10. It was a draft of the next day's statement to Parliament by the Chancellor, to be cleared by the Prime Minister immediately and by Cabinet first thing in the morning ... We were well down the statutory incomes policy path again and the Prime Minister was apparently convinced that there was no alternative.[29]

Haines comments that the draft implied that

The Chancellor would be asking Cabinet to consider an unabashed announcement of a statutory incomes policy, with no mention of sanctions against employers—which, if any statutory policy was embarked upon, Ministers insisted was essential—and proposing nothing effective on prices.[30]

Donoughue continues: 'Joe Haines and I sat down together in the Press Office and ... decided to make one last approach to the Prime Minister. We drafted, signed and sent upstairs a joint minute.'[31] The text of the joint minute is given by Haines. Its burden is that the Treasury was stampeding the Government into a statutory pay policy. 'We are reinforced in this belief by the knowledge that no money at all was spent in defence of the pound on Monday.' The proposed statement by the Chancellor did not specify that action would be only against employers. It was inadequate on prices. They emphasized that they had been formulating another alternative, part voluntary, part statutory, which stood a much better chance of success. The Treasury draft also included a serious commitment on public expenditure in advance of any proper consultation or discussion. The Treasury draft would lead to resignations from the Cabinet and the Government.

This was the message that, according to Donoughue and Haines, the Prime Minister found persuasive and which turned him away from a statutory policy.[32] But there was never any likelihood that a Labour government, or Harold Wilson specifically, would impose statutory penalties on workers, and Healey could never have expected it, desirable though it may have been. The Donoughue/Haines minute naïvely adopted a conspiracy theory about Bank of England behaviour in managing the exchanges. Apart from that, what it said was that the flexibility of Ministers' consciences would extend so far but no further. It argued that however statutory the policy was to be, it must remain arguable that it was not statutory. To that extent their minute was about presentation, not about substance. However, presentation is important, especially perhaps when policy is being changed, and the Prime Minister, though not invariably, could be a good judge of presentation. He had already drawn the line beyond which the policy would unquestionably be fully statutory, and the Chancellor had already accepted it. This is confirmed by the fact that, on 30 June, when Wilson and Healey saw Len Murray and Jack Jones, they had assured them that any sanctions would be against employers. It is absurd to suggest that, that same evening, Healey would have gone back on a pledge given to the TUC leaders in his presence by the Prime Minister.

The Donoughue account does suggest a question. Why did Healey allow a draft statement to go forward to No. 10 that did not make it clear that the statutory policy that was being proposed was to be directed against employers? The first point to note about this alleged Treasury 'bounce' is that if Harold Wilson is to be believed, Healey at midnight was not at the Treasury but at No. 10.[33] Whether or not Wilson's memory is accurate, the second point to note is that the draft was sent to No. 10 only. It would have been normal for a Treasury paper, approved by Treasury Ministers, to be circulated direct to the Cabinet. This one was not. Clearly the draft had been prepared in the Treasury, at official level, for discussion between the Prime Minister and the Chancellor. It was probably prepared on the basis of a briefing from the Cabinet Office to the Treasury following the ministerial meeting earlier that day.

The third point is that, by not specifying that sanctions were to be directed solely against employers, it drew attention to an unresolved problem. A statutory policy directed exclusively against employers raised questions of practicality as well as of policy. The Lord

Chancellor, Elwyn Jones, had repeatedly advised that a strike to force an employer to break the law would be a criminal conspiracy. To ensure that sanctions would operate against employers only, it would therefore be necessary to legislate specifically, as had been done in 1966, to exonerate strikers.[34] In other words as the law stood *at the time* legal sanctions against employers implied the possibility of legal sanctions against workers. The problem could not, in law, be avoided without further legislation. Did the Cabinet wish to introduce such legislation which, apart from being 'statutory', would look highly discriminatory even though the CBI might support it?

Donoughue implies that Healey, and possibly even the Prime Minister, were trying to drive Michael Foot to resignation, and backbenchers into revolt, despite the fact that this would almost certainly bring about the break-up of the Government, and that they would have succeeded in this intention but for the watchful eyes, and persuasive arguments, of Donoughue and Haines. Neither Healey nor Wilson was so naïve nor had they any such intention. They had agreed on a strategy under which the policy would be defensible as 'voluntary' although backed by statutory sanctions. They had agreed that the sanctions should be limited to employers. Donoughue's account makes it questionable whether, close as he was to the Prime Minister, he yet understood Wilson's position.

Cabinet on 1 July and the debate about powers

In any case there was much still to be decided. The battle over the balance of voluntary and statutory elements to be included in the policy was still being fought. Another outstanding problem was whether a Bill should be introduced at once or kept in reserve. Healey and the Prime Minister would have preferred the Bill to be enacted at once subject to implementation by regulation. At Cabinet the following morning, 1 July, Harold Wilson argued for the enactment of reserve powers which would not become effective except by regulation. Foot wanted the Bill kept in reserve as he felt that the less the legislation the more he could claim that the policy was still voluntary. Healey had begun the discussion by briefing the Cabinet on the sterling crisis and on the discussions in progress with the TUC. 'The pound, he told us', Barbara Castle reports, 'had fallen 1 per cent yesterday and this morning it had reached its lowest devaluation ever: 29.2 per cent. The worst thing was that it was now going down versus the dollar, and we could face a disastrous withdrawal of funds at any time'. Benn adds that Healey made particular reference to the danger of Nigeria, Kuwait, and Saudi Arabia withdrawing their money if sterling fell below a stated level. For the Kuwaitis that level had already been reached and the Nigerian figure was just below it.

Then Healey and Wilson reported on the meeting the previous day with Len Murray and Jack Jones. Healey said that both Murray and Jones had accepted an inflation target of 10 per cent by September 1976 and single figures by the end of 1976. But Jones had warned about the problem of compliance.[35] Wilson had assured them that there was no intention of imposing criminal sanctions on workers but then added that he 'thought the answer lay in the 1966 precedent: we should take general powers, but they would not become law except by regulation'.[36] He felt that a viable policy would be acceptable to the TUC and that the CBI would accept legislation against employers. British Leyland and other firms that received public money should be compelled to conform and there should be an insurance scheme to fund firms that held out against strikers.[37] Healey's recall is that on 1 July 'I had a big majority in Cabinet: besides the Left, the minority included Jim Callaghan, Eric Varley and Elwyn Jones, with Shirley Williams and Bob Mellish on the fence'.[38]

On the afternoon of 1 July Denis Healey made an interim statement in the Commons the purpose of which was to avert a run on sterling. He announced the Government's determination to get the rate of inflation down to 10 per cent by the end of the next pay round and to single figures by the end of 1976. A limit of 10 per cent was to be set for wages, salaries, and dividends. On 1 July it was not yet certain that a credible voluntary policy with sufficient statutory elements could be agreed. Therefore, when Healey made his statement in the House, he was still threatening legislation though indicating a preference for a voluntary policy. He made clear that the Government would take action through the Price Code to encourage compliance from private employers and added that, if agreement could not be arrived at, 'the Government will be obliged to legislate to impose a legal requirement on both public and private sector employers to comply with the 10 per cent limit'.[39]

With the respect for Cabinet secrecy typical of the Wilson/Callaghan governments, Benn arranged the following day to brief Ian Aitken of *the Guardian* on his personal position.[40] Meanwhile the Left caucus was meeting to cry out against the inevitable. Benn records such a meeting on 3 July at which Barbara was in typically eloquent flow, condemning the Left for always being beaten because in the end it never fought and never had any credible alternative. 'Boy, was she shrieking, throwing her arms in the air.' Benn concluded that Castle was really no longer of the Left. 'Although she argues against a statutory policy, she would accept it if it would prevent public expenditure cuts in the DHSS.' Which, if true, does not actually appear an unreasonable stance for the Secretary of State for Health and Social Services. Oddly, Castle does not report the 3 July meeting of the Left caucus.

She does record that, on 5 July, 'Denis is still hankering after taking his precious statutory reserve powers and this would make Mike's position impossible'.[41] Michael Foot was threatening to resign.[42] But perhaps he would not resign if the statutory powers were kept in reserve. By 6 July Benn has concluded that 'the Foot–Healey–Jones–Wilson group is running the Government, and that explains why I am on the outside'.[43] Barbara's diary for 7 July records a meeting, on which Benn is silent, at which Foot, Shore, Benn, and Varley met in her room at the House to discuss how negotiations with the TUC were progressing and whether a statutory policy, or a policy with statutory elements, would be acceptable to them. It appears that neither would have been absolutely unthinkable.[44] None of this sounds much like Donoughue's self-serving account of the decisive influence of his Policy Unit.

Winning the TUC

The next stage of the operation was to win round the TUC. Jack Jones was at the TGWU's biennial conference at Blackpool. He had succeeded in securing from his union an overwhelming vote in favour of a flat-rate policy. Donoughue says that the Prime Minister and the Chancellor met with Jack Jones and won him round to supporting a pay norm as part of a voluntary policy. This hardly does credit to Jones's role in the development of the incomes policy. Donoughue also says that Jones suggested a £6 norm instead of Joe Haines's original £5, and that this was acceptable as a small price to pay for such valuable support. Jones, however, emphasizes that £6 emerged from a tough negotiation with Healey.

[T]he Treasury preferred a percentage for wage increases and only grudgingly gave way to a flat rate approach. Healey . . . stuck at £5 while I had been pressing for £7 to £8. I came down to £6 reluctantly ... We then pressed for the increase to apply only to wages and salaries under £7,000 a year. Healey insisted the figure ought to be £10,000 and we finally settled on £8,500.[45]

Jack Jones quickly converted Hugh Scanlon and, 'with the calm support of the ever helpful Len Murray', the TUC, on 3 July, accepted the principle of a voluntary policy.[46] It will be observed that the various accounts are contradictory. MacDougall has Jack Jones proposing a £6 policy in discussions with the CBI on 24 June. Donoughue has Jack Jones, introduced late to the question, proposing a £6 policy, instead of Joe Haines's £5, on 2 July. Jack Jones, according to his own account, was haggling with Healey for £7 or £8 after 1 July. Memories are unreliable. But it is the Jones account that has the air of authenticity.

Harold Wilson now made his appeal as Prime Minister to the trade union movement. It was made in the course of a speech to the National Union of Mineworkers at Scarborough:

It is now *Labour*'s Prime Minister, your Prime Minister, at a critical hour in the nation's history, enjoining this community, once again, to assert loyalty *for* the nation. It is not so much a question of whether that loyalty, that response, will be forthcoming in sufficient measure to save this Labour Government. The issue now is not whether this or any other democratic socialist government can survive and lead this nation to full employment and a greater measure of social justice. It is whether any government *so* constituted, *so* dedicated to the principles of consent and consensus within our democracy, can lead this nation.[47]

This evocation of Abraham Lincoln would have been more impressive but for the irresponsibility and neglect of economic policy during the previous fifteen months.

At Cabinet on 10 July, Denis Healey gave an account of the discussions with the TUC and CBI thus far. There had been agreement with the TUC on £6 though there was still disagreement as to whether the cut-off for increases should be at £10,000 or £7,000. The TUC had at first not been prepared to discuss any legislation at all but had later agreed to penal sanctions through the Price Code, legislation to relieve employers of their contractual obligations, and the selective application of the rate support grant. The CBI had finally agreed to the use of the Price Code, but were urging the need for reserve powers against the employer. They did not like the £6 and still preferred a percentage figure.

The last battle

Then began in Cabinet the battle whether there should be immediate legislation on reserve powers against employers. Healey, with support from Wilson, claimed they were needed for the credibility of the policy. Credibility was threatened by the narrow vote in the General Council of the TUC. The policy had only been carried by nineteen votes to thirteen. Len Murray had been told that the Government had the right to take its own decisions after considering the views of the TUC. The CBI, on the other hand, had actually *asked* the Government to legislate against employers. Michael Foot pressed for the removal of any reference to reserve powers. After long discussion during which Healey was brought to the point of resignation and warned that, if the battery of weapons was not strong enough, it would make a full statutory policy inevitable, the Cabinet was almost equally divided.

Denis Healey then accepted, as a compromise, that there should be an announcement that a Bill was already prepared and would be introduced immediately there was a breach of the policy. If that happened, it would be a question of legislating, not reserve powers, but powers for immediate implementation. The same recourse would be necessary if the package failed to restore confidence in sterling. As Benn justly comments, it 'was just playing with words'. Healey thought he might get away with his compromise because the market did not really believe in incomes policies. What it really wanted was cuts in public expenditure. Indeed there might have to be tougher cuts as a result of the compromise. In his statement to the House on 11 July, Wilson used the phrase 'powers in reserve' rather than 'reserve powers'.[48] Later, perhaps inadvertently, he was to refer to a Reserve Powers Bill.

The additional powers which were prepared for introduction if needed had four main features. First they would have given the Government legal powers enforceable against individual employers who exceeded the pay limit. Secondly, and to meet the point made by the Lord Chancellor, there was to be provision that would prevent the prosecution of work people for criminal conspiracy. Thirdly there would be provision for compulsory notification of all wage settlements. Fourthly, it would enable the Government to reduce to the agreed level any settlements made after 1 August 1975.[49]

Battle for a Statutory Incomes Policy 171

The Left hugs its fig leaf

Clearly the compromise made the Left feel a little better. Benn felt able to tell his diary 'today has been a success in the sense that we fought off the complete abandonment of our policy. That is not to say we have won, because the White Paper is still very grim.'[50] Healey records:

> Jack Jones said he would do his best to discourage Michael Foot from resigning over legal sanctions . . . Michael did not resign. On the contrary, he became an indispensable supporter in the negotiations with the TUC over pay, which took up so much of my last three years as Chancellor.

The tribute to Michael Foot is entirely deserved. On the other hand there was now no occasion for him to resign. The line had been so drawn that Michael Foot would still feel able to defend the policy as being consistent with Labour's commitments to the TUC. The reason for this was that the sanctions were not, contrary to Healey's mistaken claim, 'embodied . . . as reserve powers in the legislation'.[51]

On 10 July, when this Cabinet meeting was taking place, I was in Brussels, at a Finance Ministers' Council. I was told what had been decided in Cabinet. I was shaken how little statutory backing there was despite Healey's strong words and threats of resignation. However, the backing to the policy was, as it turned out, very powerful. All that the opponents of a statutory policy really achieved was a fig leaf to cover their embarrassment. Moreover the Government was committing itself to a virtually permanent incomes policy. The July 1975 White Paper said that 'The Government intend to maintain policies which, over a number of years, will control domestic inflation and prevent any resurgence of the present rates of price increase. We have to get down to inflation rates no higher than those of our competitors and stay there.'[52]

Only by a long-term commitment could any safeguard be provided against a further inflationary crisis at the end of the policy. Even this Government found it necessary to announce, as a back-up to its 'voluntary' policy, that legislation had been prepared and that, if the pay limit was endangered, further and stronger legislation would at once be introduced into Parliament, though Michael Foot made clear in the House that, if such legislation were introduced, he would not be the proper person to do it. Indeed in one important respect, it *was* overtly a statutory policy. The Remuneration, Charges and Grants Act, enacted at the end of July, relieved employers of any contractual obligations that would otherwise compel them to pay more than the £6 and threatened the use of price control wherever an employer broke the limit.[53] This, together with the co-operation of the TUC, the contingency powers in draft, and the use of the Government's powers to control settlements in the public sector, made it as effective as a fully statutory policy could have been, possibly even more effective.[54]

Managing the policy

All incomes policies throw up problems not all of which are foreseen. ECP now carried a lighter load but it still had work to do. There was, for example, the question whether, in the public sector, the £6 should be a maximum or an entitlement. It was clear that it was supposed to be a maximum, not an entitlement, in the private sector. Indeed by a kind of curious logic it was being argued by some people in the TUC that if the £6 was to be paid in all cases it was getting near a statutory policy.[55] When the Prime Minister made his statement on 11 July he said that the £6 was a maximum, not an entitlement. It would have to be negotiated by established collective bargaining procedures.[56] No doubt his tongue was firmly in his cheek. In practice there was little doubt how the decision would fall.

As the year ended we had to decide how to deal with the question of how increments should be controlled within the incomes policy. Increments, it was argued, were acceptable provided that they were self-financing, that is, did not add to a company's salary bill. I observed that it was a curious idea that what worried people who did not have increments was whether increments were self-financing. In fact what worried them was that other people had increments. Somehow we found answers to all these problems without threatening the survival of the policy. It had been foreseen that the actual operation of the £8,500 cut off in incomes policy would work in a very anomalous way and would cause difficulties. In practice there was nothing that could be done about it. It was a matter to note for the second stage of the policy after July 1976 when we would have to make sure that we did not worsen the anomalies.

The Policy Unit

On Thursday 3 July I attended Cabinet. Beforehand Donoughue told me that at a meeting the previous evening Treasury officials' contempt for

Ministers had been deployed with exceptional clarity. I replied that it was a pity that Treasury officials had reason for such contempt. There was, at the time, deep suspicion of the Treasury and its motives in No. 10. It was thought to be conspiring against the Government. Even its intervention policy on the foreign exchanges, a matter regularly discussed with Treasury Ministers, was held out as evidence that the Treasury wanted the fall of the Government, or at least to force it into the adoption of policies that would threaten the future of the Government. Haines's account of the events of June/July 1975 ends with a vigorous attack on the Treasury.

Looking back at it now, and on other past crises, I find it incredible that we so readily accepted that the Treasury machine might try to upset the policy of an elected Government. It was as if we conceded the right of the permanent financial advisers to the Government to have a policy of their own in competition with the cabinet's.[57]

Donoughue considers that the June/July 1975 crisis underlined weaknesses in the machinery of government for handling economic policy. It allowed the Treasury to hold its cards close to its chest and to 'bounce' crisis packages through Cabinets of Ministers who had not been briefed with alternative ideas. 'In July 1975 if we in the Policy Unit had not had the time and the resources to construct our alternative voluntary policy, the Treasury's statutory policy would certainly have gone through' when a voluntary policy was negotiable and was likely to be successful.[58] Donoughue therefore regards the story of how incomes policy was reintroduced in July 1975 as justification for the existence of his Policy Unit. By its intervention, it ensured that Jack Jones and Hugh Scanlon, and the other TUC leaders, were fighting for the policy rather than against it.

The existence of the Policy Unit at No. 10 does not need any such justification and, indeed, the history of June/July 1975 does not provide it. What stood between the Labour Government and a fully statutory policy was not the Policy Unit, whose influence on events Donoughue and Haines grossly exaggerate, but an armful of commitments to the trade union movement. There are always weaknesses in the machinery of government and it needs to be adapted to changing circumstances. It is right, for example, that the Prime Minister should have advice from some such body as the Policy Unit. But it was not any weakness in the machinery of government that left inflation to soar month after month, nor did the existence of the Policy Unit bring the problem seriously on to the agenda before total collapse was facing the Government.[59] The truth is that it was not discussed because Ministers did not want to discuss it. It would have faced them with the breakdown of their own policy and with the necessity of cutting public expenditure and introducing an incomes policy. Better than these dreadful options was to hope that the problem would go away. Unfortunately it did not.

There can be no doubt that the failure of Ministers, over many months, to confront the mounting inflationary dangers alarmed officials in the Treasury. The great merit that could be claimed, and indeed was claimed, for a Labour Government was its relations with the trade unions whose monopoly power had, in 1974, as they saw it, threatened the survival of constitutional government in Britain. Treasury officials had placed great value on that relationship for want of any other aspect of the Government's policy on which any value could be placed at all. They were even willing to accept that such a government would have to take steps along the lines of the Social Contract to keep the unions sweet. Some had even persuaded themselves that it was sensible of the Chancellor to conduct an over-expansionist economic policy if, as a result, the co-operation of the unions against inflation could be ensured.

What the Treasury now wanted was an effective government mounting an effective attack on inflation. Yet, for month after month, the Government had sat back watching inflation rise, frightened, apparently, of the political cost of confronting the unions with the inflationary consequences of their actions, listening uncomplainingly to the self-exculpatory nonsense emerging from the lips of one trade union leader after another. At a time of dangerous and mounting inflation, the Cabinet meeting at Chequers on 20 June was, as Donoughue himself puts it, 'the first time pay policy had been considered formally and collectively by Cabinet Ministers'. This statement is not literally true. Pay policy and the working of the Social Contract had, on a number of occasions, been discussed in the Ministerial Committee on Economic Strategy. It would be fairer to say that neither there, nor in Cabinet itself, had it ever been discussed with sufficient urgency. Nevertheless there is more truth in the statement than any government should have been comfortable with. It is difficult to imagine greater irresponsibility, and if the Treasury was for once pushing Ministers as hard and as far as it could, it was only doing its duty. If, then, Treasury officials annoyed Haines and Donoughue, they can, in these exceptional circumstances, be forgiven.

A government that lacked the courage or the political strength even to threaten a partly statutory policy, with the sanctions directed only against employers, would not have been in a position to negotiate even as good a hybrid policy as was in the end obtained. It was the tough stand by the Treasury and the Chancellor of the Exchequer that secured a credible policy even if it was not quite all they would have preferred. The insistence on its being a voluntary policy not a statutory policy was a matter of face saving, not reality. The insouciance of the top TUC leaders in face of rising inflation until quite shortly before the crisis hardly gave confidence that they would help if not under the threat of some statutory action. Barbara Castle in her diary for 7 July records a comment that she made at a private meeting with Shore, Foot, Benn, and Varley: 'I said that the threat of statutory powers had obviously concentrated the unions' minds wonderfully.'[60]

Would a fully statutory policy have been better?

In a situation in which sterling was under enormous pressure and the alternative was almost certainly the fall of the Labour Government, and in which therefore the TUC would have hesitated before taking up a stance of outright opposition, it was at least arguable that a fully statutory policy would have been a better option than the hybrid policy that was in fact adopted. A statutory policy based on 10 per cent might have been more effective in reducing inflation and would have provided a softer re-entry than did, eventually, the £6 policy. The White Paper *The Attack on Inflation*, 11 July 1975, announced the Government's intention to bring inflation down to single figures by the end of 1976. This was not achieved. The RPI rose by 15 per cent during 1976 compared with over 25 per cent in 1975. It was still rising at an annual rate of 15 per cent in the second half of 1976. The £6 policy was initially variously estimated to add 10–11 per cent, or 12 per cent, to earnings. A year later it was being calculated that it had in fact added 14 per cent to earnings even at a time of rising unemployment. One reason for the discrepancy between estimate and out-turn may have been devices such as re-grading used by employers to protect the differentials of skilled workers.[61]

Virtue rewarded

On 24 July, I was told privately by a source likely to be in the know that the Prime Minister intended to resign in the autumn. I did not believe it but, in my diary, I commented that, if true, it would enable him to escape the developing economic problems and go out with the achievement of the Common Market referendum behind him. It would also enable him to leave a government reborn, equipped with a reconstituted incomes policy, and therefore, as his final bequest to the nation, the prospect of inflation defeated. In fact, however, it was Healey who, with major help from Jack Jones, had saved the Government. It was to be expected, therefore, that at the annual conference of the Labour Party, the following September, the Left should have organized to remove him from the National Executive Committee of the party, and not unexpected that they should have succeeded.

But for some Ministers at least the crisis was over and everything could go on as normal. After the traumatic Cabinet on 1 July, Barbara Castle recorded in her diary that she was making sure that the really important things were not forgotten.

Meanwhile I am still doing battle with Ted Short about the inclusion of my Pay Beds Bill in next session's programme. Doesn't the Government realize that this is an essential political sweetener for the unions?[62]

Notes

1. For example, on 9 May I made a speech to the National Savings Assembly in Bournemouth and on 20 May spoke to the National Union of Mineworkers Summer School at Barlaston.
2. *Daily Telegraph*, 21 May 1975.
3. William Keegan, *Financial Times*, 21 May 1975, and Samuel Brittan, *Financial Times*, 22 May 1975.
4. MacDougall 218.
5. Reported in *The Times*, 24 Apr. 1975.
6. *NIER* (May 1975), 6.
7. Haines 47–8.
8. Castle 421.
9. Benn 403.
10. Haines 46.
11. Crosland 296.
12. Donoughue 63.
13. Benn 404–5, and Donoughue 63.
14. The Chequers meeting is described by Castle 425–30.
15. MacDougall 221.
16. Jones 299–300.

17. Jones 296. Benn had been advocating a flat rate 'which would deal with the problem of inflation' since June 1974. Benn 166.
18. Jones 296. See also Castle 436.
19. Barbara Castle reports a meeting of the Liaison Committee on 9 July at which Alex Kitson was still arguing for a flat-rate policy and against a statutory policy while Denis Healey was not prepared to rule a statutory policy out of court. Castle 452.
20. Donoughue 63–4.
21. Donoughue 66.
22. Haines 50.
23. Donoughue 67.
24. Haines 55.
25. Healey 394–5.
26. Donoughue 67.
27. Haines 55.
28. Haines 56.
29. Donoughue 68.
30. Haines 57.
31. Donoughue 68.
32. Wilson (1979), 115 acknowledges receipt of this message in wording that is, perhaps, significant. He says: '*In this respect* [emphasis added] Mr Joe Haines's book reproducing his note to me on the midnight Treasury *demarche* is accurate.' One can only speculate on the respects in which Mr Haines's account is thereby condemned by Lord Wilson as inaccurate.
33. Wilson (1979), 115.
34. Castle 442. In 1966 there had been other penalties against strikers.
35. Benn 411.
36. Castle 439–40.
37. Benn 411.
38. Healey 395.
39. HC Debs., 1 July 1975, cols.1189–90. See also Castle 443.
40. Benn 413.
41. Castle 447.
42. Healey 395.
43. Benn 413.
44. Castle 448–9.
45. Jones 298.
46. Donoughue 69–70. The TUC was not, as a whole, enthusiastic about a flat-rate policy. In a comment in July 1975 it said that the flat-rate approach was 'not envisaged as a permanent policy for continually eroding differentials either between or within negotiating groups'. *The Development of the Social Contract* (London, July 1975).
47. Wilson (1976), 90 n.
48. HC Debs., 11 July 1975, col. 904.
49. These powers were outlined by Denis Healey to the Commons on 21 July. HC Debs., 21 July 1975, col. 58.
50. This account of the Cabinet on 10 July is based on Castle 454–6 and Benn 414–16.

51. Healey 395.
52. Cmnd. 6151.
53. See Harold Wilson's statement, HC Debs., 11 July 1975, cols. 903 ff.
54. The Government directly employed 2m. people and a further 2m. were employed by the nationalized industries.
55. Castle 470.
56. HC Debs., 11 July 1975, col. 902. This was repeated in the Commons by Denis Healey. HC Debs., 21 July 1975, col. 53.
57. Haines 49–50.
58. Donoughue 72.
59. Donoughue discusses the implications of the June/July 1975 crisis for the machinery of government in Donoughue 71–8.
60. Castle 448.
61. *NIER* (August 1976), 8. See also *NIER* (Feb. 1977), 14.
62. Castle 443.

S·I·X·T·E·E·N

Treasury Advice and Cabinet Responsibility

The problems of the UK economy are never solved. They are merely handled more or less successfully with instruments of policy that are frequently inadequate to the task. Economic management requires a balancing act between conflicting priorities. In July 1975 the defeat of inflation was unquestionably the dominant priority. But no priority dominates indefinitely. The July measures left many other serious economic problems which might in their turn demand priority status.

Treasury advice

At a lunch with Treasury Ministers on 15 October 1975, Denis Healey said he was very worried about the Treasury's advice. Much of it, he said, did not stand up to examination. He displayed his distrust more devastatingly in his meetings with Treasury officials by probing the advice he was receiving. So difficult did Treasury officials find these encounters that they appeared to consider my presence a useful diversion as Denis was as likely to attack me as them. On one occasion a very senior Treasury official told me of a meeting with the Chancellor to which I had not been invited. He suggested, half seriously, that I should get myself invited. But I gained the impression that when I was not invited to one of the Chancellor's meetings it was no mistake. I was seldom able to deflect the lightning unless Healey himself wished me to serve that purpose.

There was, unfortunately, too much justification in Denis's criticism of Treasury advice. Too frequently, advice was brought forward without adequate preparation or, for that matter, conviction. Yet there was also a great deal to be said on the Treasury's side. What exactly did the Chancellor want? He knew that the Treasury was divided and had asked that the divisions should not be concealed by monolithic advice. Yet, by the summer of 1975, he had still not made up his mind between the different schools of thought. What the 'deflationists' were proposing was always too tough and what the Keynesians were proposing was often too risky. Treasury officials had lived for eighteen months with a Chancellor whose intellectual powers they admired but who still seemed to lack a policy of his own. Healey, it seemed, wanted to be known as a 'political' Chancellor. But, whatever their differences on other matters, Treasury officials knew that it was not a time for political Chancellors.[1] Treasury officials felt themselves entitled to look to the Chancellor for leadership, not just for criticism of their own proposals. But Healey's difficult position in Cabinet inhibited him from giving that leadership. He had to satisfy the Cabinet, the TUC, the party, the market. Treasury officials probably had more sympathy with his problems than he had with theirs.

The Chancellor and the Cabinet: a conflict of attitudes

Healey was under considerable pressure from Cabinet colleagues to be more open with them in making economic policy. This was, in part, an inheritance from the earlier period of Wilson Government. Some, with experience of the 1960s, claimed that never again should a Chancellor be permitted to make economic policy in a political vacuum. Chancellors must be made responsible to Cabinet just as were other Ministers. As economic policy is the foundation of all other policy, it was hardly surprising that other Ministers and their supporting back-benchers should look jealously at the extraordinary powers possessed by any Chancellor, at least as long as he has the support or the tolerance of the Prime Minister.

Distrust of the Treasury is endemic in all governments. It is not confined to Ministers. Sir Antony Part, a distinguished Permanent Secretary of the Department of Trade and Industry, has referred to the Treasury's 'tendency to centralise too much' and of its over-estimate of the degree to which the high intelligence and imagination of Treasury officials can substitute for the experience of officials in other departments.[2] In part the distrust has been earned by the Treasury's own uncertainties and misjudgements. In part it follows, however unjustly, from the failures of British economic performance which have left this country lagging in economic growth.

The Chancellor has two interlinked responsibilities, for the control of public expenditure and for economic policy. Within the Cabinet, the Chancellor is heavily outnumbered by spending colleagues. Unless he can rely on very strong support from the Prime Minister, he is likely to be defeated in any attempt to control public expenditure. Control is most likely to be lost under governments pledged to major increases in public expenditure. It was my view that the only way of managing a controlled increase rather than an explosive increase was to leave decisions as far as possible to the Chancellor and the Prime Minister. That is very difficult to achieve under the British system because all Ministers in Cabinet have an undeniable interest. So far as economic policy generally was concerned, it was my view that Cabinets had too much influence, not that they did not have enough. Moreover what might have been conceded in normal times without great risk would have become a real danger at that time. We had lived through eighteen profligate months. We had not yet emerged successfully from an extreme crisis which could easily have brought down the Government. To concede more power to Cabinet at that moment would have been to face further unacceptable hazards.

Healey, on the other hand, who actually had to play the Treasury cards in Cabinet, was more sympathetic to the querulous complaints of his colleagues that they were being constrained by economic policies to which they had never consented, which had never in their view been adequately explained, and for which in theory they were ultimately responsible. Many thought they were simply in the presence of an old-fashioned, and obscurantist, Treasury orthodoxy. They thought that the Treasury was not on their side and that it ought to be on their side. They were, after all, supplied with enough economic advisers to be persuaded that, with different policies, the constraints on their departmental expenditures could be relaxed. Healey, no doubt, saw then the danger to which he has since given expression, that the procedures of collective responsibility will lead only to 'a soggy compromise'.[3] But he had to live in close proximity with colleagues who, being bound by collective responsibility, wanted a voice even if they did not really know what to say with it.

When Cabinet did win opportunities to comment on economic policy, the time was largely wasted with the deployment of fantastic alternatives which lacked the essential element of credibility. At Cabinet on 6 November 1975, Benn was given another opportunity to argue for import controls.

> I have urged protection in one form or another for eighteen months: first, a policy of rescuing firms in 1974, then temporary employment subsidies and selective import controls. But I am now convinced that to protect the balance of payments and protect jobs we need a major wall of protection around us because senile industries, like infant industries, must be protected.

He ended, 'We must reject the deflationary and monetarist policies we are now pursuing.'[4] But no Prime Minister would have entrusted economic policy to Benn. His arguments had nothing to do with the formation of policy. They were simply for the record.

Pressure for reflation came from the Right as well as from the Left. At the same Cabinet, Harold Lever proposed 'a rolling deal with the trade unions'. He said, 'If through being over-cautious . . . over reflation we lose the cooperation of the unions, nothing could be more catastrophic. Reflation ought to be pursued by a series of smaller steps'. Barbara Castle comments: 'I can only hope our nagging away on these themes will have some effect in weaning the Chancellor from his pressure for those desperately deflationary public expenditure cuts he is planning.'[5]

Even this Cabinet was just about to conclude that substantial cuts in planned public expenditure were necessary. The lack of realism in what was being said at this meeting of Cabinet illustrates how little benefit there can be in Cabinet discussion of economic policy. As the area of discretion in the making of economic policy narrowed, the wider was imagination allowed to range.

Notes

1. Castle 485.
2. Part 187–8.
3. Healey 376.
4. Benn 458.
5. Castle 542–3.

S·E·V·E·N·T·E·E·N

Public Expenditure: The Fight for Control

By the autumn of 1975, some forecasts foresaw the current account deficit for 1975 as low as £750 million, a dramatic improvement on the previous year. The improvement was due to the recession in the UK economy rather than to any advance in competitiveness. The world recession was proving deeper and more prolonged than many had expected and the UK could no longer hope to isolate itself from it. To some Keynesian minds outside government, success in establishing the incomes policy combined with the greatly improved current account suggested that the Government's priority should now be the reduction of unemployment.' The latest Treasury figures showed unemployment reaching 1,200,000 during the winter of 1975/6. Michael Foot thought this forecast optimistic and that the rising tide of unemployment would do great damage to the anti-inflation policy. In December Healey would react to the concern about unemployment. But for the Treasury, two other problems had priority. One was the need for substantial cuts in public expenditure. The other, despite the improved figures, was the funding of the current account deficit.

There was now no disagreement at official level within the Treasury on the subject of public expenditure. This agreement simplified the task of briefing Ministers and setting out a policy. Public expenditure was on the Treasury agenda even before the incomes agreement with the TUC had been finalized. Healey had been pressing for public expenditure cuts at least since March.[2] He had, in May, allowed himself to be deflected on a £3 billion package of cuts and higher charges. Discussion was deferred to July. He had been opposed by Tony Crosland, Tony Benn, and Barbara Castle and he had received scant support from the Prime Minister.[3]

Cash limits

In his statement on incomes policy on 11 July, the Prime Minister ruled out 'panic cuts' in public expenditure but, with a significance not fully understood at the time, he emphasized the pledge given by Healey on 1 July 'to employ the system of cash limits more generally as a means of controlling public expenditure in the short term'.[4]

> We have made clear our intention to apply cash limits, as opposed to limits based on resources measured at theoretical constant prices, as a means of ensuring financial discipline . . . Urgent work is in hand to ensure the extensive use of cash limits in the coming financial year.[5]

Healey on 1 July and Wilson on 11 July both referred to cash limits as an instrument in the battle against inflation. Changes, of which the use of cash limits was one, were being planned to bring public expenditure under better technical control. At the end of 1975, Sir Leo Pliatzky became Second Permanent Secretary at the Treasury in charge of public expenditure. The changes, which were to have unexpected effects, have been described by Pliatzky himself. First, the contingency reserve was to place a limit on additional expenditure. Once it had been spent there was to be no more money that year unless by decision of the Cabinet itself. A shortfall against planned expenditure was not to be relevant to the consideration of new, unplanned, expenditure. Secondly, to reinforce this control, Treasury Ministers were not to be overruled in Cabinet Committees. Pliatzky has described this as 'a very important constitutional change'. It made Cabinet itself the monitoring authority on the contingency reserve.

The third change was cash limits. These put a ceiling at the beginning of the financial year on the degree of indexation of programmes (except some which were open-ended in character) which the Government would be prepared to finance.[6] The effect was 'to convince departments that if they overspent they would run out of money and there would be no more . . . And so at each level in departments, those responsible for controlling budgets were holding something back and not committing it.'[7] These measures did not actually come into effect until the beginning of 1976 but, when they did, there was a significant increase in shortfall against planned expenditures.

Questions of presentation

Public expenditure was, at the time, presented in a way which exaggerated the proportion of gross domestic product it constituted. The figure of 60 per cent of GDP devoted to public expenditure was one to strike horror in the heart of the most valiant social democrat. Healey has argued that the Treasury's definition of public spending was 'unforgivably misleading'. When, in 1976, public spending was redefined in the same way as in other countries, UK spending was reduced by £7.7 billion at a stroke. And when GDP was costed, like public spending, at market prices, the ratio of public spending to GDP fell from 60 per cent to 46 per cent. Healey convicts the Treasury of 'sado-masochism'. He comments:

> I could find it in me to forgive the Treasury for the inaccuracy of its forecasts . . . But I cannot forgive it . . . for misleading the Government, the country and the world for so many years about the true state of public spending in Britain. Indeed I cannot help suspecting that Treasury officials deliberately overstated public spending in order to put pressure on governments which were reluctant to cut it.[8]

Pliatzky has described how the UK Government's presentation of its public spending statistics was brought into line with those of other OECD countries.[9] During a visit to Canada, he had discovered the different presentation adopted and this had led him to question many aspects of the UK presentation, including cases where there was actual double counting. Two questions arise. The first is whether, as Healey alleges, the Treasury was guilty of deliberate falsification with a view to influencing Ministers. The second is what difference of substance was made by the difference in presentation which was adopted during 1976.

On the first point, it can be pleaded in mitigation that it was a Treasury official, Sir Leo Pliatzky, who was primarily responsible for changing the presentation. If the Treasury's main purpose had been to exert pressure on profligate Ministers, it could have been achieved by showing, on *any* consistent definition, the rapidly increasing proportion of GDP devoted to public expenditure. The ratio of public expenditure to GDP in current market prices rose from 39 per cent in 1973 to 44.2 per cent in 1974 and to 46.2 per cent in 1975.[10] Only then did it start falling again. These are very substantial increases at any time and especially at a time of high inflation and reduced real national income. They are quite enough to make the Treasury's point. It is more likely that the Treasury's failure to review its definition earlier was the result of inertia rather than of design. On the second question, the exaggeration could certainly influence foreign opinion, and thus have real market effects. On the other hand there were many other characteristics of the UK economy which alarmed foreign opinion without the aid of this particular statistic. There was the record of its performance over many years, its high rate of inflation, and its current account deficit.

Moreover the difference in *presentation* did not in any way affect the reality of the sums actually being spent. It is not persuasive to argue that a level of public expenditure in the UK is justified because it represents a proportion of GDP comparable to that found in some other country. The difference in economic performance of those other countries has also to be taken into account. The question was not whether the UK proportion was comparable with that of other countries but whether its level was acceptable in the UK context. Healey himself points out that all economic management is a matter of judgement. Evidently Healey himself judged that the upward drive of public expenditure had become, in the UK context, unsustainable. Writing of the decisions following the IMF crisis, he says: 'By 1978/9 my successive cuts had brought it down to about forty-two per cent—about the same as West Germany but far below Scandinavia and the Netherlands.'[11] The decisions that led to this result were taken *after* the presentation of UK public expenditure had been changed. Presumably he found the cuts he had negotiated with his Cabinet colleagues necessary irrespective of the previous errors in presentation. In the same way, in July 1975, he had concluded that, as a matter of substance, not of presentation, cuts were necessary if his policies were to succeed.

Priorities

On 8 July, there was a meeting at the Treasury to discuss the medium-term assessment. Substantial cuts in public expenditure were necessary if room was to be left for any increase in private consumption or industrial investment. There were the usual clashes between Healey and myself. Healey perhaps thought that I had been insufficiently appreciative of his efforts to secure the incomes policy and, if he felt that, he had every justification. There followed on 4 August a special Cabinet at Chequers to discuss public expenditure priorities. The priorities that appeared to emerge were housing (but not housing subsidies), industrial training, and inner cities. The lowest priorities were transport and higher education.[12] In fact, nothing was being decided. The real battle was still to come.

Wilson's concern, on this as on other occasions, was to give Cabinet Ministers the illusion of having been consulted. But because everyone wanted to speak, members of Cabinet were limited to 'speeches' of ten minutes each. Crosland, Lever, Jenkins, and Shore all attempted to widen the argument beyond departmental concerns but the occasion illustrated the problems of constituting a consensus on public expenditure, or on economic policy, among a Cabinet of over twenty Ministers, most of them burdened by departmental interests, and few of them equipped to comment on wider issues.

Tony Crosland argued that the UK was far from being the most lavish of countries in the proportion of its GDP devoted to public expenditure. Crosland was a professional economist. He felt that he, rather than Healey, should be presiding over the Treasury. The Prime Minister had preferred Healey perhaps because he detected in Crosland a lack of the toughness necessary at the Treasury. Moreover Crosland was not at his most effective in Cabinet. He never showed the determination in opposing Treasury orthodoxy for which Barbara Castle looked. Reporting on a later Cabinet meeting, at which there was a discussion of the public expenditure survey, she says: '[I]t is clear to me that the majority of our colleagues will always toe the Treasury line—including Tony C. for all the oratorical gestures he likes to make.'[13] Of course Barbara Castle at DHSS and Crosland at Environment were rivals in the allocation of public expenditure and watched each other's manœuvres like hawks.

The PSBR soars again

In the autumn the Treasury produced the regular National Income Forecast (NIF) which showed the PSBR for 1975/6 rising from £9 billion to £12 billion which, at around 5 per cent of GDP, was alarmingly high. The external deficit was forecast to be over £1 billion and rising. Wilson immediately summoned an inner group of Ministers. Donoughue reports:

At the meeting Chancellor Denis Healey presented three options. Unless Ministers significantly cut public expenditure the alternatives facing the Government were either to introduce import controls (this was floated mainly to frighten Ministers); to devalue sterling by 7 per cent (to frighten the Prime Minister); or to apply to the IMF for a major loan (revealing how early on, still under Harold Wilson's premiership, an application to the IMF was on the agenda). The Ministers did not reach any precise decision at this meeting . . . However, they did indicate that of the three options they preferred the IMF loan . . . Mr Callaghan himself said: 'Let us do the tough things now and get them out of the way.'[14]

It would become the continuing cry of those Ministers who saw the need for doing *something* that enough should be done to get away from the recurrent public expenditure crises that were so disruptive politically and so damaging to morale. Unfortunately the Cabinet's judgement of 'enough' repeatedly fell short of what really was enough.

Resources: Crosland versus Healey

At the regular Treasury Ministers' lunch on 15 October, we reviewed the position on a number of issues: public expenditure, cash limits, and whether we should make an application to the IMF for borrowing under the oil facility. Later that afternoon I had a meeting with Harold Lever. He referred to the conflict between Healey and Crosland on public expenditure. Crosland had asked Lever to tell the Prime Minister that he and Healey were on a collision course.

The intellectual argument about the demand for public expenditure cuts swirled around the concept of 'resources'. Was public expenditure placing so high a demand on resources as to deny sufficient increases in private consumption and in private investment, and to be in itself inflationary? Crosland's position was that it was absurd, at a time of high unemployment, to claim that resources were under pressure. On the contrary, it was unlikely that there would be any danger of economic over-heating as far ahead as could be seen. The most he was prepared to concede were total cuts of £2 billion in the increases planned for the two years 1977/9. He no doubt hoped that if his resources argument proved correct any cuts could be restored.

At Cabinet on 13 November, Healey emphasized the risks the country and the Government were facing. He began with hope. He was talking, he said, about the return to full employment. He rejected immediate cuts which would only increase unemployment. But he called for total cuts of almost £4 billion in planned future increases covering 1977/9. His reason was that by then the world economy would be recovering. Room would have to be made for investment and exports plus a modest improvement in living standards.

To this end, the demands of public expenditure on resources had to be reduced. The public sector was at present borrowing 20 pence for every pound it spent and the burden of debt was becoming crippling. Public expenditure was still not being properly controlled. The increase in 1975/6 would probably be 4 per cent instead of the planned 1.5 per cent. If Crosland's advice was followed, the necessary resources would not be released. There would be a need for further borrowing but the borrowing necessary in any case might not be possible without larger cuts.[15] The only alternative would be a substantial increase in taxation which was already too high.[16] Denis insisted that it was essential to achieve balance in our payments by 1978/9. Otherwise the burden of debt interest would wipe out the gains from North Sea oil and gas. In this he was demonstrating what he regarded as one of his peculiar political skills. Any argument would do if it served his purpose. Certainly he had never accepted from me that the Government's conduct of policy was likely to wipe out the prospective gains from North Sea oil.

Economic forecasting was not then and is not now sufficiently reliable to provide a firm basis either for the Crosland argument or the Healey argument. One problem was that the measure of available resources was itself highly unreliable. The fact that there had been an increase in unemployment did not necessarily imply that there had been a proportionate release of resources. Economic policy ideas are as free as the wind and indeed often consist of little else. The question always is can deficits be funded? If not, Ministers with expansionary ideas should save their breath to cool their porridge.

Industrial policy

Healey strongly supported industrial policy. Not to support industrial policy would have been to deny all that was left that was distinctive in a Labour government's handling of the economy. More decisively, Healey was very sensitive to the TUC's demands under the head of industrial policy because he knew how dependent he was on them in the battle against inflation. He always attempted to do something for them when he was contemplating other, less popular, steps. The result was that each time he proposed a round of public expenditure cuts, he sought for some increase in expenditure on industrial policy. On this occasion about £2 billion *extra* was allocated to trade, industry and employment over the period 1975/9. It included £225 million a year for the NEB.[17]

It is always more difficult for a Chancellor to secure control of public expenditure when he has his own favourite objects. Healey won little credit with his colleagues for putting the industrial strategy ahead of social expenditures, particularly as it was his priority rather than theirs. His audience was sceptical not because they doubted the efficacy of an industrial strategy but for two other contradictory reasons. On the one hand they believed that the industrial strategy did not go far enough, was not expensive enough, and did not include enough public ownership. On the other, they criticized Healey because his increases in expenditure on industrial policy carried with them the threat of yet further cuts in social expenditure. Yet priority for the industrial strategy was, supposedly, the policy of the Labour Party.

Healey triumphs

The debate in Cabinet continued on 9 and 11 December.[18] Healey won without too much difficulty. Wilson summed up in his favour, although Barbara Castle calculated that there had been a slight majority in Cabinet for a smaller cut. 'Eric [Varley] whisper[ed] to me that he thought Denis would have resigned if he had been beaten.'[19] This illustrates the importance of having a Prime Minister who can count, though if a Prime Minister supports his Chancellor, there is seldom any need to count. The Public Expenditure White Paper Cmnd. 6393, eventually published in February 1976, showed cuts as compared with Cmnd. 5879, the previous year's White Paper, of £1.6 billion in 1977/8 and £3 billion in 1978/9. The White Paper declared the Government's intention to freeze the level of public expenditure from then on. On the other hand the comparison with Cmnd. 5879 also showed increases in public expenditure of £1 billion in 1975/6 and nearly £500 million in 1976/7.[20] To critical observers, increases in the short term were bound to induce scepticism as to the longer term.

Donoughue comments: 'This exercise was actually quite a triumph for Chancellor Denis Healey, who perhaps for the first time since 1974 displayed his true calibre, showing great stamina and powers of sustained argument.'[21] Healey had obtained substantially what he had asked for. It did not ease his position in subsequent rounds that he was coming back for more. Healey was perhaps assisted by the feeling in

Cabinet that what was being taken away from future years might later be restored, and that meanwhile current over-expenditure was being accepted. There was the further feeling that it was better to bite the bullet now and get the whole miserable business of public expenditure cuts over with once and for all. Moreover an application had been made to the IMF for a stand-by facility and it is always more dignified to do in advance what one's lender of last resort might have it in mind to suggest.

Though he had won this public expenditure round there was little comfort in *NIER*'s forecasts. '[H]igh unemployment, high inflation with a mere hint of further slowdown, substantial current balance deficits, and high public sector borrowing requirements. Even if we look to the very end of 1977, there are few hints of an improvement on any of these fronts'. Of course, as *NIER* recognized, this was only a forecast and many things could affect it for better, or worse.[22] No doubt some at least of those asked to fund the UK's current account deficit would have noticed that though the out-turn might be better than this forecast, yet, bad as it was, it could be still worse.

Notes

1. See *NIER* (Aug. 1975).
2. Benn 356.
3. Donoughue 62. Donoughue regards this defeat as justification for the Treasury's failure to bring forward earlier measures to deal with the critical economic situation. The Cabinet meeting is described in detail in Castle 398/401 and Benn 379/81.
4. HC Debs., 1 July 1975, col. 1190.
5. HC Debs., 11 July 1975, cols. 905–6.
6. Pliatzky (1982), *passim* and *Contemporary Record*, 3/2 (Nov. 1989) (hereafter CR).
7. CR.
8. Healey 401–2.
9. Pliatzky (1982), 161 ff.
10 Pliatzky (1982), 212–13.
11. Healey 401.
12. Castle 482–6.
13. Castle 542, 6 Nov. 1975.
14. Donoughue 83–4.
15. Benn 461.
16. Healey claimed that Crosland's proposed cut of only £2b. would imply an increase in the standard rate of from 5p to 9p. Castle 546.
17. HMSO 32–3 and 143.
18. Benn 475–7 and 478–9.
19. Castle 548–9.

20. HMSO 143.
21. Donoughue 84–5.
22. *NIER* (Nov. 1975), 5.

E·I·G·H·T·E·E·N

The Current Account: Forecasting a Crisis

An IMF funding?

At a meeting on 5 August 1975, Treasury Ministers were warned that, despite the improvement in the current account, it was unlikely that it would be possible to finance the 1975 deficit from private flows of capital. A confidential approach to the IMF to signal that we would probably need to borrow against the oil facility was advised.[1] The estimates for 1976 showed that by then we would be within the conditional tranches of our IMF quota.

Discussion during the autumn was dominated by concern how the current account deficit was to be funded and what policies should be adopted to correct it. On 7 November the Government decided to apply to the IMF for a loan of SDR 1 billion under the oil facility and SDR 700 million as the UK's first credit tranche.[2] The IMF had been watching the UK predicament closely. The Fund staff observed that although the trade deficit was running at half the rate of the previous year, the reasons for the improvement did not provide comfort for the longer term. Nor had the improvement inspired much confidence. 'Instead of accumulating further holdings of sterling . . . the governments and private entrepreneurs of oil exporting countries began to sell large amounts of pounds sterling.' The current account had benefited from a favourable shift in the terms of trade due to a fall in commodity prices. There had been a large drop in imports due to depressed domestic demand and the depletion of inventories.[3]

However, in the course of the following two months, encouraged no doubt by the cuts to be made in public expenditure, the Fund staff concluded that the policies already adopted were those appropriate to the UK's problems, that they were already having some success, and that the UK's application, officially made on 15 December, should be approved. With that recommendation, the UK's application was referred to the Executive Board meeting on the last day of 1975. Though often critical of UK policies, and even more of its post-war economic record, the IMF staff regarded the UK with a certain affection. Normally called upon to discipline developing countries, it added to their prestige that they could augment their client list with a developed country.

Debate about the deficit

To correct the deficit, two policies were being advocated, depreciation and import controls. The IMF was strongly opposed to general import controls. Nevertheless they were widely advocated within the Government. At a meeting of the Liaison Committee with the TUC on 22 September, Michael Foot urged an import surcharge of 10 per cent to save £1 billion of imports. At a meeting of the NEC on 26 September, he said he did not believe import controls to be 'anything like a full answer to the problem of unemployment'. Clearly he felt that reflation was required as well.[4]

The short-term forecast discussed by Treasury Ministers on 17 October showed the balance of payments in 1976 in deficit to the same extent as in 1975 but both at a much higher level than the more optimistic forecasts of about £750 million emanating from some outside observers.[5] After 1976, there would, according to the forecast, be a severe deterioration to a £3 billion deficit in 1977 which could not be financed. The forecast deterioration was due to a rise in commodity prices expected as the international economy recovered.

The forecast was credible. There was concern about under-investment in commodity supply in developing countries. Various schemes were being propounded to improve the supply. But none would change the situation in the short term. If demand increased, a substantial rise in prices was inevitable. All this would be happening despite that great saviour, North Sea oil, supplies of which would, by 1977, be gathering pace. After the meeting I had a word with Denis Healey and suggested that it would be wrong to rush to import controls. The forecasts for

1975 had also been bad but the out-turn, bad as it was, looked like being far better than forecast. Denis said that was right but we could hardly be happy with the reasons, lower imports and a deeper depression than expected. That, I said, was true but it did not mean that we should rush to import controls on the basis of a forecast of what was going to happen more than twelve months hence. Nothing demonstrated the fragility of the UK economy more than the susceptibility of Treasury confidence to these unreliable forecasts.

Nicky Kaldor came to see me, that same day, on a renewed lobbying expedition. He wanted me to urge Denis to go for import controls. Nicky, who, during the 1960s, had been the father of devaluation, was now its sternest critic. It would stoke up inflation and the benefits would rapidly be dissipated. While I shared his anxieties about devaluation, I resisted his arguments on import controls. They grossly underestimated the risks of retaliation. They appeared to me to come nowhere near the fundamentals of our problem. There was already too much pressure for import controls within the Government and not from Nicky alone. Nicky, however, was a prime academic source of the pressure. His advice was, as usual, available to anyone who would listen including Tony Benn who hardly needed it.[6]

The medium-term forecast, now available, was discussed on 28 October. It again showed the 1976 balance of payments deficit at the same level as 1975 followed by a substantial deterioration in 1977 due to commodity price increases and despite the import saving from North Sea oil. The Treasury proposal was for a substantial sterling depreciation. It was estimated that this would lead to an improvement in the balance of payments after about eighteen months, that is after the ill effects of the J-curve had worked themselves out.

Denis was scathing about this proposal. He said that if he adopted a policy of depreciation he would at once have the Governor coming to him to complain that everything was out of control. Such a policy must take account of the effect on the holders of the sterling balances, notably Nigeria. It could turn into a rout. I also had considerable doubts but insisted that we should consider seriously what was to be done. The forecast appeared to me to reinforce the case for the substantial cuts in public expenditure then under consideration. But such was Denis's scorn for the Treasury proposal that the meeting broke up without a thorough discussion of the options. After the meeting Gordon Richardson and Kit McMahon came to my room because they feared that I was committed to the Treasury proposals. I explained that I was not and that I saw the problems with them. I said that if there was to be a deliberate devaluation, we would need a statutory incomes policy.

On 29 October, Sir Brian Hopkin and Michael Posner came to me to defend the Treasury proposal which we had not properly discussed the previous day because of Denis's scorn. They said that the inflationary effects of the depreciation should be dealt with by tax remissions despite the effect this would have on the PSBR. The trouble with all this, it seemed to me, was that policies would act in conflicting ways and the outcome would be very uncertain. Tax cuts would have a direct effect in increasing the PSBR. The stimulus to the economy might reduce the PSBR. At the same time, however, tax cuts would tend to increase the current account deficit, the reduction in which was the object of the exercise. If the 1977 forecast current account deficit was reliable, we certainly could not afford anything worse. Hopkin and Posner said that further papers coming forward would reveal the whole strategy, would reconcile the contradictions so far as they could be reconciled, would hopefully answer my questions, and would no doubt be discussed in due course if the Chancellor was prepared at least to suspend judgement on the depreciation policy.

I had thus, in the course of two days, received the conflicting advice of the 'New' Cambridge School in the shape of Nicky Kaldor, and of the 'Old' Cambridge School in the shape of Michael Posner. Nicky Kaldor now had little support in the Treasury at official level for his import control policy. The Keynesian leadership in the official Treasury was turning towards depreciation as its preferred option. With the PSBR threatening to reach £12 billion and inflation still high, there was a limit to what could be done by reflation. Therefore a stimulus via the exchange rate seemed an option worth examination. It would raise output and employment, it might even encourage co-operation from the unions in the next stage of incomes policy, as well as attacking the forecast problem of a £3 billion current account deficit in 1977.

Less than comforting advice from NIER

In November we had the benefit of the advice of *NIER*. *NIER* had now abandoned earlier optimism about the current account. It said that 'The financing problems posed by both the current deficit and the public sector borrowing requirement are not to be dismissed as potential sources of instability in the forecast. The problems are essentially those of credit-worthiness.' Financing the deficit might 'require a continued rise in the UK's covered interest differential, assuming no borrowings from the IMF beyond those announced already'. Given the high degree of uncertainty attached to current account forecasts, the best policy, it said, was to let the exchange rate depreciate 'rather faster than assumed in the forecast . . . and not to hold it up with even higher interest rates than may be necessary for internal monetary reasons'. *NIER* continued that

while this would add slightly to inflationary pressures, this cannot be avoided, and there is no reason to believe that the mere fact of a faster depreciation would cause destabilising capital outflows, since the expected exchange loss will be more than balanced by the interest rate differential in favour of sterling. Further borrowing from the IMF (another £1.2 billion is available beyond the first credit tranche already asked for) could also be helpful, if it can be assumed that the policies required by the IMF would be broadly the ones set out here.

However, *NIER* warned, appropriately, that the conditions demanded by the IMF for additional borrowings might 'be more stringent than the policy assumptions made in this forecast'. *NIER* then turned to a consideration of the import control option.[7]

These quotations bring out the complexity of the UK dilemma. Interest rates had to be high enough to encourage capital inflows, low enough to allow sterling to depreciate, high enough to ensure that it did not depreciate too much thus stimulating inflation. *NIER*'s recommendations about import controls were comparably demanding. They were ruled out on any scale but could be considered selectively. But if ruled out on any scale, they had nothing to contribute to a solution unless the contribution expected was purely presentational. Policy instruments did not exist that would solve concurrently all the problems then facing the UK economy, inflation, current account deficit, high unemployment. Yet though they did not exist, it was a political imperative that they be found. *NIER*'s principal achievement had been to guide us to this point and then abandon us to a mixture of incompatibles.

The snake?

On 15 December I attended an informal meeting of Finance Ministers in Brussels. I was accompanied by Gordon Richardson, Kit McMahon, and Sir Derek Mitchell. After the meeting, we flew back to Stansted where, due to fog in London, we had to wait two to three hours for our cars. This created an opportunity for an informal discussion on the Government's economic dilemmas. From our discussion there emerged the idea, not one to which anyone present was committed, that, if we wished to use the exchange rate aggressively, we should devalue to a fixed rate or to the snake. By becoming a member of the snake, we would give the market confidence that we were determined to keep sterling at the new level. To carry conviction there would have to be a number of other associated policies such as a very strict incomes policy and very severe cuts in public expenditure. It would be pointless if, having devalued, we threw away such competitive advantage as the devaluation gave us.

The following day, 16 December, there was a formal meeting at the Treasury on economic strategy. Denis noted that he was not being pressed to take action at that point even on accelerated depreciation. Treasury officials now wanted the discussions on the second stage of incomes policy to be further advanced before any price effect of accelerated depreciation came through. Nicky Kaldor was still arguing that depreciation would not help and both the overseas finance side of the Treasury and the Governor of the Bank were arguing that accelerated depreciation was not feasible. Healey said he would therefore defer consideration until further studies had been made.

I said we were continually deferring decisions. If we were told that the policy advocated by Treasury officials was not feasible, perhaps we should go back to a policy which we had looked at earlier in the year but had then rejected, that is a devaluation but a devaluation not to a floating rate but to a fixed rate. This would have to be associated with a very strong incomes policy and substantial cuts in public expenditure but we just could not sit back if there was a real prospect of a deterioration such as was forecast in the balance of payments. To my surprise Denis Healey, having argued with me briefly, said, 'As a matter of fact I agree with you. Are you surprised?' I said: 'No, I am not surprised. It does sometimes happen.' With that the meeting broke up, the only decision being to defer a decision for the time being but to look at the matter again towards the end of January or perhaps February.

The IMF decides

Our anxieties did not prevent Healey announcing, on 17 December, a modestly reflationary package relaxing hire purchase conditions. I had hoped that the warning he had received about the problems of funding the deficit might discourage such action. I was disappointed in that hope but, fortunately, not in any major degree. It was a small Christmas present for the trade union movement. Healey no doubt calculated that by showing willing on the subject of unemployment, he would assist the negotiation of a second round of incomes policy.

On the last day of 1975, the Executive Board of the IMF met to consider the UK's application.

William S. Ryrie, Executive Director appointed by the United Kingdom, emphasized that had the cost of imported oil not gone up, the United Kingdom would not have had great difficulty financing the balance of payments deficit. Authorities of the United Kingdom had wanted to avoid Draconian measures to curb the payments deficit, partly because of political differences in the United Kingdom as to how far the authorities ought to go with deflationary policies that increased unemployment and reduced the real income of the work force, and partly in line with the request of Mr Witteveen and the Committee of Twenty in January 1974 for countries to avoid excessive deflation.

The IMF approved new credit arrangements with the UK of SDR 1.7 billion though several executive directors from developing countries were concerned that the UK's large drawings would leave less in the kitty for drawings by developing countries. In addition, on 16 January 1976, the UK purchased the full amount of its gold tranche, equivalent to SDR 700 million.[8] Thus was the additional time for fundamental decisions purchased.

Notes

1. An oil facility had been established by the IMF by August 1974, financed primarily by oil-producing members. Its object was to add to the IMF's resources ready to help fund balance of payments deficits.
2. At a rate of exchange of SDR1 = $1.2, the total value of the loan would be about $2bn. *NIER* comments that the UK could expect no further loans under the oil facility. *NIER* (Nov. 1975), 11.
3. Garritsen de Vries (1985), 465.
4. Castle 502 and 507.
5. The actual deficits on the current account were £1,855m. in 1975 and £1,137m. in 1976. *Economic Trends* (Nov. 1978), 46.
6. Benn 481.
7. *NIER* (Nov. 1975), 4–5 and 8.
8. Garritsen de Vries (1985), 465–6. The SDR 1b. under the IMF oil facility was purchased in Jan. The SDR 700m. under the stand-by agreement was purchased on 12 May.

Part IV

Catharsis

N·I·N·E·T·E·E·N

Sterling in Free Fall

The Treasury gains confidence in the Government?

On 12 February 1976 Healey announced an unemployment package, involving a gross expenditure of £220 million. His estimate was that it would save 70,000 jobs.

Official circles within the Treasury were learning to love the Government they were paid to serve. The outlook for the current account was still worrying but the worst excesses of the post-election period were over. Attempts were being made to control public expenditure. An incomes policy was in operation. As its success was dependent on the co-operation of the trade union movement, it might well seem sensible to feed it some few morsels, such as the £220 million package, particularly as, in the view of much expert authority, there was enough deflation in the system already. What was not sufficiently appreciated was the effect on international opinion of this continual tinkering in a reflationary direction when inflation was still very high by international standards, when there was a large current account deficit to fund, and a prospective PSBR of £12 billion.

Sterling still holds

During the first two months of 1976 sterling was reasonably stable at around $2.05. OPEC money was still being attracted. Britain's banking and political links with the Middle East were still more influential than the adverse evidence about its economy. Sterling was also supported by a 3 per cent uncovered differential against the dollar. BP's giant Forties field had been 'unveiled' at Aberdeen on 3 November 1975. This evidence of oil from the North Sea actually being delivered seems to have allayed some doubts. Successive governments had looked for some way of freeing the UK from its balance of payments constraint. Floating exchange rates had been expected to do it but they had not. The bonanza of North Sea oil must surely ensure what all other policy measures had failed to ensure. This belief discounted too much both the size of the indebtedness and the danger that the UK could achieve the seemingly impossible—a full, refreshing, flow of North Sea oil and at the same time a current account deficit. This miracle, of which I gave frequent warnings, was not actually achieved until 1988 under a Conservative government. It was delayed by the doubling of the oil price in 1979.

So, a combination of factors sustained sterling. Why should the UK Government worry if foreign holders of sterling did not? It would, nevertheless, have been prudent to assume that the holders of the sterling balances were viewing UK economic policy with an apprehensive eye. So large was now the UK's indebtedness and its dependence on further foreign borrowing that, if disbelief in the UK's economic policies passed an unknown threshold, there could be a sudden and devastating collapse in confidence.

Depreciation or import controls?

NIER, in its February 1976 edition, repeated its view that there was little prospect of the UK attaining full employment and current account balance by 1980 'without substantial further improvements in its international competitiveness, or equivalent measures to shift resources into the external balance'.[1] At the same time it reiterated its warning against generalized import controls. Readers looking for a Keynesian prescription would observe that confronting the continuing current account deficit, not by import controls but by achieving substantial further improvements in competitiveness, could only imply a significant depreciation of sterling.

Forecasters have a habit of making two-way, and even three-way, bets. *NIER* claimed that while 'The deficit for both years [1976 and 1977] still gives cause for concern ... The deficits may not, however, be as difficult to finance as in 1975'. This expectation was not simply a deduction from the fact that there was now an IMF loan in place. It arose also from a judgement that 'The greater stability expected in the exchange rate may reduce the speculative intra-company flows that occurred in the first half of 1975, and may make easier the continued attraction of the short-term funds which financed much of the 1975 deficit.'[2] Thus *NIER* had recommended depreciation and yet expected greater stability.

Weak economies, and weakly managed economies, are highly sensitive to adverse forecasts. It is impossible to say how far *NIER*'s forecasts and policy recommendations influenced the market or how far the market noticed its warning of traumas to come: 'It is . . . reasonably clear that the slower the rate of reduction in the deficit the greater the risks of a foreign exchange crisis - a sharp discontinuity in the exchange rate or interest rates - precipitated by some unexpected development which shakes the confidence of creditors.'[3] *NIER* had managed, in one issue, to recommend depreciation, to forecast greater stability in the exchange rate, and to warn of a foreign exchange crisis.

The discontinuity

The discontinuity was about to occur. On 4 March, the Bank of England sold sterling, not an unusual action and one which did not necessarily imply an intention to devalue the currency. It may simply have been selling sterling to prevent a *rise* in its exchange rate. Or it may have been intending to use the strength of sterling to increase the foreign currency reserves. On 5 March minimum lending rate was reduced by 0.25 per cent to 9 per cent. This marginal adjustment again hardly indicated that the Government had adopted a settled policy to devalue sterling. The market may have misinterpreted the Bank's intentions because of action, at the same time, by the Nigerians. On 9 March, the Nigerians announced that their foreign exchange holdings had been diversified from their previous predominantly sterling content. The Nigerians may have been selling sterling at the same time that the Bank was selling sterling. The combination of Bank sales and Nigerian sales may have unintentionally created the false impression that the UK Government was no longer prepared to support the existing exchange rate.

It is possible that the Bank's actions suddenly opened the eyes of the market to what it should have been perceiving for months before, that sterling was overvalued given the state of the UK economy, the policies of its government, the rate of inflation, and the prospects for its current account. Nevertheless, a much more substantial effect on market psychology would result from the Nigerian announcement. The Nigerians, presumably, had read the tea leaves and were acting on what they saw. What really has to be explained is why the market ignored so many signs for so long rather than whether this or that action by the Bank, or by the Nigerians, actually triggered its belated response.

With a loss of confidence in the market, sterling began to weaken and intervention by the Bank of England, reported to be at one time at the rate of $500 million a day, seemed incapable of stopping its inexorable decline. The drain on the reserves caused by the attempt to support sterling had its influence later in the year in forcing the application to the IMF. Later in March the French left the snake, thus achieving an effective devaluation of the franc. It may well have been assumed in the market that what the French had been forced to do overtly would also be affecting thinking in Whitehall. Once the run on sterling had started, 'leads and lags' added to the downward pressure. As a currency widely used in foreign trade, sterling was highly vulnerable to trading decisions by its holders. If they were going to need foreign currencies, they might buy them earlier before they became dearer in sterling terms. If they were were going to need sterling, they might leave the purchase as late as possible in the hope that it would by then have become cheaper. 'Denis Healey was later to blame leads and lags for about a third of the outflow; what he did not say was that two-thirds was caused by a wholesale withdrawal from the sterling balances.'[4]

A mishandled devaluation?

Donoughue tells us that 'The Prime Minister was understandably angry with the Treasury because of what he saw as an amateurish technical mishandling of the attempted devaluation.'[5] The Prime Minister failed to realize that the actions of his government over two years bore the major responsibility rather than any technical incapacity in the Treasury or the Bank of England. The trouble was that UK economic policy had the appearance of a tightrope walker about to lose his balance.

Donoughue says: '[T]he Treasury was still seeking currency competitiveness: it did not want the rate above $1.95 and in the medium term hoped it would settle around $1.88.'[6] Keegan and Pennant-Rea tell us that the Treasury wanted a devaluation of 5 per cent down to the $1.90 area.[7] Pliatzky says:

It is true that the pound, at above $2, had been overvalued . . . and that a prevailing economic view in the Treasury favoured progressive depreciation in order to offset the escalation of our domestic industrial costs. But nobody had wanted or bargained for the slide in the exchange rate which now took place and could not be halted.[8]

By July, sterling had depreciated by 12 per cent. These accounts, two from insiders, suggest that the Treasury had decided on a devaluation and that those in the Treasury who favoured it were thinking of something of the order of 5 per cent. A 5 per cent devaluation would have been quite insufficient to deal with the current account outlook now forecast for 1977.[9]

There is also a view that the Treasury insufficiently understood the effect an attempt at a controlled depreciation was likely to have on the market. David Smith says: 'The Treasury's attempt to achieve a controlled depreciation of the pound had reckoned without the killer instinct of the markets.'[10] Keegan and Pennant-Rea, in giving support to this view, say: 'The Treasury—and the Bank as its agent—had been playing with fire, and the more stability-conscious Bank knew it . . . . the Government's strategy was rumbled'.[11] Yet, within the Treasury, it was perfectly understood how dangerous it could be to play with the exchange rate, and no one was more persuaded of the dangers than Denis Healey.

In fact, the Government's strategy was not rumbled because there was no plan for a controlled depreciation, not even a misconceived or mishandled plan. The Prime Minister, contemplating resignation, would have been unlikely to assent to deliberate depreciation, and no such decision could have been made without his concurrence.[12] The only sense in which the Treasury was playing with fire was that it was conducting unsustainable economic policies, but it had been doing that for many months. That was what the market now at last perceived. As Healey puts it: 'When a currency is felt to be weak, the markets will put the worst possible construction on any piece of news which might affect it—economic, political, or even industrial.' Healey now blames 'two major mistakes' made by the Bank of England, first in selling the pound when it was already under pressure and then in lowering interest rates the following day.[13] It would be remarkable if Healey was not himself consulted about the drop in interest rates even though it would be normal for him not to be consulted about the day to day details of operations on the exchanges.

Pliatzky says 'The immediate cause which inadvertently triggered off the decline was said to have been a move by the Bank of England to "cream off" dollars at a particular juncture when the pound was thought to be relatively strong.'[14] As this extract indicates, at the time the pound was thought in Government to be relatively strong, not weak as claimed by Healey, and there was no plan, there was only 'inadvertence'. This inadvertence only triggered the rout because the market became concerned about the state of the UK economy and about its management. The Deutschmark does not collapse each time the Bundesbank sells it.[15]

The market had taken the decision about competitiveness out of the hands of the Government because the Government had proved unable to make it. With so many difficult decisions which *had* to be taken, for example on the future of incomes policy, why make decisions which, apparently, could be postponed? Healey argues that any decision to depreciate was unnecessary because the real economic situation was improving substantially. The current account deficit that year, he says, was under £1 billion and inflation was falling steadily.[16] It is certainly true that the current account was improving and that inflation was falling. In retrospect Healey appears more complacent about the situation than he can have felt at the time. Moreover it had proved impossible to extract a firm decision not to depreciate. Healey had felt unable to make a decision *not* to depreciate because inflation had not met the targets set out the previous July and he was threatened with a substantial current account deficit one year ahead. The only decision had been to postpone a decision.

Pre-conditions for a planned depreciation

A planned depreciation would, in March 1976, have been impossible to formulate but, if it had existed, it would have had certain essential characteristics. First would have been a devaluation, more substantial than 5 per cent, to a level which the Government had the resources and the determination to support, assisted perhaps by membership of the snake. In fact, Britain's official reserves, at less than $5 billion, were quite inadequate to give that assurance to the market. This implies a requirement for a large international loan plus, probably, international central bank co-operation to help defend any new value for sterling against the very real danger that a devaluation would start a run on the sterling balances.

Secondly, there would have had to be yet more cuts in public expenditure to release more resources for export. But this was politically impracticable. The Cabinet had given Healey what he had asked. The ink on the Public Expenditure White Paper was hardly dry. It would have been impossible without strong pressure from external events to come back for more. Even the cuts in previously planned increases which were made in the 1975 public expenditure round led to defeat for the Government in the Commons by its own supporters who, on 10 March, refused to approve the White Paper. Thirdly, it would have involved a declared, and probably statutory, extension of the incomes policy in a form which would have produced a more rapid fall in inflation to international levels. Yet negotiations with the TUC regarding the next phase of incomes policy were still in progress. All these desiderata of a planned devaluation had been discussed in the Treasury and with the Bank of England during the months preceding March 1976. None of these elements was present in March 1976 and two of them would have required stronger political leadership than the Government was then in a position to give. There was no plan and there could be no plan.

Wilson resigns

On 11 March the Government secured a vote of confidence in the Commons for its economic and financial policies. Denis Healey made a violent attack on those members of the left wing of the Parliamentary Labour Party who had secured the defeat of the Government the previous day. On 15 March my source in the Prime Minister's office rang me to say that Harold Wilson would be resigning the following day. I replied that any such idea was absurd and had not become less absurd over the months during which my source had been giving me notice of it. The following day Harold Wilson announced his resignation, a resignation apparently long planned. It was an appropriate time for him to go. His Government had lost the confidence of the market and of other Western governments, notably that of the USA. A new Prime Minister might restore that confidence on which the future of the Government, and even of the United Kingdom, depended.

In the subsequent leadership election, I supported Healey. He had the intellectual powers and the physical stamina. He had, I thought, at last begun to appreciate the nature of the UK's economic problems. Any other candidate might have to pass through the same learning curve. I did not rate his chances very high and my second choice was Callaghan but that was not a choice to be made without considerable reservations. As it turned out, Callaghan took seven dangerous months to learn the job and was then, once the IMF crisis was out of the way, an excellent Prime Minister until he ducked the general election decision in the autumn of 1978.

James Callaghan became Prime Minister at the beginning of April 1976 facing economic problems that must have reminded him of his own period as Chancellor of the Exchequer. In early 1967 I had been a guest at a dinner at Nuffield College, Oxford, at which Callaghan, then Chancellor of the Exchequer, was also present as a Visiting Fellow. He took me aside and told me that he was now confident that the economy was emerging from its troubles. He expressed gratitude to Harold Wilson for standing by him during the crises of the previous two and a half years when he might so easily have been made a scapegoat for failure.[17] As Prime Minister, Callaghan would be aware both of the uncertainty of economic prediction and of the importance to any Chancellor of the confidence of No. 10.

Notes

1. *NIER* (Feb. 1976), 3. According to the IMF's index of relative unit labour costs in manufacturing, British industry's competitiveness has deteriorated by about 7.5% in 1974 and 6% in 1975.
2. *NIER* (Feb. 1976), 13–14.
3. *NIER* (Feb. 1976), 70.
4. Keegan and Pennant-Rea 162.
5. Donoughue 86.
6. Donoughue 85–6.
7. Keegan and Pennant-Rea 161.
8. Pliatzky (1982), 148.
9. Gavyn Davies has asserted that there was a debte in a Cabinet Committee about a sterling devaluation of 10%. Only the Economic Strategy Committee, or an *ad hoc* committee called specially for the purpose, in either case with the Prime Minister in the chair, could have had such a discussion. But Wilson would certainly have opposed any such plan. CR.
10. Smith 64.

11. Keegan and Pennant-Rea 161.
12. CR.
13. Healey 426–7. Callaghan 414 makes a similar allegation.
14. Pliatzky (1982), 148.
15. See Keegan and Pennant-Rea 162.
16. Healey 427.
17. Callaghan 203–4 describes events which throw a light on this conversation of which I was not aware at the time.

TWENTY

Callaghan's Inheritance

Secretary of State for Trade

During the election to the leadership of the Labour Party, I told Denis Healey that if, under the new Prime Minister, I was not appointed to the Cabinet, I would leave the Government. Being Number 2 in the Treasury had its attractions but I wanted my own Department. Whether I would get it was less certain. I had no political pull and I had never attached myself to any leading figure.

I had been promised membership of the Cabinet many times by Harold Wilson. James Callaghan performed what Wilson had so many times promised. He appointed me to his Cabinet as Secretary of State for Trade. It was like coming home. I had been in the Board of Trade as Minister of State under Tony Crosland in the 1960s. I liked the Department and the people in it. My historic title of President of the Board of Trade, though in modern practice demoted to a mere addendum to 'Secretary of State for Trade', carried for me a warm resonance.

Although I was now myself political head of an economic department, I had never believed that any other economic department should attempt to rival the Treasury or to second guess it. I considered the creation of the Department of Economic Affairs, of which, briefly, I had been a Minister in the 60s, not just as a failure but as having been counter-productive. It was for Treasury Ministers to get their policy right and it was for me to be as helpful as I could be. Theirs was a lonely role. I could make it a little less lonely. By this stage in the life of the Government, Healey's policies and my views were coming closer together, not as a result of my persuasiveness but due to increasing external pressure. For a short time, occupied with my own departmental matters, I was out of touch. But, as the gathering economic clouds darkened, I became more and more involved as Healey's principal, or at least most reliable, supporter in Cabinet. That should have been the Prime Minister but he was still finding his way.

Problems and critics

Thus far in the life of the 1974 Labour Government, Callaghan had not played a central role in economic policy formation. He was rapidly given the grim picture. 'Gavyn Davies, one of Bernard Donoughue's team who had good contacts in the City . . . reported to me on the day I became Prime Minister that sterling holders believed a further devaluation of between 5 and 10 per cent in the value of sterling was inevitable.'[1] He records his first official conversation as Prime Minister with Denis Healey. 'I was shocked when he told me how much had been spent by the Bank of England to support the sterling exchange rate since 1 January 1976. Denis added that we might need to make an approach to the IMF during the summer to replace the reserves we had spent.'[2] The dismal message was compounded by the Governor of the Bank of England and 'had I taken it all at face value the only thing to do would have been to throw myself out of an upper-floor window on to the Downing Street pavement'.[3] Any such temptation was stoutly resisted but Callaghan was, as yet, uncertain in his own mind as to what policies should be followed, and he had a problem of party management as well as of Cabinet management. His tasks of management were not made easier by an end March 1976 forecast by Wynne Godley that unemployment would rise to 1.5 to 2 million by the end of the decade unless imports were controlled.[4] He was very soon to lose his minimal overall majority in the Commons. As he was surprised to have become Prime Minister, he probably did not curse his fate that he had not become Prime Minister in better times.

It was not difficult to list the problems, together amounting to a crisis, which faced the new Government. Following the events of early March, the exchange rate of sterling was falling, apparently out of control. The current account deficit had to be funded at a time when international confidence in the UK economy and its management appeared to have been finally lost. Inflation was still high, higher than had been forecast, and there was no certainty that it would not start rising again. A further stage of incomes policy had to be negotiated, although influential trade union leaders were sceptical of the need. Public expenditure commitments had been reduced, but the Government's proposed cuts had led to defeat in the debate on the Public Expenditure White Paper on 10 March. Such defeats levied their own toll on the international credibility of the Government. One problem, of which the new Prime Minister was very conscious from his time as Chancellor, was that of the sterling balances, an embarrassment for a weak economy at any time. His solution was to fund them, but he could only fund them if there was confidence in the British economy and its management, and that confidence was lacking.[5]

Callaghan was careful to keep informed the key leaders of the international community. He was in frequent telephonic communication with Chancellor Schmidt, President Giscard d'Estaing, and President Ford. He had been greatly cheered by a phone call from Helmut Schmidt congratulating him on the new pay agreement with the TUC. Nevertheless, influential overseas critics of UK economic management, particularly in the USA, were becoming pressing. They feared that panic action by the UK could threaten the international trading system. Trudeau, the Canadian Prime Minister, believed 'the state of the British economy is a matter of intense concern to all in the industrialized world'.[6] On the other hand, within the Parliamentary Labour Party, the idea was taking hold that the UK could use its supposedly central position in international economic relations to negotiate assistance on favourable terms by the threat of disruptive action. Such views were not just held on the Left. They were to be found in all wings of the party and the Government. It was maintained that international opinion about the British economy was wrong, and that if it could not be persuaded that it was wrong, the threat of disruptive action might be one weapon with which the UK could bring it to its senses.

I exclude Harold Lever from any such disruptive intention. He was a dedicated supporter of the international economic system, regretful only that major forces within it did not understand how mistaken were their policies. I criticize him only for persuading colleagues that the UK could borrow its way to solvency, for his exaggeration of the UK's power to borrow, and his failure to understand that the UK, if it wished to borrow, had to accommodate itself to international financial pressures rather than the other way about. In a speech to the House before the defeat of the Government on 10 March, I had replied to arguments raised by the Labour back-benches extolling the virtues of borrowing.

> The next proposal which some of my hon. Friends have made . . . is that we should borrow. How we have borrowed—(Interruption) If borrowing is a test of Socialism, we have been very Socialist. It leads me to wonder whether my right hon. Friend the Chancellor of the Duchy of Lancaster [Harold Lever] is not the greatest Socialist of all.[7]

Inflation

James Callaghan had long-standing relations with the trade union movement. He had opposed Barbara Castle's White Paper *In Place of Strife*. Now that he was Prime Minister, he dropped Barbara from the Cabinet. He had spent, and, as Prime Minister, continued to spend, a great deal of time cultivating his relations with trade union leaders.[8] Yet because of his long relationship with them, and because he felt more comfortable with them than had Wilson, he was more ready to stand up to them where he felt it to be necessary. Callaghan now hoped for some return from the trade union movement for his past assiduous attention to their views.

He could by no means be confident that there would be such a return. Jack Jones was not yet convinced of the need for a further year of restraint. Moreover the TUC-Labour Party Liaison Committee was making further demands on the Government. A new joint statement entitled *The Next Three Years and the Problems of Priorities* included proposals for a massive expansion of training, a wealth tax, selective import controls, food and fuel subsidies, industrial democracy legislation, and the expansion of planning agreements, with pensions to be raised to 50 per cent of average earnings for a married couple and one-third for a single person. Other ideas were for the extension of public works schemes to relieve unemployment, and the introduction of a national transport planning authority.[9] There was little sign there of a realistic appreciation of the Government's problems.

The Treasury was debating the structure of a second year of incomes policy. A flat rate for a second year would further compress differentials. A 1977 'norm' expressed in percentage terms would therefore be desirable and would allow for systematic progress in restoring wage differentials. If it was impossible to secure TUC agreement to a percentage norm, a compromise might be that part of the norm was expressed in percentage terms. The first year's incomes policy was not, owing to 'slippage', achieving the reduction in inflation that had been hoped for. This implied that the new norm should be set as low as possible. Three per cent appeared the appropriate figure. If this did not prove feasible, higher unemployment could become the only alternative incomes policy.[10]

The Policy Unit took a rather more relaxed view of the target incomes norm. 'Within three weeks of taking office, the Policy Unit warned Mr Callaghan that a sterling crisis was highly likely and that if the next pay round settled at above 5 per cent he would almost certainly have to go to the IMF for a loan and accept the painful conditions such a move would entail.'[11] This was a more realistic assessment of what could in practice be negotiated and was closer to the eventual outcome. But Healey needed to leave himself negotiating room and therefore adopted, as a starting point, the Treasury position.

The tax-pay proposal

On 6 April 1976 Healey introduced his Budget. In it he offered to link a reduction in personal income tax to a union agreement on incomes policy. Inflation, he argued, had to be reduced to international levels by the end of 1977. To secure union agreement to the necessary restraint, he offered to increase income tax reliefs in two stages, the first £370 million unconditionally and the second £1,000 million conditional on agreement to limit wage increases in the following year to an average 3 per cent. This was the first time any such offer had been made to the trade unions. Tax rates were to be negotiated with trade union leaders and then, presumably, rubber stamped by the House of Commons. But however objectionable in principle, there was no doubt about the political realism of this approach.

In my own speech in the Budget debate, a few days before I moved from the Treasury, I compared Healey's tax-pay proposals with the similar policy then being conducted by the Norwegian Government. Frank Johnson, in a 'sketch' in the *Daily Telegraph*, wrote: 'one very much doubted whether Mr Dell had been roaming the fiords ascertaining how they [the Norwegians] sort out their incomes policy. Face it, some creep in the Treasury told him that it was what they did in Norway and he accordingly told us'. In fact, I had been in Norway the previous

September, and had discussed incomes policy with the then Finance Minister. Frank Johnson made no attempt to find out whether what he proposed to write was true. He preferred his joke.

Joe Haines complains that Healey's announcement was never discussed in detail with his colleagues and that, as a result, it was badly received by the trade unions whereas, if it had been discussed within government beforehand, it would have been well publicized and the reception might have been more positive.[12] I have referred elsewhere to evidence that Haines did read the press. Healey had made clear well in advance that his budget judgement had to be linked to what the trade unions were able to offer for the next stage of the incomes policy. This was well known to attentive observers.[13] If Haines thought he had useful advice to tender on the presentation of this policy, he could have offered his services.

Jack Jones seems to have taken a less sour view of Healey's proposal. 'It was an ingenious approach, and to Healey's credit it was the first time that the tax elements of a budget had been the subject of previous public debate.'[14] Thus encouraged, Jack Jones, eventually, gave his reluctant agreement to 5 per cent with a minimum increase of £2.50 and a top figure of £4 plus the income tax concessions that had been offered. On 5 May Healey made a statement to the House reporting agreement with the TUC on the next pay round. Michael Foot expressed his warm admiration of Healey's 'Herculean' feat in persuading the unions.[15] No one would wish to deny Healey the attribute 'Herculean'. But whether, despite his twelve labours, Hercules shared the qualities of perseverance and sufferance that enabled Healey to cajole trade union leaders into acquiescence on this and other occasions must remain doubtful.

It would eventually appear that Jack Jones and the trade union leadership had more influence over government policy than over their own membership. As a result, the Government's counter-inflation policy was always at risk. Healey described the new policy as implying 'about 4.5%' on the pay bill. *NIER* estimated in May that the incomes norm would add about 8 per cent to average earnings between the third quarters of 1976 and 1977 made up of 5 per cent through the permitted rise in wage rates and 3 per cent to allow for additional earnings from piecework, overtime, and slippage. By August, *NIER* had amended its estimate of the earnings effect upwards to 9 per cent (August 1976 to August 1977). It observed that 'the £6 policy which was expected on early estimates to add 10–11 per cent to earnings now seems likely to result in a 14 per cent rise during a period of rising unemployment'. It was the judgement of *NIER* that inflation 'seems likely to run at around its current rate of 14 per cent until mid-1977, because of exchange rate developments'.[16]

Public expenditure

On 21 May, Paul Martin, the Canadian High Commissioner, paid a visit to the Chancellor.

Denis was obviously pleased with having reached an agreement with the trade unions for the second phase of the incomes policy ... [He] hopes to cut the rate of inflation by half—to six per cent by the end of next year .... he pooh-poohed my suggestion for important cuts in public expenditure. Nevertheless, he would not want his colleagues to exceed present expenditure ceilings.[17]

Denis Healey had good reasons to resist the idea of further public expenditure cuts. It would be ill advised to stir up expectations in the market-place that might well be disappointed. Many members of the Cabinet continued to disbelieve market signals. The technique of bringing pressure on colleagues by leaking an intention to cut public expenditure, and then threatening them with a sterling crisis if they did not submit, could be used once too often. If it was to be used at all, the Chancellor needed to be absolutely sure that he had the support of the Prime Minister and could carry his Cabinet colleagues and the Parliamentary Party with him however reluctantly.

Yet there were more authoritative sources of advice on the level of UK public expenditure than Paul Martin. They included the US Treasury. In May an IMF team arrived in London for routine annual consultations with the Government. They too felt that public expenditure was too high. In the courteous way that retired officials have in writing about retired Ministers, Pliatzky refers to one source of Healey's hope that, despite all this pressure, he had now done enough on public expenditure. 'One opinion which was urged upon the Chancellor with characteristic persuasiveness was that the most sensible and also the most painless course was to borrow our way through the situation: we should raise loans enabling us to put funds in the shop window on a scale large enough to demonstrate that there was plenty of backing for the pound and that speculators against it would burn their fingers.'[18] The disguise is inadequate to conceal the person of Harold Lever, as always at the

Chancellor's side to offer comfort in difficult times. And, indeed, a further stand-by facility was about to be made available without any overt requirement that public expenditure should be cut.

The June stand-by

In May sterling had hit a new low of $1.70. On Friday 4 June Dr Jelle Zijlstra, President of the Netherlands Central Bank and of the Bank of International Settlements, intervened. He believed that the £ was undervalued and should be supported. The Bank of England was itself prepared to put its name to the proposition that sterling had been carried to 'an unjustified level'. Dr Zijlstra proposed to Gordon Richardson that a stand-by credit, which could be used to support the pound, should be put together from friendly central banks. In a statement in the House on 7 June, Healey was able to announce that the Bank of England had negotiated a short-term stand-by credit of $5.3 billion with central banks, of which about $2 billion was from the United States and the remaining $3.3 billion from central banks in other Group of Ten countries and Switzerland and from the Bank of International Settlements. France and Italy did not make any contributions because of their own problems.

A normal stand-by would have been for three months, renewable indefinitely for further periods of three months. That was Dr Zijlstra's intention. This standby, however, was for three months, renewable only once for a further three months, making the final date of repayment 9 December 1976. Healey had had to promise Bill Simon, the US Secretary to the Treasury, that if, on the due date, he could not repay out of the reserves, he would go to the IMF.[19] An unconditional facility thus became conditional. This requirement was, according to Lever, an 'afterthought'. He claims that those in the Treasury who wished to force the Government into the hands of the IMF secured the insertion of this condition.[20] There is no doubt that, as Pliatzky puts it, 'There were some on both sides of the Atlantic who wanted the UK to have to go to the Fund . . . so that we would come under the financial discipline of the IMF's terms . . . . William Simon . . . was said to regard the British nation as on a par with the insolvent municipality of New York City.'[21]

It did not require a conspiracy by Treasury officials to ensure the insertion of this humiliating condition. There was a widespread view among those in a position to insist that the stand-by was the UK's last chance to get its affairs in order and that, if it failed once again, no course should be left open to it other than IMF conditionality. Two billion dollars was being provided by the United States. When therefore Edwin H. Yeo III, US Under Secretary for Monetary Affairs, arrived in London to enforce the condition, neither Callaghan nor Healey nor Lever should have been surprised.[22] Callaghan and Healey had no alternative but to concede.

Healey allowed himself to hope that the stand-by would reduce pressure on sterling without a further attack on public expenditure. Indeed he felt able to say in his statement to the House that 'This is not a situation in which any responsible British Government could allow themselves to be pushed into hasty and ill-considered changes of policy on public expenditure.'[23] Unfortunately the market proved less impressed by the stand-by credit, and by the assurances from eminent central bankers that the pound was now undervalued, than Healey may have anticipated. Not unreasonably, it was not the fact that help had been received that influenced the market but that, once more, it had proved necessary and, quite soon, would have to be repaid.

Bill Simon and friends

The need for effective action should have been reinforced when Callaghan and Healey met President Ford and Bill Simon at the economic summit in Puerto Rico on 27 June. Bill Simon was frequently referred to, in British government circles, accurately but disparagingly, as a bond salesman. He did not understand that the magical economic theory in vogue in some parts of Britain required him to lend his country's money to support the enlightened policies of the UK Government. At the OECD Ministerial Conference in Paris in June, he said: 'Lenders will become increasingly reluctant to finance expanding current account deficits unless borrowing nations make fundamental changes in their domestic economic policies'. Simon showed considerable delicacy in not actually mentioning the UK but his reference was widely understood, the more so as one of his officials, Gerald Parsky, Assistant Secretary of the US Treasury, had taken care to specify the UK as a country where further measures were required.[24]

Simon was not without knowledge of the British economy. Throughout 1976 W. Greenwell & Co., with the knowledge of the Bank of England, was giving the US Embassy in London daily gilt-edged market reports which Simon, as a bond salesman, might be expected to understand.[25] Possibly other City institutions were similarly employed furnishing Simon with reports on other parts of the market. Unfortunately for his British critics, this bond salesman had now more influence over the future of the British economy than economists merely equipped with theories, or politicians equipped with a democratic vote. They should not have complained. It is too late to discover, when you have made yourself dependent on foreign borrowing, that you are dealing with a mere bond salesman with old-fashioned ideas about the repayment of debt.

Supporting Bill Simon in the US Treasury was Ed Yeo who believed that the British economy was being led to perdition and that it might take with it the whole of the international trading system. His habit of dropping in on London did not evoke the warm feelings of hospitality normally aroused in British ministerial breasts by official visits from the United States. Yeo is quoted as saying, 'We feared that if a country like Britain blew up, defaulted on its loans, and froze convertibility, we could have a real world depression.'[26] Neither Simon nor Yeo were politicians in the British mode. They were appointed officials. Their experience even with the American electorate was limited. They had no understanding of the political problems of a British Labour government with a minimal majority in the House of Commons.

Indeed they were about to help their President lose his own election by their failure to conduct the more expansionary policies which might have helped the UK. Nevertheless, even if not an elected official, and lacking the sensitivity of a Minister with a constituency, Yeo began with one advantage over most of those who hold ministerial office in British governments. He was a professional, if not in government, then at least in the field that he had come to Washington to manage, monetary affairs. It is a field in which professionalism is far from being the be-all and end-all. But it is something. Healey refers affectionately to Simon in his memoirs. He found him a good colleague even though 'he was far to the right of Genghis Khan'. With regard to Yeo, Healey is less warm. '[H]e could always enliven a difficult meeting with a ponderous but pointed joke.'[27] In their concerns about the British economy, Simon and Yeo were supported by Arthur Burns, Chairman of the Federal Reserve. Repute has it that Arthur Burns was once asked whether a certain nation should not be refused a loan. His response was that that sort of charity no longer existed in the world. It was clearly not his view that any kind of favour is done by lending money to nations that seem unable to balance their own accounts.

The market continues sceptical

It is arguable that the market should not have lost confidence at this time. There was optimism in British industry. Its liquidity position had become much more favourable. There had been an improvement in the rate of inflation and in the current account deficit. The current balance in the first quarter of 1976 was far better than had been expected, a deficit subsequently calculated at about £70 million. There was evidence of overseas recovery. Competitiveness had benefited from the large devaluation of about 10 per cent. The effective exchange rate had fallen from Smithsonian 70 in February to 63 by early May. This held out hope for a rapid further improvement in the current account once the J-curve effect had been surmounted. Following 4 March, the deficit rose markedly. Even so, the figures issued at the time exaggerated the deficits that were accruing. Whereas at first it appeared that the current account deficit for the year was about £1.4 billion, this was subsequently revised down to about £1.1 billion. By mid-1977 the current account was in surplus.

However the market is moved by what it knows at the time. What was known at the time included Healey's failure to achieve in negotiation with the TUC the incomes norm which he had demanded in his Budget. The UK was still running a current account deficit. There had been withdrawals from the sterling balances which would have absorbed the loans from the IMF. The inflation rate was higher than that of its main industrial competitors. The Government was shaky and too susceptible to trade union pressure. Public expenditure and the PSBR were too high. Economic management, even though at last more sensitive to the concerns of the market, was the subject of intense disagreements within government, accompanied by threats of general import controls and attempts to borrow with menaces. Moreover, hanging over the Government was the need to repay by December any drawings on the June stand-by. If the UK had to make drawings, it would suggest that the market was not yet appeased. If it made drawings and then appeared unable to repay out of the reserves, pressure on sterling must be expected to redouble.

Once more sterling was on a knife edge. In these circumstances, the Prime Minister reluctantly accepted advice from the Treasury and the Bank of England that a further major round of public expenditure cuts was needed. Donoughue recounts that

> although Mr Callaghan had outwardly resisted the Treasury package of cuts, he privately told me 'We have to do it . . . . We will have to have more cuts and we had better get it over with soon.' From that moment in the summer of 1976 Mr Callaghan effectively took over the conduct of the Government's economic policy.[28]

Notes

1. Callaghan 418.
2. Callaghan 414.
3. Callaghan 415.
4. Castle 679.
5. Callaghan 419–20.
6. Martin 142, 2 June 1976.
7. HC Debs., 10 Mar. 1976, cols. 554–5. Margaret Thatcher referred to this crack in HC Debs., 11 Mar. 1976, col. 642.
8. Martin 161–2.
9. Jones 310.
10. Similar arguments can be found in *NIER* (Nov. 1975).
11. Donoughue 88.
12. Haines 66–7.
13. See e.g. *NIER* (Feb. 1976), 4.
14. Jones 305.
15. Healey 397.
16. *NIER* (Aug. 1976), 4, 8.
17. Martin 138–9.
18. Pliatzky (1192), 148.
19. Bernard Donoughue writes, curiously, that the Prime Minister, when informed of the need for further public expenditure cuts, initially resisted and told the Treasury to go first to the IMF for a stand-by credit facility of £5 billion. 'We therefore received assistance from the IMF well before the major crisis broke.' Donoughue 88. Donoughue's book shows every sign of having been written at great speed.
20. CR.
21. Pliatzky (1982), 152.
22. Fay and Young, 14 May 1978.
23. HC Debs., 7 June 1976, col. 915.
24. *Financial Times*, 22 June 1976.
25. CR.

26. Fay and Young, 14 May 1978.
27. Healey 419–20.
28. Donoughue 88.

TWENTY ONE

The Third July

The Prime Minister's conduct of the Cabinet

'Mr Callaghan's management of this economic debate in July' says Donoughue, 'was superior to anything I had observed earlier . . . the Treasury was compelled to refine its arguments and did indeed eventually make them much more convincing.'[1] There is no need to question Callaghan's skill. The most persuasive argument the Treasury could produce was that, if public expenditure was not cut, sterling would continue its decline with incalculable consequences. There were other arguments but none with the direct persuasive effect of that simple truth.

Callaghan ensured that he himself was thoroughly informed.

Mr Callaghan . . . specifically asked the Governor: 'Will £1 billion off the expenditure target for this year be enough to hold the currency? If not, let us not duck it, let us face it, do more, and get it over as soon as possible.' Gordon Richardson assured him that with £1 billion of cuts everything should be all right, although nobody of course can guarantee the behaviour of currency.[2]

The Governor, presumably, was being questioned not about a cut of £1 billion 'this year' but in 1977/8. That was what Treasury Ministers were proposing.[3] Richardson's reported response is, on the face of it, unlikely. He himself had been arguing for some time that the Government should go to the IMF and it would have been optimistic indeed to imagine that the IMF would be satisfied with a £1 billion cut in 1977/8.[4] There was a minority Treasury view and a strong Bank of England view that much more would be required.[5] Later, the Cabinet itself came to the conclusion that more was required than a £1 billion cut in public expenditure, and it would be remarkable if Richardson had taken a more optimistic view.

According to Donoughue, Callaghan was open with colleagues. He allowed full discussion in Cabinet. Although Healey had his support, the Chancellor had to understand that he must persuade. This, however, was not Tony Crosland's view. Towards the end of June, Crosland was complaining: ' "Callaghan and Healey are skilfully and unscrupulously preparing the ground", Tony said . . . "By leaking the desire and intention, they're going to bounce Cabinet. If the Treasury is defeated in PESC, there now really will be a frightful run on the pound." '[6] So Crosland thought the Cabinet was being manœuvred into a decision on public expenditure by leaks authorized from No. 10.

It is, indeed, difficult to believe that Callaghan, having been persuaded himself, was willing to leave the decision, and hence his occupancy of No. 10, to his Cabinet colleagues. Callaghan was a new Prime Minister, determined to get his way. There are questions too serious for Cabinet government.

Cabinet cabals

Donoughue, in his account, divides the Cabinet into four camps. The first camp was the Treasury group consisting of Healey, the Chief Secretary Joel Barnett, not himself a member of the Cabinet but present at all Cabinet meetings on public expenditure, and Dell 'an able ex-Treasury Minister who had the instincts and pessimistic character of a natural Treasury man'.[7] 'This loyal group was essential for the success of the Chancellor, whose position is inevitably a very lonely one when proposing unpopular policies.' The second camp consisted of the 'Keynesian dissenters'—Crosland, Lever, Hattersley, Williams. Donoughue's third camp were the 'alternative strategy' men led by Benn with Foot, Silkin, Orme, and Shore. The fourth camp were the 'King's Party' who 'owed their position in Cabinet mainly to the personal favour of the Prime Minister'.[8] In this analysis Donoughue is really looking forward to the November/December crisis rather than to the events of July 1976. In July neither Hattersley nor Orme were members of the Cabinet. Perhaps this paragraph became displaced in Donoughue's account.

The serious problems for the Prime Minister lay with Michael Foot, Tony Crosland, and, to only a slightly lesser extent, with Peter Shore. It was Michael Foot who could break up the Cabinet. He was the darling of the Left and had come second in the ballot for Prime Minister. He was the voice of the TUC in the Cabinet. The TUC was critical but it wanted to keep the Labour Government in office. This also was Foot's position. But he had to be handled with care. He was concerned that the TUC would be upset at the cuts and he was concerned not to upset the TUC. Barnett says that the Prime Minister 'would invariably agree with Denis . . . but at times he would insist that Denis could not go as far as he wanted because of the political dangers'.[9] The Prime Minister was also unwilling to press Peter Shore too far. The relationship between Callaghan and Shore had something of the flavour of that between Wilson and Barbara Castle. Shore could be almost as long-winded as Castle had been, though certainly more persuasive. But he appeared immune from Prime Ministerial impatience.

The other stumbling block was Crosland, the ideologist of revisionist socialism, now, to his own surprise, Foreign Secretary. Callaghan had long been close to Tony Crosland. Indeed it would not have been surprising if he had appointed Crosland to the Treasury and Healey to the Foreign Office. Evidently he planned the switch for some future date. Clever, moody, disappointed, arrogant, often ineffective in Cabinet, Crosland

> probed Denis Healey and Treasury officials about the further cuts in public spending which would be presented to Cabinet . . . they made no serious attempt to sustain any proper economic argument . . . . When alone with Tony, Callaghan was candid: the cuts were being made to retain confidence in the pound. "So we relapse into total economic orthodoxy," Tony replied drily.[10]

The orthodoxy that Healey would argue was that, if there were insufficient cuts, sterling would slide. He could add that, with the UK economy and the world economy expanding, cuts in public expenditure would be necessary in 1977/8. Thus the cuts he was suggesting for 1977/8 were not to be regarded as deflation but as making room for demand that would be exerting pressure on resources in the following financial year.[11] On that argument he had based the case for the cuts announced in the February White Paper. This was an argument on which I supported him, with some sympathy even from Harold Lever. At Cabinet on 6 July Lever passed me a note: 'You made easily the best case on the crucial and *necessary* area of resources.'

This argument did not satisfy Crosland. How could there be any strain on resources when unemployment was so high? There was a sad exchange in Cabinet between those two old friends, Callaghan and Crosland. Callaghan asked Crosland sarcastically whether he was proposing some cuts in the Foreign Office vote in substitute for other proposed cuts that he was criticizing. Crosland replied that, as the Foreign Office vote was small, he could offer very little as Callaghan would have done when, three months before, he had been Foreign Secretary. The Cabinet laughed and Callaghan replied angrily that at least he would have supported the Chancellor.[12]

What was done

As usual cuts in public expenditure were made more difficult by Healey's determination to accompany each package with a gesture towards the trade union movement. Again there was to be a modicum of industrial policy 'selective assistance'. This took the form mainly of increased resources through the NEB and the Scottish and Welsh Development Agencies. In the theology of contemporary industrial policy, selective assistance was superior to general assistance. To fund these increases, cuts were made in general assistance. The net result was still a saving of about £100 million in 1977/8 in the trade, industry, and employment programme. But the saving could have been greater.

Shirley Williams was still Secretary of State for Prices and Consumer Protection. The invention of this Department by Harold Wilson in 1974 was a gimmick. Unfortunately, it made Shirley the defender of food subsidies. The phasing out of food subsidies had been delayed, for political reasons, in July 1975. Barnett records: 'the subsidies were disproportionately costly for the small effect they had on the retail price index . . . . they were not an effective way of making desirable switches to the more deprived members of the community'.[13] A political gimmick had turned a serious politician into a defender of counter-productive absurdities. In this battle the Treasury made some headway, to the extent of a cut of £80 million in 1977/8.

The 2 per cent national insurance charge

There were seven Cabinet meetings between 6 and 21 July climaxing with two on the 21st. The Cabinet was unwilling to go beyond a cut of £1 billion in 1977/8. Pliatzky says: 'one look at a £2 billion package was enough to rule this out of consideration. Though £1 billion might be the minimum from one point of view, it looked like the maximum from the point of view of acceptability to the Cabinet.'[14] A few months later, the Cabinet found it possible to go well beyond cuts of £1 billion in 1977/8.

The cuts did not actually amount to £1 billion. The net reduction, after allowing for the increased selective assistance, came to £952 million. The biggest single item was of cuts of £157 million in the capital expenditure of the nationalized industries, excluding BNOC which was exempted. If the extra capital expenditure required for BNOC had been brought into the arithmetic, the net total of reductions would have fallen well short of £1 billion.[15] Moreover, real public expenditure appeared to have been little altered because the cut was offset by the higher public spending reported in recent quarters.[16]

This background accounts for the sudden decision to increase employers' national insurance contributions. A mystery exists as to whence emerged the proposal to add 2 per cent to the employers' national insurance contribution, a decision which infuriated employers but was not reversed for many years thereafter. The opinion among those not present at the Cabinet meeting on the evening of 21 July is that this was another example of Treasury cunning. It is accused of getting its public expenditure cuts agreed first, and then slamming an increase in taxation on a tired and bewildered Cabinet. Donoughue comments: 'The Chancellor thanked his colleagues and then promptly put on the table a second proposal—for £1 billion of National Insurance surcharge. This promised to bring the PSBR down to £10 billion, although at a social cost of 200,000 extra unemployed.'[17] Actually the promise of the measures announced on 22 July was to reduce the estimated 1977/8 PSBR to £9 billion, not £10 billion.

Pliatzky says that 'At a late stage, and to the chagrin of the industrial strategy side of the house, the Chancellor decided to top up his proposals ... with an addition of 2 percentage points to the employers' national insurance contribution, which would yield around a further £1 billion.'[18] Keegan and Pennant-Rea have the Cabinet furious at this trickery. 'By adding another £1 billion at the last minute in the form of higher employers' national insurance contributions, Healey infuriated the Cabinet ... and only underlined, in the eyes of overseas opinion and the financial markets, the Government's reluctance to cut public expenditure.'[19] Even Joel Barnett, who was present, has allowed his memory to stray. 'Denis decided, with the Prime Minister's approval, to say nothing at this stage about his intention of going for a 2 per cent increase in Employers' National Insurance.'[20]

Treasury trickery was, as usual, less than alleged. Healey's intention to ask for an increase in employers' national insurance contribution in the final stages of the discussion was known to Callaghan. In order to protect Cabinet and himself, Callaghan had felt it necessary to enter into an agreement with Healey that he was not to be 'bounced' by proposals put forward by the Treasury with little notice. It was an agreement which, in retrospect, he considered to have been implemented 'on all major occasions'.[21] But Healey's intention, conveyed to the Prime Minister, was an increase of *1* per cent. Healey proposed it in view of the Cabinet's failure to achieve persuasive public expenditure cuts. In his customary lackadaisical way, Crosland asked Healey why, if it was so important to reduce the PSBR, he was not proposing to increase the contribution by 2 per cent rather than 1 per cent. I then argued that if we could do so little on public expenditure, we *should* make the increase 2 per cent rather than 1 per cent. This was opposed by both the Prime Minister and the Chancellor. However, so strong was the feeling in Cabinet that an end should be put to these everlasting economic crises and rounds of public expenditure cuts, that I won the argument. Roy Mason came up to me after the meeting. 'Well, you have beaten the Prime Minister this time. Do not do it too often.'

Keegan and Pennant-Rea are right. The 2 per cent increase was counter-productive. If we had reduced the 1977/8 PSBR to £9 billion by public expenditure cuts, it is possible that there would have been no autumn crisis. That it had to be done by a £1 billion tax increase convinced the market that there really was no way of persuading this Government to come to its senses.

The money supply

In his statement of 22 July, Healey said 'For the [1976/77] financial year as a whole money supply should amount to about 12 per cent. Such an outcome would be fully consistent with our objectives for reducing inflation.... I do not intend to allow the growth of the money supply to fuel inflation this year or next.'[22] This statement has been taken as evidence of Healey's conversion to monetarism. At a later date I was honoured by Ian Mikardo in being linked with Healey as one of two people who introduced monetarism to UK policy.

I have never been a monetarist. This does not mean that I believe that governments which wish to borrow large sums of money can ignore the opinions of the lenders. Nor do I think it sensible to show complacency at any explosion in the money supply. Attempts to constrain it may exert some beneficial counter-inflationary effect. The more important question is whether Healey had been converted to monetarism. In a lecture to the Council for Foreign Affairs in Washington in October 1979, shortly after he left office, Healey said:

Almost the only uncontroversial statement about money supply is one on which Keynes and Friedman would agree: 'No continued and substantial inflation can occur without monetary growth that substantially exceeds the rate of real growth.' We can all say yes to that. And I think most people would agree that if monetary growth exceeds the rate of real growth as much as it did for two years under my predecessor, Lord Barber, galloping inflation is bound to follow. But beyond that, all is uncertain. We do not know how monetary growth influences inflation, or with what time-lag. We do not know how to measure the relevant monetary growth or how best to influence it. And some economists still believe that changes in the velocity of circulation may make monetary growth an unreliable indicator in any case.

Later in the lecture he said: 'All this is not to argue against the necessity for controlling monetary growth . . . It is to argue for a more sceptical and pragmatic approach than is now in vogue.'[23] All this would appear to show a healthy agnosticism rather than the customary fanaticism of the convert.

According to Pliatzky, 'The Chancellor believed that the crucial reason for the failure of the July package was the omission of any money supply targets from his statement.'[24] Although the Treasury and the Bank of England had been framing money supply targets for several years, they had not been published. They were first published in Britain by Denis Healey. Yet it seems improbable that Healey really believed that the 22 July statement failed because he had not given a money supply target. The difference between his words and the actual statement of a target was minimal. The package failed because the target for public expenditure cuts set by Treasury Ministers was itself insufficient to satisfy the market and the Cabinet failed to accept even the Treasury proposals and, instead, increased taxation.

The Parliamentary Labour Party

The Parliamentary Labour Party, partly through exhaustion, partly through the imminence of the summer recess, accepted the 22 July

232   *Catharsis*

package without too much difficulty. Its morale was not assisted by finding itself technically in a minority because two Labour MPs resigned the whip, fed up with public expenditure cuts. Crosland's explanation of the easier than expected reception by the PLP was:

Partly because the Left is now totally demoralised . . . The Centre and Right are much more solid now that Europe is out of the way . . . There's a general swing to the Right among 'informed' public opinion in the West, and certainly there's a strong reaction against high public expenditure: Schmidt, Giscard, Ford all sermonise about it. And I'm in a minority in this conservative Cabinet. Still, nothing unusual about that.[25]

Crosland was not too unhappy. Though he had not won, he had helped to prevent the worst. He liked to think he was alone but that, nevertheless, he was right. But, as events would rapidly show, he was not right and he was not alone.

Notes

1. Donoughue 91.
2. Donoughue 89.
3. Donoughue is perfectly aware that the cuts proposed were in respect of 1977/8. See p. 91.
4. CR.
5. In June 1976, Kaldor was urging a 5% payroll tax that would yield £3 billion. Thirlwall 253.
6. Crosland 342. PESC was the acronym often used for the annual public expenditure survey covering a five-year period, but the cuts made in July 1976 were a separate *ad hoc* exercise applicable only to 1977/8, the next financial year.
7. Who would not be pessimistic after two years' experience of this Government? Donoughue describes Barnett as Financial Secretary, another slip. Barnett was Chief Secretary, a more senior post.
8. Donoughue 89-90.
9. Barnett 90.
10. Crosland 343.
11. HC Debs., 22 July 1976, col. 2012. He asserted that public expenditure was now under control and that there was 'no economic or financial case for further reductions in public expenditure or the PSBR this year.'
12. Barnett 93. Crosland 353.
13. Barnett 91.
14. Pliatzky (1982), 149.
15. Pliatzky (1982), 151.
16. This point is made in *NIER* (Aug. 1976), 7.
17. Donoughue 91.

18. Pliatzky (1982), 149.
19. Keegan and Pennant-Rea 164.
20. Barnett 93.
21. Callaghan 415.
22. HC Debs., 22 July 1976, col. 2019.
23. Quoted by Pliatzky (1989), 123. See also Healey 383.
24. Pliatzky (1982), 150.
25. Crosland 354.

T·W·E·N·T·Y T·W·O

No Alternative to the IMF

Disappointment again

In a matter of weeks, Healey knew he was to be disappointed once again. He had not persuaded the market that he had done enough. He suggests these days that part of the trouble was with Treasury forecasting. The Treasury, he argues, was putting out figures that threw doubt on the proposition that the economic fundamentals were at last right. What he discounts in this judgement is the extent to which doubts had been created by previous policies and statements. Overkill was made necessary by the need to persuade even if it was not necessary according to some more relaxed economic judgements.

In any case the current figures were worrying. Inflation was still running at 14 per cent and showed little sign of falling further.[1] Commodity prices were rising. The current account, after improving in the first quarter of 1976, was once more deteriorating. The money supply figures were poor. The market was resistant to buying gilts. Healey found himself compelled to use interest rates for the combined purpose of selling gilts and sustaining sterling.[2]

During August, the pound, with support from the Bank of England, held steady at about $1.77. Healey took a holiday in Scotland. It was a location that served to refresh the spirit but also provided for easy communications with the Treasury and any necessary return to London without undue publicity. From there he authorized the Bank of England, during one flurry against sterling, to spend up to $150 million on intervention but then to let it fall. Stability returned the following day.[3] But the outlook was uncertain, sensitive to the least bad news, and therefore raised many questions. What weight should Healey place on the alternative ways of sustaining sterling, interest rates at increasingly embarrassing levels and purchases in the market? If it was true that at last he had the fundamentals right, purchases in the market would be a valid strategy. It was on the stand-by, together with whatever he could borrow long-term in the Euro-dollar market for public sector bodies, that he depended for reserves if he wished to support sterling by buying it. But how long could he hang on against the market's disbelief when the stand-by was repayable not later than 9 December? Then there was one more harrowing question. Was the market so wrong? As he now knew, the estimate of the prospective PSBR had risen since the July measures.

On 1 September, the Federal Reserve in New York confirmed that up to 30 June Britain had withdrawn about $1.1 billion from the $5.3 billion stand-by agreement. While there were no drawings in July, this information strengthened the belief in the market that Britain would have to make an application to the IMF in time to meet its repayment obligations.[4] On 10 September, the minimum lending rate was raised by 1.5 per cent to 13 per cent. A day later the Cabinet was reshuffled. Roy Hattersley, Bill Rodgers, and Stanley Orme joined it in a reconstruction, politically well balanced in Labour Party terms, but not of the kind that would suggest a government united around any particular economic policy. Shirley Williams became Secretary of State for Education. About the same time, the Bank stopped supporting sterling in the foreign exchange market. As Pliatzky puts it: 'The Prime Minister and the Chancellor put the Bank on an increasingly short rein as to the extent to which they could use the reserves for intervention.'[5] On 16 September, the Bank of England called for £350 million of special deposits from the banks and finance houses because monetary expansion was proceeding too rapidly.

The retreat from Heathrow

The Labour Party Conference, with all its potentiality for embarrassment, drew near. At the beginning of September sterling was still at about $1.77. Healey warned the Economic Strategy Committee of the Cabinet, during the week before the Conference, that a sterling crisis was impending and that the Government must quickly apply to the IMF for another loan. This was agreed but no announcement was made as Healey did not wish it to be known before he attended the annual IMF

Conference which, that year, was to be held in Manila. With his usual readiness to advise, Ed Yeo stopped in London on his way to the IMF meeting. He saw Healey and Richardson. On Monday 27 September, the first day of the Labour Party Conference, sterling dropped 3 cents and fell below $1.70. Intervention by the Bank of England was having no effect. On the morning of 28 September, as Healey and Richardson were at Heathrow, just about to leave for Manila, they learned that panic had broken out on the exchanges. There was a further 4.5 cents fall to $1.64. Healey returned to London. At a meeting at the Treasury it was decided to announce the application to the IMF for a loan within the conditional tranches. Callaghan, at Blackpool for the Labour Party Conference, agreed. It can be debated whether Healey would not have been better advised to proceed with his journey.[6] The immediate market reaction to the return from Heathrow was to increase the panic even further. Another effect was that Healey and Richardson lost an opportunity to discuss the terms of a stand-by arrangement directly with Witteveen, the IMF Managing Director. 'The lack of frank, face to face, talks at this stage may have added to the difficulty of later negotiations.'[7] But it was a responsible decision and politically wise.

The Callaghan speech

It was in these circumstances that, the same day, Callaghan, in a passage in his speech to the Labour Party Conference, partly drafted by his son-in-law Peter Jay, signalled to the world that the Labour Government was coming to terms with the constraints on policy imposed by the world economic crisis.

For too long . . . we postponed facing up to fundamental choices and fundamental changes in our society and in our economy . . . The cosy world we were told would go on for ever, where full employment would be guaranteed by a stroke of the Chancellor's pen . . . We used to think that you could just spend your way out of a recession . . . . I tell you in all candour that that option no longer exists, and that in so far as it ever did exist, it only worked . . . by injecting a bigger dose of inflation into the economy, followed by a higher level of unemployment . . . That is the history of the last twenty years.[8]

It has been said of this speech that it 'effectively sounded the death-knell for post-war Keynesian policies, and ushered in the new era of monetarism'.[9]

This misinterprets the significance of the speech. Its significance was not in the field of economic theory for indeed it said nothing new. In a speech to a Conference on Business Strategies seventeen months before, for which I claim no originality, I had said much the same. I was engaged in the selfless activity of defending the Treasury wherever, in good conscience, I could.

In the eyes of its critics, the Treasury's main fault appears to be an addiction to elementary arithmetic. If, on adding up the likely demands on resources, it finds these to exceed the likely supply . . . the Treasury is hardly to be blamed if it draws this fact to the attention of the Chancellor . . . Some Chancellors . . . have preferred the relative security of such arithmetic as a basis for policy. Others have preferred the so-called dash for growth, a sort of economic equivalent of the charge of the Light Brigade. It is magnificent but it is not economic management. In the short term, the dash for growth, though inflationary, is easier for industry. It is a kind of macro-economic lame-duckery . . . The dope of expansionist demand management brings forth investment even in our low investment economy . . . . But it brings it forth ever more slowly and more reluctantly . . . Experience indeed undermines any confidence in the durability of such policies. They have led in the end only to the disappointment of expectations.[10]

Of course there was a substantial difference in significance between words such as these in the mouth of the Prime Minister and their significance in my mouth. Nevertheless my words illustrate that what Callaghan said was what every government, other than the British, had known for at least two years. Callaghan's speech was welcome because it suggested that light was at last pouring into the mind of British government as well. Yet it would become clear before long that Callaghan himself had not understood the full significance of what he was saying.

The IMF to the rescue

On 29 September a formal application was made to the IMF for support amounting to $3.9 billion, the largest sum ever requested of them.[11] It was so large that it would force the IMF itself to seek supplementary resources under the General Arrangements to Borrow.[12] This meant that countries like Germany and the USA would be asked to contribute. The announcement having been made, Healey flew to Blackpool on 30 September. He still felt able to claim that the economic fundamentals were already right and that, therefore, it was primarily a matter of getting an IMF certificate of good housekeeping in order to convince the markets. He therefore told the Conference that he would go to the Fund 'on existing policies'. 'I mean things we do not like as well as things we do like. It means sticking to the very painful cuts in public expenditure . . . It means sticking to the pay policy.'

Healey briefed me at a private meeting on 1 October. He called me to another unscheduled meeting at No. 11 at 7 p.m. on 6 October. I at first took this to be an example of his wish to keep me informed. But he had a more specific purpose. There had been a period of rapid growth in the money supply between the spring and autumn of 1976.

The Governor persuaded me that we needed to raise interest rates to 15 percent, which was unheard of in those days, in order to sell enough gilts to get money under control. But I was also persuaded by him that we could then get them down again within a year to 12 or 10 percent, which was roughly the level of inflation.[13]

Despite the Governor's advice, Callaghan at first refused his consent to the increase in interest rates. He warned that if Healey raised the matter in Cabinet he would not have the Prime Minister's support. Healey discussed the situation with the Governor and decided that he would call me in as he would feel bound to press the matter in Cabinet. In his memoirs Healey explains his approach to me as 'the only member of the Cabinet on whom I could count'. Healey had got thus far in telling me his story when the Prime Minister's Principal Private Secretary, Ken Stowe, put his head round the door and said that the Prime Minister had decided that if Healey was really determined, he should go ahead. This incident must have created considerable doubt in Healey's mind as to how far he could rely on the Prime Minister's support. The increase in interest rates was accompanied by a further call for special deposits, this time for £700 million.[14] These measures succeeded in producing a sharp slow-down in monetary growth. Sterling M3 grew by just 7 per cent in 1976/7—below the bottom end of the 9 to 13 per cent target range.

The increase in interest rates stimulated discussion at Cabinet the following morning. Peter Shore argued for import controls. Tony Benn also advocated protection, admitting that he was talking of a siege economy and that it would involve sacrifices. Callaghan by no means ruled these suggestions out. Benn's account is that Callaghan summed up by saying, 'The longer I am Prime Minister, the less sure I am that I know what is right and what is wrong.'[15]

On 11 October, the Commons returned from the recess. There was a debate on the economic situation during which Denis Healey defended his actions during the recess. Once the application to the IMF was made, and interest rates raised to 15 per cent, sterling remained uneasily steady apart from a panic stimulated by a report in the *Sunday Times* on 24 October that the IMF and the US Treasury had agreed conditions for a UK drawing from the IMF which included the pound at $1.50. The report was emphatically condemned both by Bill Simon and by William Dale, the Acting Managing Director of the IMF.[16] Nor was it UK government policy.[17] Indeed, it was obviously nonsense. Currencies were floating and, after an agreement between the IMF and the UK Government, sterling was likely to appreciate, not depreciate further. Nevertheless, sterling reacted sharply, falling 7 cents on the Monday morning almost to $1.50. The fall led to renewed attacks on Healey not just from the Conservative press but also from Samuel Brittan of the *Financial Times* who wrote of Healey's loss of credibility.[18] Sterling, it was argued, would not have fallen 7 cents in response to a newspaper article, if it were not for the parlous condition into which the UK economy, under Healey's stewardship, had fallen.

Dell for Chancellor

The autumn of 1976 could well have been the nadir of Healey's career from which he might never have recovered. In fact, it became the apogee because he survived, and fought and won through for a policy that restored his and his country's credibility. Callaghan was too just, or not sufficiently ruthless, to remove Healey, or perhaps he saw that he lacked a suitable alternative. His own experience might have restrained him. He had felt obliged to move from the Treasury to the Home Office following the 1967 devaluation and Roy Jenkins had won the credit for the subsequent recovery. As things were, the credit justly accrued to Healey. Healey may, many times, have been mistaken in his policies, he may have been too much of a 'political' Chancellor, but now that his back was to the wall, he fought like a lion. If he and the Government were to survive, the next few months would require all his considerable courage and moral and intellectual strength. He had been two and a half years in his job, but had very little to show. Since he had begun the retreat from the profligacy of his first year, nothing he had done, it seemed, was enough. In surviving and winning through during the next few months, nothing less than the courage of a lion would have sufficed.

During the autumn of 1976 there were repeated newspaper calls for me to take over from Healey as Chancellor. It was argued that I, alone among my Cabinet colleagues, understood the necessities of the situation. The principal problems associated with my nomination were, apparently, that I was little known in the country, and that I would be unacceptable to wide tranches of the Parliamentary Labour Party. On the occasion, in late October 1976, when Healey was particularly under attack, I thought I detected his own voice in a Press briefing which led to the comment that I was the 'favourite' for the succession of 'several senior Ministers', was 'awfully good in Cabinet', but that I was 'a bit grim'.[19] If I am right in detecting the voice of Healey, I can only suppose that in his own defence he thought it necessary to set me up as the only possible, and yet obviously impossible, alternative to himself. He probably had rather less reason to worry than he may have thought. His position was protected not just by the Prime Minister's loyalty but by the lack of *any* credible alternative Chancellor provided only that his health held out. I confess not to have realized at the time that this could not be taken for granted. He records: 'In October 1976 the strain of dealing with these problems was almost too much for me.' If they had proved too much, the Prime Minister would have faced an almost insoluble dilemma. Yet someone would have been appointed and would have grown rapidly into the job. It was highly unlikely to have been me.

Calls for my succession came mainly, but not entirely, from newspapers supporting the Opposition whose preferred alternative was not Dell for Chancellor but an entirely new Government. I realized that the attempt by the Tory press to promote me was merely a way of getting at Healey. I knew that, in fact, there was not the least chance of my becoming Chancellor at that time, and little enough at any subsequent time. While Crosland was alive the question did not arise. Callaghan would not have wanted to offend Crosland by appointing anyone else to succeed Healey, and yet Crosland had ruled himself out for the time being by his attitude to the economic crisis. Crosland's attitudes had become Healey's guarantee that he could hold the job as long as he wanted it.

I knew all this and had no illusions. I decided that I would give Healey my full support. Indeed I demanded even tougher measures, so that at least he should not appear to be advocating extremes. This was not simply tactical. I would have preferred tougher decisions than emerged eventually from the crisis Cabinets. But it had a conscious tactical element. After the crisis I continued to support Healey as the best available Chancellor. My worries emerged again when in his 1978 Budget he appeared to me to be imperilling the gains of the previous fifteen months.[20] In November 1978, during my final conversations with James Callaghan before my resignation from the Government, he told me, unprompted, that I had been on a 'very' short list of people he was considering as successor to Healey. I take it this was true because I had not come to him to press for promotion but to present my resignation. Nevertheless it had been my own view at the end of the IMF negotiations that the stand I had taken had finally ruled me out of the succession to Healey, even if I had ever been a serious possibility.

The problem of imports

In Callaghan's view I was a political innocent. I was not, for example, sufficiently understanding of the need for consulting the TUC, and for appearing to respect their views. I never thought that I was quite as politically innocent as Callaghan believed. I did not regard it as political innocence to judge, as I did, that the increasing power of the trade unions was profoundly unpopular. But I knew Callaghan's view as he did not take much care to conceal it. In his eyes my political innocence was confirmed by my criticism of expenditures on industrial policy and by my opposition to import controls. For example, on 4 November, I opposed additions to industrial aid and was rebuked by the Prime Minister. He told me that we could not be totally 'pure'.[21] But industrial policy was not my responsibility and I did not waste too much time on a lost cause. Trade policy *was* my responsibility and, in the autumn of 1976, it was headline news. I came under considerable pressure to act like a politically sensitive Minister, and submit to the increasing protectionist pressures. In the view of distinguished journalists, all was now not merely fair but sensible in trade and war. 'Dell needs a dirty tricks department', proclaimed Mary Goldring.[22]

The Government considered that our economically stronger trading partners were not doing enough to help us achieve balance. The size and increasing volume of the UK's short-term debt was adding to instability. It would be helpful if the UK's return to balance could be speeded. Such thinking was encouraged by *NIER* in its editorial dated 18 August 1976.

[F]or this to happen some other balance or balances must be allowed to worsen more quickly, which means that some countries should pursue less cautious management policies . . . allow their exchange rates to rise, or else waive the rules concerning import restrictions for the deficit countries. It may be unrealistic to envisage a world wide system of compensating expansions and contractions, but at the EEC level the institutions do exist for working out what would amount to a partial mutual adjustment of economic policies; a principal object of this would be to reduce the level of unemployment in all member countries.[23]

NIER did not itself advocate wider import controls at that stage. But it was obvious that its editorial could be turned by advocates of import controls into an argument for them, or for their use as a threat to achieve co-operation from our trading partners.

My reply to such arguments is to be found in my lecture 'The Politics of Economic Interdependence', which I delivered in February 1977. The lecture was a compendium of the arguments I was using during the autumn of 1976.

We should not conduct our policies on the assumption that the world is in love with us and our problems. They are fed up with us and our problems. They have their own problems and their own national self-interest. One important interest of the strong powers is that the world should not relapse into protectionism . . . They will have little sympathy for this country . . . if we give an impetus to a relapse. We should not start battles we are likely to lose.[24]

At the OECD Ministerial Council in June 1976, I had signed the OECD pledge to avoid import controls. In accordance with previous government policy, reasserted following further collective discussion, I had made the proviso that other major economies should grow faster to help the weaker economies. I said the UK Government had noted with satisfaction that the stronger economies had led the way towards recovery but that they also had a particular responsibility to ensure that expansion continued. I briefed journalists that the UK would like to see a faster rate of expansion in world trade over the coming years than the 8 per cent to 9 per cent forecast by OECD and that the British Government did not share the fears of some experts that expansion was already too fast.[25] It did not seem to me possible, and certainly not desirable, after making such a pledge, to renege on it a few months later when nothing substantial had changed.

My opposition to widespread import controls was strengthened by forecasts that we would emerge from deficit over the following year or eighteen months.[26] North Sea oil would help. But, fundamentally, my opposition arose from my conviction that, in our situation, import controls would do more harm than good. They would bring retaliation or, at least, emulation. They might give temporary relief but they would not enhance the competitiveness of British industry, quite the opposite, and they would give even more power to the trade unions.

On my appointment as Secretary of State for Trade, the Prime Minister had asked me my attitude to general import controls. He had been pleased by my negative response but he himself had only just emerged from the Foreign Office, a department even more committed to *laissez-faire* than my own Department of Trade. In his Memoirs Callaghan expresses views on import controls that parallel my own at the time.[27] I cannot say that, at the time, I felt I had in him a particularly determined supporter against the pressures for import controls coming from the TUC and from the CBI. He seemed irritated by my apparent unwillingness to act. He invited me to undertake a departmental study on what could be done to limit imports. What, for example, could I do to increase the effectiveness of non-tariff barriers? I reluctantly undertook this study but little followed. The idea that through this route there was any relief from our problems was, in my view, sheer counter-productive self-deception, and I had no alternative but to fight it.

Fortunately in this battle I was not alone. Denis Healey supported me in my problems at least as strongly, and probably more effectively, than I supported him in his. This does not mean that I would have opposed a scheme of *import deposits* in all circumstances. Donoughue records that, in mid-September, 'The Chancellor also had plans for import deposits placed on seven-day readiness.'[28] According to Callaghan, the idea of import deposits also had the support of the Governor of the Bank of England.[29] I discussed the idea with Denis Healey at a private meeting at No. 11 on 16 September. Such a scheme had its supporters among officials and it would have been possible to imagine circumstances in which its introduction would have been appropriate. In any case such schemes cannot be introduced in an emergency without having been prepared in advance. But Samuel Brittan and Adrian Hamilton recorded my views accurately when they reported, not without taking evidence on the matter, that

Despite growing support among some financial officials for import deposits, a number of key Ministers and their advisers, including Mr Edmund Dell, Trade Secretary, remain utterly unconvinced and are fighting hard against them . . .

Some Ministers, notably Mr Dell believe that the country is still living beyond its means and that the proper course is a further reduction in public expenditure.[30]

I was not unwilling to make gestures to ward off the pressure from the TUC and CBI. They called for selective controls and I gave them selective controls. My actions were described in one paper as a 'sop to the left', but they were equally a sop to the CBI. There was a long list of selective import controls which I could brandish. In September, I wrote to Len Murray to explain and justify the selective import control policy. I strengthened the section in my Department concerned with anti-dumping and when, as bound to do under the Treaty of Rome, I passed anti-dumping control to the European Commission, I made well-publicized visits to see Sir Christopher Soames, vice president of the Commission, in order to ensure that Brussels was adequately equipped for this new responsibility. I also exerted what pressure I could on the Japanese Government and industry in the hope of achieving some measure of reciprocity, but I realised that, in practice, UK pressure would not achieve much unless supported both by the USA and by the European Community as a whole.

But the drug of selective controls proved too weak to satisfy the cravings of the protectionists. What was diplomatically described as 'selective' import controls was meant by them to convey a demand for general import controls. What I was doing was considered totally inadequate, by the TUC, the CBI, and also by the Prime Minister. The TUC proposed an import penetration ceiling for each of the thirty five key industries identified in the industrial strategy. In *The Times* of 25 September, David Basnett, General Secretary of the General and Municipal Workers' Union, contributed an article calling for an import deposit scheme and restrictions on the free outward flow of capital. On 29 September, I spoke at a fringe meeting at the Labour Party Conference and attacked the idea of general import controls. But the subject was not ready to go away.

On 13 October 1976, the TUC and CBI presented a joint memorandum on imports. They did not ask for general import controls but the list of products for which they demanded selective controls was sufficiently long to amount to it. At a press conference, Len Murray attacked me. 'Don't lets be mealy-mouthed about this . . . We think that Ministers who have been in charge of trade . . . have been far too diffident about tackling this real problem.' He was not the only critic. I learnt from the press that the Prime Minister's immediate response to the memorandum had been 'fulsome'. The impact of the memorandum was strengthened by the poor trade figures announced the following day. Even the *Financial Times* gave editorial comfort to the policy of selective controls by describing them as 'working reasonably well'.[31]

I counter-attacked with an interview on BBC TV and in a speech at a dinner on Merseyside on 15 October. I argued that

> Wide ranging import controls, whether a general scheme or a much greater accumulation of selective controls ... would not ... solve unemployment. They would not offer a quick and painless means of correcting the balance of payments. On the contrary ... they would have to be accompanied by substantial deflationary measures. And we cannot just shrug away the danger of retaliation.

I ended with a cool welcome to the CBI–TUC memorandum as 'a basis for discussion and consideration'.[32]

The contrast between the Prime Minister's reaction to the CBI–TUC memorandum and mine provoked press comment. It indicated, it was claimed, a clash between him and me.

Disagreements about import controls became absorbed in the wider crisis. At NEDC on 3 November I tabled a response to the CBI–TUC memorandum. It listed once more all that the Government was doing and proposed to do by way of selective restraints, anti-dumping action, in the GATT Tokyo Round, and in bringing pressure on the Japanese.[33] There was little, if anything, new. Its main significance was that, with Healey's help, I had not yet lost the battle against general import controls.

Notes

1. *NIER* (Aug. 1976), 4 and 5.
2. *NIER* (Aug. 1976), 9.
3. Healey 428.
4. By the time the application for the IMF stand-by was made, it was not possible for the IMF to complete until towards the end of December whereas drawings under the June stand-by were repayable on 9 December. It was therefore necessary, as it turned out, to repay the drawings from the June stand-by from the reserves and to replenish the reserves from the IMF stand-by when it became available.
5. Pliatzky (1982), 151.
6. James Callaghan debates it in Callaghan 428.

7. Garritsen de Vries (1985), 468.
8. Callaghan 426–7.
9. Smith 65.
10. Speech at Conference called by *The Times*, the CBI, and the Administrative Staff College, Henley, 16 Apr. 1975.
11. The previous January the IMF had enlarged by 45% the amounts that could be drawn under the credit tranches. This meant that the UK could have a stand-by arrangement up to 245% of quota. This amounted to SDR 4,060m. which, less the SDR 700m. of the first credit tranches already drawn, left SDR 3,360m. Garritsen de Vries (1985), 467. For the technicalities of the application see Pliatzky (1982), 151–3.
12. In December 1961, ten leading countries agreed on the General Arrangements to Borrow. The object was to provide additional support for the international monetary system. However the funds would be contributed to the IMF only if the Group of Ten agreed collectively to do so.
13. Denis Healey in *Institutional Investor* (June 1987), 68.
14. In fact, the call for the last half of this was repeatedly postponed. On 13 January 1977, the Bank of England released £1.1b. of special deposits, and on 27 January a further £360m.
15. Benn 620–2.
16. Healey 434.
17. Callaghan 428. Donoughue appears to put this event in late September. He says: 'There had been a leak from the Treasury direct to the newspaper as I quickly learned from my own *Sunday Times* contacts.' Donoughue 92.
18. *Financial Times*, 26 Oct. 1976.
19. Alan Watkins in the *Observer*, 24 Oct. 1976.
20. 'There was probably too much optimism already, and even the ultra-cautious Edmund Dell could not dampen it.' Barnett 141.
21. Barnett 102.
22. *Investors Chronicle*, 8 Oct. 1976.
23. *NIER* (Aug. 1976), 6.
24. The fifth Rita Hinden Lecture.
25. *Financial Times*, 22 June 1976.
26. See e.g. *NIER* (Aug. 1976), 5. See also *NIER* (Nov. 1976), 3–4.
27. Callaghan 424.
28. Donoughue 93.
29. Callaghan 422.
30. *Financial Times*, 24 Sept. 1976.
31. *Financial Times*, 18 Oct. 1976.
32. 15 Oct. 1976 Department of Trade Press Notice.
33. *Trade and Industry*, 12 Nov. 1976.

T·W·E·N·T·Y T·H·R·E·E

The IMF in London

Paul Martin wrote in his diary on 29 October: 'There is much talk about the possibilities of an election here.'[1] A fortnight later, Mrs Thatcher said to Martin that 'she felt she had Callaghan and company on the ropes'.[2] She underestimated the Cabinet's instinct for self-preservation.

The agonies of James Callaghan

From his own experiences, Callaghan was distrustful of the Treasury and he could hardly distrust the Treasury without also distrusting its political head. Hence Healey's constant worry. How far could he rely on the support of his Prime Minister? Healey speculates that 'Jim Callaghan . . . had been badly bruised by the Party Conference, and seemed uncertain whether it was economically right or politically possible to make more cuts in public spending.'[3] Joel Barnett reports:

Around the end of October there was a Press leak hinting that Jim was fed up with Denis. I told Dr Bernard Donoughue . . . that the Treasury view was that the leak came from him. He denied being the source, but said that whether or not Jim was dissatisfied, he himself was fed up with the Treasury.[4]

Callaghan was behaving rather oddly. The approach to the IMF had been made at the end of September. On 1 November the IMF team arrived in London. It was led by Alan Whittome, who had worked in the Bank of England. It was to spend six weeks in London, 'three times longer than the customary two-week period for such negotiations'.[5] By the time the team arrived, there had been no collective decision on the Government's negotiating position. Callaghan kept them waiting in their hotel for almost a fortnight before he would allow Treasury officials to talk to them.⁶ As a result, formal negotiations were not opened until 19 November. The fact that they were kept hanging around so long led to some asperity on their part when serious discussion did at length begin. Pliatzky had what he has described in personal conversation as a non-meeting with Whittome on 11 November but nothing of substance was discussed. He comments: 'I had not been anxious to become involved in detailed discussions . . . since it seemed to me that my function was to advise Treasury Ministers rather than the IMF on cutting public expenditure.'⁷

Division in the Treasury

The Cabinet, on 26 October, agreed that officials should look at 'the scope for savings'.

The package that was beginning to take shape inside the Treasury involved bringing the PSBR down to £10 billion in 1977/78. It was thought that we might do this by the sale of some British Petroleum (BP) shares, combined with changes in the financing of export credit, and about £1 billion from a deflationary mixture of public expenditure cuts and VAT.⁸

Normally the IMF team would have expected to receive guidance from the Treasury as to the measures necessary to restore the economy to equilibrium. The divisions in the Treasury made it difficult for the IMF team to decide its negotiating position. It is a problem for a visiting team, however expert, to determine in a matter of weeks what measures are necessary. The IMF team found that many Treasury officials believed that nothing further needed to be done. They were told that 'all that was needed was an announcement by the Fund of financial support so that confidence in sterling would be quickly restored'.⁹ For political reasons alone, they were unlikely to agree with that view. They would have had some difficulty persuading Witteveen of such a proposition, let alone the US Treasury and others in the Federal German Government and Bundesbank who were to be asked to fund any borrowing through the GAB. If the IMF team was forced to make its own guess, it was likely to agree with the overseas side of the Treasury which was recommending substantial cuts in public expenditure.

The IMF team proposed reductions should be made of £3 billion in 1977/8 and £4 billion in 1978/9 at 1976 survey prices. Any cuts which could be made in the current year, 1976/7, would be a bonus. They accepted that it was for the British Government to choose between different ways of reducing the PSBR, but emphasized that expenditure reductions would have a better effect than tax increases on financial opinion and on the economy. These figures represented cuts of 6 per cent rising to 8 per cent on public expenditure programmes totalling something like £50 billion. Pliatzky comments: 'It was never on the cards that Treasury Ministers would put such proposals to Cabinet, let alone succeed in getting approval for them . . . . This did not mean that . . . nothing could be done . . . . But the negotiating gap was immense.'[10]

Despite the immensity of the gap, the IMF proposals could be described as almost moderate as compared with the £5 billion cut in the 1977/8 PSBR demanded by *The Times*.[11] On the other hand, when told that their proposals, which they recognized as having been calculated on crude assumptions, were unrealistic and were likely to have serious political effects, the IMF team indicated that these were not their final terms, that they were looking for information, and that they would carefully consider whatever was disclosed.

This was a negotiation and a negotiation in which the IMF team, confronted by a divided Treasury, was well advised to take the line it did. If its objective was to shake a recalcitrant UK government into offering something sensible by way of cuts, it was successfully achieved. If the Treasury had had a united and realistic view and had been authorized to give guidance to the IMF on what the Cabinet should be expected to accept, the IMF team might not have needed to put forward such an extreme opening position. But the Treasury did not have a united and realistic view, had not been so authorized, and there was at the time no knowledge of what, if anything, the Cabinet would accept.

The story that some officials from the divided Treasury were briefing the IMF and the US Treasury to impose tough terms on the UK Government was spread among others by the Liberal MP John Pardoe. 'At least one senior Minister felt he had evidence that this was true. It also became clear that some of the Prime Minister's advisers, if not Jim Callaghan himself, believed it.'[12] Callaghan may well have believed it and it would not have made him more in love with the Treasury. The existence of such a conspiracy is certainly believed by Donoughue who claims to have evidence of it in a meeting to which he was 'privately summoned' by 'a very senior official' at the United States Embassy in London. At this meeting he was told that 'parts of the Treasury are in very deep cahoots with parts of the US Treasury and with certain others in Germany who are of very right wing inclination.'[13]

Those less conspiratorially inclined may feel that as the views of 'parts of the Treasury', of the US Treasury, and even of 'certain others in Germany' were perfectly well known, no conspiracy between them was necessary. They were all acting on their known convictions and, in the end, to the great benefit of the UK Government. An unpatriotic conspiracy by 'parts of the Treasury' is, however, a much more appetizing explanation of the IMF crisis than policy failure. This conspiracy theory did not lose in persuasiveness from the fact that it pandered to deep feelings of hostility within the Government not just to the Treasury but to all those who were being asked to do the UK the favour of lending it money. The IMF was not loved in the British Labour movement. The deep suspicion towards it was a major handicap in arriving at a sensible solution to the UK's self-induced crisis.

Within the Treasury there were those who, not just on economic grounds, were worried by the possibility that a Labour government might be destroyed by international financial pressures. In 1974 the same people had been worried about the ungovernability of Britain and had regarded the election of a Labour government as an ill omen suggesting that no government could stand up to the unions. Now they were worried about the implications if a Labour government collapsed through refusal to meet IMF conditions. Pliatzky has written of the initial terms demanded by the IMF:

Anyone who remembered how the terms thought necessary for foreign loans and financial survival in 1931 had led to the break-up of Ramsay MacDonald's Labour government could not doubt that comparable damage would be done if these terms were imposed in order to get the IMF loan.[14]

There was indeed, at the time, a great deal of wild talk about the dangers in Britain of totalitarianism of the Left or Right.[15] I was myself approached by a senior Treasury official who was in a state of great alarm. He believed that the Government might fall, that this would lead to social strife, and even threaten the survival of constitutional government in the UK. He asked me what he could do to assist the Government to resist IMF demands. I replied that he would be well-advised to leave this subject to the Cabinet. The pressure from the IMF would do nothing but good both to the economy and to the government.

Callaghan and the influence of Tony Crosland

The importance of Tony Crosland at this time lay in his influence on the Prime Minister. During his August holiday, Crosland had reflected on the wider economic climate and the costs of the cuts he so much detested:

(a) Demoralisation of decent rank-&-file: Grimsby L.P. . . . (b) strain on T.U. loyalty . . . Outstanding success of last 2 yrs, has been implication & involvement of T.U.'s in national economic policy. If this survives, will struggle thru.: if not, disaster. (c) breeding of illiterate & reactionary attitude to public expenditure—horrible. (d) collapse of strategy which I proposed last year . . . Now no sense of direction and *no* priorities: only pragmatism, empiricism, safety first, £ supreme. (e) and: unemployment, even if politically more wearable, = grave loss of welfare, security, choice: very high price to be paid for deflation & negative growth . . . Import controls probably necessary to ease *politics* of situation, tho' doubt if will make much difference to the reality.[16]

With much of this, Callaghan would sympathize. To him, too, relations with the trade unions were important. He had not ruled out import controls and, as for deflation, he thought it had gone far enough. He was unwilling to do anything that hit industry, prices, or employment, though any package seemed bound to hit all three. He appeared to believe that the only real problem was the sterling balances. Crosland's influence was illustrated during the early days of November. I was talking to Denis Healey in the corridor behind the Speaker's Chair off which runs the passage to the Prime Minister's rooms. Callaghan came up to us and said: 'Tony Crosland tells me that it is all a bankers' ramp like 1931. I think I agree with him.' Before Healey could make any response, Callaghan walked off into the Chamber. Healey turned to me in near despair: 'What can I do now?' Yet, despite Crosland's influence, I remained persuaded that in the end the Prime Minister would be forced to tell the Cabinet that there had to be an agreement with the IMF and that that would involve substantial cuts in public expenditure programmes. I did not expect him to endorse the IMF's original terms. But I thought he would be bound, in the end, to support his Chancellor in negotiating the best terms he could. It was the only way of saving the Government.

In any case, there were, by this time, too many doubts about Crosland himself. Crosland had undermined the confidence of his former friends and supporters by his refusal to regard as important any question that involved him in difficulty. Gradually most of those who had supported him drifted away. While still at the Treasury, I was outraged by his refusal to intervene in the illiberal attack against the lump which John Silkin, a senior Minister in his Department, was pushing through the Government.[17] It could have made it virtually impossible for any construction worker to be self-employed. I raised the question with Crosland. He told me that the matter was not sufficiently important for him to intervene. This did not prevent his pressing me to alter my stance when he was to make a speech to the construction workers' union, or intervening in support of Silkin when the matter came to Cabinet where, after a difficult battle, I won. His attitude is perfectly caught by Tony Benn in his account of the discussion when the industrial strategy White Paper was before Cabinet. 'Clever Tony Crosland knows it all, very much dislikes the policy, of course. He pretends it is meaningless; it doesn't matter; it has got nothing to do with anything.'[18] It was his lack of interest in matters which to others were important that resulted in his humiliation in the leadership election in March 1976.

The Economic Strategy Committee gets to work

With the IMF team waiting in London, the Economic Strategy Committee of the Cabinet was at last discussing what should be its attitude to the negotiations which it had, inescapably, to authorize. At a meeting on 3 November, the Committee was presented with a series of unpalatable forecasts which suggested higher unemployment and higher inflation, together with a substantial cut in living standards. Though output was now more buoyant, unemployment was still rising and seemed likely to remain above 1 million for a long time.[19] The world economy, which had appeared to be growing fast in July, now seemed to be slowing down. The PSBR was now estimated at £11 billion.[20] It had not yet been realized what an impact cash limits were having even in 1976/7.

These forecasts would confirm Callaghan in his view, earlier shared by Healey, that enough had been done by the July measures, and that the IMF should now be prepared to make its loan on the basis of 'existing policies'. In his memoirs Callaghan states that he agreed with Healey that the PSBR for 1977/8 'must not exceed £9 billion', the figure that the Cabinet had thought had been achieved by the July measures.[21] But that was not the way he at first behaved. According to the latest Treasury estimates of the PSBR, a £9 billion target would require further substantial cuts in public expenditure. Callaghan was very uncertain about the need for further public expenditure cuts and remained uncertain until near the end. He did not consider that a refusal of such cuts was inconsistent with his Blackpool speech. The difference now between Healey and Callaghan was that whereas Callaghan was not yet prepared, even under *force majeure*, to do anything more, Healey had appreciated that something more had to be done to satisfy the IMF and the market. To Healey, the price that had to be paid was unfortunate, and should be kept as small as could be negotiated, but it had to be paid.

There was a feeling that Healey's policies were leading nowhere. Foot, Benn, and Shore argued for import controls. According to Benn, Shirley Williams rejected public expenditure cuts, rejected import controls, and favoured a large loan; and Hattersley argued for some sacrifices of social priorities in order to save employment but was sceptical about import controls, without ruling them out. I supported Healey's call for public expenditure cuts. There was no conclusion to the discussion because what Healey was proposing was unacceptable to a majority of the Committee, and yet there was no agreement about alternatives. Joel Barnett comments of the situation at this time: 'Denis's credibility with Cabinet... was pretty low.'[22]

The best that the meeting could produce was a suggestion from the Prime Minister of a national recovery programme. That idea was taken up again at a further meeting on 10 November when the CPRS had attempted to put some flesh on dry bones. The CPRS presented a suitably searing document, listing all the problems without too much joy even at the end of two difficult years. If Callaghan had hoped for some relief from his problems in the idea of a national recovery strategy, he must have been disappointed. His only reward was to find that the Left regarded the CPRS's draft as nothing but a coalition strategy.[23] Thus the Cabinet's senior economic committee whiled away its time while the IMF negotiators waited in their London hotel.

Callaghan does not seem yet to have realized that Jack Jones, the most influential trade union leader, had taken a remarkably realistic view of the situation. Benn and Stan Orme went to see Jones at Transport House to lay before him the latest dispiriting economic forecasts and to seek his advice. They left with a flea in their ear. They had been told not to resign, not to believe the forecasts, and to make the best of a bad job so far as public expenditure cuts were concerned.[24] Callaghan would discover the practical attitude of Jack Jones toward the Government's difficulties when he consulted him and Lionel Murray just before finally declaring his own hand in Cabinet on 2 December.[25] It would have been better if some of that practical spirit had entered into the Government's discussions.

Only at a third meeting of the Economic Strategy Committee on 17 November were the negotiations with the IMF seriously addressed. Even then Callaghan at first appeared to believe that the Government could dictate to the IMF the terms on which they were to lend to us. Although he had come to accept that the PSBR was the key, it was Healey who had to insist that there had to be a reduced target for the PSBR and that, if he was given authority to negotiate, his aim would be a PSBR no lower than £9 billion. It was then that Callaghan gave a signal that he might be prepared to accept the figure of £9 billion as a minimum. Later he was to write: 'I was not willing to go below the £9 billions that the Cabinet had agreed as recently as July.'[26] But he still hoped that the implications of that figure could be avoided. He was conducting discussions with his friends Helmut Schmidt and President Ford.[27] What is friendship worth if it does not bring succour?

Callaghan woos Ford and Schmidt but they do not love him enough

Despite experience gained from occupying so many great offices of state, Callaghan retained a streak of naïvety. There is a long-standing diplomatic tradition, now abandoned, that it is inadvisable to allow heads of government to talk to one another. They will not understand the real significance of what is said. Heads of government are reluctant to be too tough with their colleagues. They may appear more understanding than they can afford to be. When they return to their capitals, and officials resume work, it is likely to be found that nothing has changed.

Callaghan believed that in the USA and in Germany he had friends who would help him. Helmut Schmidt, Chancellor of the Federal Republic of Germany, was an old friend of Britain and, as a Social Democrat, presumably a friend too of its Labour Government. Callaghan briefed Benn on 7 October about discussions he was having with Helmut Schmidt at Chequers the following weekend:

Helmut Schmidt and I are going to have a long, comprehensive financial talk with nobody present from the Foreign Office, nobody from the Treasury, they'll wreck it. But Helmut Schmidt has got $32 billion dollars in reserves. They could fund the entire sterling balances. He's from Hamburg and they all like the English.[28]

Yet if a foreigner has made the effort to like the English, he should not also be required to pay for it. Schmidt was personally more sympathetic than his own government allowed him to be. He was encouraging at the Chequers meeting with Callaghan and later made somewhat extravagant promises of German support when required.[29] British Ministers sometimes seemed unable to grasp that personal friendship, and even political ideology, were insecure bases upon which to plead for charity. In February 1977, when the IMF crisis had been survived, I advised my colleagues in a public lecture that 'Friendship flourishes best where the demands made on it are least' and 'not to put our trust in princes, even democratically elected ones of a social democratic hue'. Callaghan saw the text of my lecture before delivery, must have recognized the reference, and made no comment.[30]

Discussions in Cabinet were delayed while Callaghan cast about for alternatives to an IMF rescue. He tried to persuade Helmut Schmidt and President Ford to offer unconditional assistance. These efforts were based on the conviction that UK policy was already sufficiently tight. But they were bound to be fruitless first because it was not true and, even more crucially, because the market did not believe it. Then he exerted his influence with his old friends to mitigate the IMF terms and to help him negotiate an international solution to the problem of the sterling balances. Harold Lever visited Washington on Callaghan's behalf to discuss the question of the sterling balances and was told off by President Ford about a speech I had made a few days before in New York in which I had criticized certain aspects of US trade policy.[31] While in Washington, Lever did not see the IMF who did not, in fact, wish to see him.

Neither Ford nor Schmidt was willing to help with the sterling balances until a deal was made with the IMF. In any case, if the UK did not bite the bullet, its problems would be recurring whatever was done about the sterling balances. The balances were a secondary problem. They obsessed Callaghan but they were not the prime issue. They were even a diversion from the main issue. The point was well made by Sir Samuel Goldman, a retired Treasury mandarin who wrote: 'let us not use the reserve role of sterling and the sterling balances as an alibi and an excuse for weaknesses which lie much deeper, and exaggerate the help which a partial funding of the balances alone would bring us.'[32] Even Lever himself said in Washington that the question of the sterling balances was not one of the 'greatest urgency'.[33] The prime issue was the management of the British economy. All Callaghan's efforts were to end in disappointment when the hard negotiations with the IMF began. Yeo flew to see Schmidt to unpersuade him if he had indeed been persuaded at Chequers. Britain could not be favoured when simultaneous IMF negotiations were in progress with Italy and were in prospect with Portugal. Yeo found that his journey had been unnecessary. Karl-Otto Pöhl, then of the German Finance Ministry, confirmed to Whittome that the German Government was not asking the IMF to soften its terms.[34]

It was clear that even the political leaders, those who understood political problems, and not just hard unelected officials of the US Treasury and Federal Reserve, believed that some terms must be imposed on the UK and that those terms must be negotiated with the IMF. Ford was by now a lame duck, since Carter had won the presidential election in November. But Carter and Blumenthal, the President and Treasury Secretary elect, shared the views of the Ford Administration.[35]

Callaghan had expected too much from the charm and persuasiveness of Harold Lever. There was, however, one matter on which Callaghan should have had no doubts following his conversations with his friends. They would not tolerate import restrictions. Callaghan himself reports a conversation in which President Ford made that crystal clear.[36] Given that indication, it is surprising how long Callaghan persisted with the idea that import deposits might be an option.

The Cabinet takes charge

The critical Cabinet discussions did not begin until 23 November though there was a brief, preliminary, skirmish on 18 November. So far as I was concerned, the first stage was a small private meeting called by the Prime Minister at No. 10. I arrived without any foreknowledge of its purpose. I found Denis Healey and Tony Crosland there together with Treasury officials. The purpose of the gathering, I found, was to discover whether there was any meeting of minds between those identified as the

The IMF in London

main contenders. Denis Healey explained why it was vital that the negotiation with the IMF should be successful. That could only mean further cuts in public expenditure. Crosland then produced the arguments against the cuts which he was later to put to Cabinet. Susan Crosland records what those arguments were, ascribing them to the meeting of the Cabinet on 23 November where indeed they were repeated in terms virtually identical to those he had used at the Prime Minister's private meeting. In due course, they were to appear in Peter Jenkins's column in *The Guardian*.

There was no economic case for the cuts, he said. He dealt with the arguments one by one. With 1.25 million unemployed, nobody could say that there was not enough spare capacity to increase exports. Far from reducing the PSBR, the spending cuts would mean higher unemployment, which would in turn mean higher social security payments and lower tax revenue, thus actually increasing the PSBR. In any case, Treasury forecasts of the PSBR were unreliable; other experts' forecasts were much lower than the Treasury's. The cuts would massacre the industrial strategy. So far as trade unions were concerned, Jack Jones might agree, but the public sector would not. Without the public sector unions the Social Contract, already deeply damaged by the effects of the cuts on rents and so on, would collapse. The only serious argument for cuts was one in terms of international confidence. But what would happen to confidence if the Government bowed down and accepted the package, and as a result the Social Contract broke, and the smouldering resentment of the PLP meant that the Government could not deliver the cuts in the House of Commons?[37]

Crosland did not, at this meeting, suggest the threats to run down our NATO commitments and introduce a siege economy which, at the Cabinet on 23 November, would so undermine the credibility of his arguments.

The Prime Minister then turned to me. Crosland had summarized his arguments by claiming that everything was now in place for the long-looked-for economic recovery. I argued, first, that he could not know whether what he was saying was true or not; and, secondly, that even if it were true, the disbelief of the market could undermine it and, indeed, bring down the Government before we reaped the benefit of having at last got everything in place. There just was too strong a basis for the market's lack of confidence for the Government to behave as he was proposing. The trade figures were still worrying, inflation was still high, and we did have commitments to meet in December. Crosland seemed to have no appreciation of the problem of financing the balance of payments, with liabilities greatly in excess of reserves and a continuing current account deficit. If the market had believed that all was in place for a recovery it would have supplied the money we needed unconditionally. Our application to the IMF had been forced on us by the incredulity of the market and therefore we had to make the choice, to negotiate successfully with the IMF, or to be swept from office.

The Prime Minister made no commitment to either side of the argument. The whole question would have to go to Cabinet. He had wanted to listen.

The cabals had been forming. On 22 November there was a meeting in Tony Crosland's room at the Commons to co-ordinate their opposition to the IMF cuts. Present were Harold Lever, Shirley Williams, David Ennals, and Roy Hattersley. Bill Rodgers came in halfway through. They all opposed cuts though for different reasons. Ennals and Williams wanted to protect their departmental budgets. Lever and Hattersley thought the whole exercise unnecessarily deflationary. Harold Lever had not changed his mind on how to resolve the crisis, any crisis. At an earlier stage, Samuel Brittan and Adrian Hamilton had reported that 'One view, long held by Mr Harold Lever, is to seek a major stabilisation loan of perhaps $7-$8bn.'[38] Barnett reports that 'Lever was confident we could borrow what we needed, without having to cut public expenditure.'[39] This was a thesis to which Lever remained loyal to the end despite hearing Yeo refer to one of his schemes as a 'lunatic notion', a term which none of his friends would have used to his face.[40] But lenders of last resort have special privileges. Crosland was not present at the meeting as he was at dinner with the President of Venezuela. Government hospitality does not stop simply because the whole fate of the government is in question. I also was at the dinner and relations with Venezuela were not the only subject of conversation among the Ministers who were present.

The other group opposed to the IMF terms consisted of the Left, Shore, Foot, Benn, Silkin, Orme, and Booth. This group was under the influence of the New Cambridge School. Francis Cripps, Tony Benn's adviser at the Department of Energy, was writing papers on the alternative strategy which would go to Cabinet if the Prime Minister agreed.[41] Nicky Kaldor, the New Cambridge School's principal publicist, now out of the Treasury but conveniently located in the House of Lords, was busy, agitating against the cuts. On 23 July 1976 Nicky had made a speech urging Healey to announce that he was seeking approval from the EEC and IMF for an import deposit scheme in view of the serious balance of payments position. He had argued that a deflationary package would not be enough and, with 1.3 million already unemployed, such a policy 'would be a complete break with the most basic tenets of the Labour Party'.[42]

This advice was extraordinary. There was not the least chance of getting international approval. But Kaldor did have the excuse that the Prime Minister himself was playing with the idea of import controls. On 22 November Nicky met with Peter Shore and Tony Benn and, with his customary impeccable political touch, told them that it was essential for the life and safety of the Labour movement that any cuts should be rejected and that Callaghan's bluff should be called.[43] He could also assure anyone prepared to listen that the Treasury had locked in its cupboard a complete plan for import controls and exchange controls.[44] How could he be wrong? He had filled those cupboards himself during his various stints in the Treasury. It would be unfair to Nicky to imagine that he was confining his briefing to Shore and Benn. No doubt he was also talking to the Crosland group in the same sense. He had been in close touch with Crosland in the 1960s when he still believed in devaluation and there was no need now to cut off the stream of advice. Nicky made no contact with me. No doubt I was, once more, out of favour. No one, however, depended on personal contact to discover Nicky's views. He was a prolific letter writer in the columns of *The Times* whose readers learnt from him that 'it would be a grave mistake to assume that either devaluation or deflation is a viable policy option in all the circumstances, and it would be an even graver mistake to think that they are the only policy options available'.[45]

The Crosland group made an approach to the Benn group to see whether they could move into an alliance. This was rejected by Frances Morrell on behalf of the Benn group who 'were not willing to play that game with the Crosland group'.[46] The position of the Benn group was that they would not ally with Crosland but would support him, except perhaps to the degree that the Crosland proposals also involved attacks on the social services such as earnings-related benefit.[47]

Healey and I were also meeting together from time to time. But when we met, we were alone.

The Cabinet of 23 November

Among economists there continued to be substantial disagreement with any further attack on the PSBR. In an article in *The Times*, opposing the protectionism then being advocated by Wynne Godley and Lord Kaldor, seven eminent economists wrote that

> a quick attempt at a massive reduction in the budget deficit would simply aggravate the recession ... so long as private savings remain high, corporate liquidity low, a collective oil deficit persists, and the economy remains slack, it is perfectly rational to plan a substantial budget deficit ... Public expenditure should indeed be cut ... But cuts adopted for this reason should be accompanied by tax reduction rather than being used to reduce the budget deficit.[48]

This argumentation appeared to assume that any money a government wished to borrow would be readily available whatever assessment lenders might make of the likelihood that they would ever be repaid. Indeed it is quite clear that many of the articles written in the heavy press in support of the proposition that the PSBR should not be cut were written in the mistaken belief that the UK's power to borrow remained intact, and that the governments of the major industrial countries would be only too willing to fund a safety-net for the sterling balances, even if not the market.[49] At least these gentlemen did agree that public expenditure could and should be cut. But if eminent economists were dissatisfied with the arguments for reducing the PSBR, it was not surprising that their scepticism should find an echo in a Labour Cabinet.

On 23 November, at a Cabinet cut short by a reception offered by the President of Venezuela, Crosland repeated his arguments against Healey's policies. But this time he had something to add. He believed, evidently, that the Government's negotiating position was much stronger than we had realized. First, he made one concession. 'The Government had made its negotiations too public to do nothing now. He was prepared to see cuts—mainly cosmetic—of one billion pounds, half a billion coming from the sale of shares in Burmah Oil [sic], the other half to be found in the least deflationary way possible.' Then he played his master card.

> The Government should then say to the IMF, the Americans and the Germans: if you demand any more of us we shall put up the shutters, wind down our defence commitments, introduce a siege economy. As the IMF was even more passionately opposed to protectionism than it was attached to monetarism, this

threat would be sufficient to persuade the Fund to lend the money without unacceptable conditions. Politically the IMF could not refuse the loan. If the Government kept its nerve, it could insist on its own terms—could limit the cuts to 'window-dressing' to appease the irritating and ignorant currency dealers. 'We have to stop paying danegeld.'[50]

Tony Benn helps us to get the full flavour of this Crosland speech which, in the Benn version, ended with the cry: 'Our weakness is our strength, it is a test of nerve, and the IMF must give us the loan.'[51]

The folly of these threats confirmed my view that Crosland could no longer be trusted. He was recommending that we should gamble with the life of the Government on the basis of wild assurances that the IMF could not refuse the loan and that we could secure support in Parliament for winding down our defence commitments and introducing a siege economy. It counted for nothing apparently that our forces in Germany were deployed in our own defence, not as a favour to our allies. His remarks showed a Crosland who had lost all power of judgement. Indeed it was difficult to know how seriously to take such proposals. I was certain they would never be implemented. They had something in common with King Lear's helpless outcry against the cruelty of his daughters. Crosland seemed unable to make contact with a world that saw no reason to do the UK favours, and demanded from it only a quality of economic performance which it was failing to deliver, but which it had to deliver if the UK was ever to be taken seriously again. Callaghan himself had been interpreted as making such threats on *Panorama* at the end of October but I was convinced that, in the end, he would understand their absurdity and the poor judgement that led Crosland to suggest we contemplate such a course.[52]

Susan Crosland gives us Tony's assessment of the Cabinet of 23 November:

The Prime Minister went round the table, then cut the discussion short. Of the thirteen people who spoke, ten took the view that the loan could be obtained on the terms set out by the Foreign Secretary—cuts largely done by mirrors. Only two supported the Chancellor: 'Reg Prentice, who is mad, and Edmund Dell who is in a very very reactionary state of mind. Both thought Denis hadn't gone far enough . . . It was a dramatic Cabinet—and a very interesting discussion. Jim didn't—as he said last night he would—support Denis. When Jim summed up, he was *excellent*.' . . . As reports of this Cabinet rocketed round Whitehall, the Treasury knew it had suffered a defeat; it still expected to win in the end. The Cabinet had agreed that before it met again on Thursday, the Prime

Minister would communicate with the American President and the German Chancellor and tell them that Britain would not accept the IMF's terms. At that very moment, a Treasury representative was in Bonn putting the case to Chancellor Schmidt before the counter-argument could be heard.[53]

Benn's account, which is dominated by Benn's contribution instead of Crosland's, confirms that there had been no clear cut conclusion. Callaghan had put before the meeting a proposition that Healey should be authorized to negotiate with the IMF on the basis of a £9 billion PSBR in 1977/8. There had been a great deal of opposition, the alternative strategy had been strongly advocated, and it was clear that the Cabinet would have to return to the question, perhaps with the benefit of advice from President Ford and Chancellor Schmidt. Crosland's fear that Schmidt's mind would be corrupted by Treasury advice before he had heard the views of the British Cabinet did less than credit to the Federal Chancellor's understanding, apart from exaggerating the amount of notice he was likely to take of a Cabinet thinking in terms of the alternative strategy. In any case he had already had the opportunity of briefing from Callaghan.

In the whole course of these largely academic discussions in Cabinet, there was really only one question. When would Callaghan declare his hand? Not everyone shared my conviction that, in the end, Callaghan would support Healey. Benn reports on 24 November that 'Michael [Foot] . . . thought that Jim was going to come down against Denis, and Denis might resign.' Benn commented in his diary: 'Of course if [Denis] does resign, the pound will go through the floor, even if we get the IMF loan. In order to keep Denis you have to have more deflation but the trick is to keep Denis and have less deflation.'[54] Callaghan had decided to give the whole Cabinet the opportunity to talk its way through the problems, hoping thereby to achieve an agreed, or at least a tolerated, solution. In a Cabinet as ideologically divided as the Callaghan Cabinet, mutual tolerance was often the highest form of accord that could be achieved.

This tactic also had the advantage of giving him time finally to make up his own mind and discover what his friends were really ready to do for him. A Labour Cabinet was in suspended judgement, praying to be saved by a lame duck Republican President and by the most right-wing (and successful) Social Democrat in Europe.

Notes

1. Martin 183.
2. Martin 187, 14 Nov.
3. Healey 430. See also Benn 623.
4. Barnett 101.
5. Garritsen de Vries (1985), 470.
6. Healey 430. See also Denis Healey in *Institutional Investor* (June 1987).
7. Pliatzky (1982), 153. See also CR.
8. Barnett 101.
9. Garritsen de Vries (1985), 467. See also Healey 430.
10. Pliatzky (1982), 153–4.
11. See *The Times*, 23 Oct. 1976, and their 'Programme for Stability'.
12. Barnett 102.
13. CR.
14. Pliatzky (1982), 153.
15. Benn 634.
16. Crosland 355–6.
17. 'Lump' was the name given to labour only subcontracting in the construction industry. It was believed to lead to widespread avoidance of income tax and national insurance payments. Such labour would therefore be highly competitive with unionized labour in the construction industry.
18. Benn 212.
19. *NIER* (Aug. 1976), 5.
20. *NIER* (Nov. 1976), 6, which was published shortly afterwards, also took a gloomier view of the economy than in August.
21. Callaghan 423.
22. Barnett 100.
23. Benn 636–8.
24. Benn 643.
25. Callaghan 438–9.
26. Callaghan 435. See also Benn 646.
27. Benn 646–7.
28. Benn 624.
29. Callaghan 431–2. See also Fay and Young, 21 May 1978.
30. The Fifth Rita Hinden Lecture.
31. Harold Lever gives an account of his visit to Washington in CR.
32. *The Times*, 10 Nov. 1976.
33. *The Times*, 17 Nov. 1976.
34. Fay and Young, 21 May 1978.
35. Healey 430. See also Keegan and Pennant-Rea 167.
36. Callaghan 430.
37. Crosland 377–8.
38. *Financial Times*, 24 Sept. 1976.
39. Barnett 100.
40. CR.

41. Benn 656–7.
42. Thirlwall 252.
43. Benn 651–2.
44. Benn 657.
45. *The Times*, 30 Nov. 1976.
46. Crosland 379.
47. Benn 656.
48. *The Times*, 15 Nov. 1976. The seven were Wilfred Beckerman, John Black, Christopher Bliss, John Flemming, Alan Peacock, Maurice FG. Scott, John Williamson. It is fair to say that what they had in mind was a £5b. cut in the 1977/8 PSBR as advocated by *The Times*.
49. See e.g. David Watt in the *Financial Times*, 26 Nov. 1976.
50. Crosland 377–8.
51. Benn 654.
52. Benn 632.
53. Crosland 378, 23 Nov. 1976.
54. Benn 656–7.

T·W·E·N·T·Y F·O·U·R

Accepting the Inevitable

Some outstanding questions

The Cabinet of 23 November left various questions open which would have to be answered over the next few days. For example, would the Cabinet really opt for the alternative strategy whether of the Benn or the Crosland variety? If it did not, on what realistic basis could Healey be permitted to negotiate with the IMF team waiting in London? Above all, when would Callaghan make up his mind? When would Ford and Schmidt give him the only advice they could give him, that if the IMF came to an inadequate agreement with the UK, any increase in confidence would be short-lived? When, in other words, would they achieve that higher level of friendship which consists in telling the truth? Bill Simon visited London on 27 November. He could be relied on to speak frankly. Ford's willingness to do so was less clear.

No doubt Ford and Schmidt both knew the nature of the debate in the British Cabinet. Everyone else did and there was no reason why they should have been excluded from knowledge of this very public controversy. Perhaps no major Cabinet debate has ever been so publicly displayed due to briefing of the media by the contending factions—even extending to the passage to friendly journalists of notes prepared for Cabinet speeches. Undoubtedly the bias of the intelligentsia, as reflected in the press and in the Commons, was in support of the Crosland arguments. The leaks delighted liberally minded journalists because they believed it helped them to influence the debate away from those they regarded as deflationists in the Cabinet and in the Treasury.

The alternative strategy rejected

Crosland and Hattersley were working out a scheme for import deposits. Among other benefits, the deposits would help with the PSBR. Crosland advanced the scheme at Cabinet on 25 November. The idea was that with such a scheme Healey could go back to the IMF and beat them down. Crosland 'was in a good mood: it was still possible that a united front would break the IMF's hold on Healey. Callaghan had still not supported his Chancellor in Cabinet, but he consistently told Tony that he expected to do so. Therefore it was imperative that Healey be shifted.'[1]

Callaghan allowed a paper from Benn on the alternative strategy to be circulated and to be discussed. The Cabinet was assisted in considering it by a neutral paper by the CPRS setting out the pros and cons. Benn's paper was treated dismissively by the Cabinet as a whole on 1 December. The alternative strategy would not even avoid the hardships associated with agreement with the IMF.[2] In the words of Susan Crosland, it was 'pulverised by Denis'. Benn's circulation of the 1931 Cabinet minutes which produced the split in the Labour Party and Government led only to vigorous denials by Callaghan that we were back in those dark ages.

Peter Shore, my predecessor as Secretary of State for Trade, had put in a paper drawing attention to the circumstances in which the GATT permitted import controls. It was discussed on the same day. Unlike Benn, Shore made a 'strong lucid case for import controls'.[3] Shore did not want to reduce imports, simply to prevent them from increasing. Shore, like Benn, was labouring under the illusion that it would be possible to get international support for the alternative strategy. This was a misconception probably derived from contact with the New Cambridge School who themselves shared it.[4] They believed that their approach would lead to a new structure of international economic relations in which international trade would be appropriately balanced and the economies of the world could expand together. They failed to see that the stronger economies had no interest in any such arrangement, quite the opposite. The New Cambridge School later came to realize that they were deceiving themselves. But they had, meanwhile, wasted a good deal of time in the British Cabinet much of which wanted to believe they were right because it would provide so convenient a means of escape from the real problems of the UK economy.

Disintegration of the Crosland camp

Shore's argument was regarded in the Crosland camp as reinforcing the Crosland paper on import deposits. 'It was this paper on which the final struggle turned. It did two things: it presented the Treasury with a viable alternative, and it kept open the way to an alliance between those opposing the Treasury.'[5] Whatever else could be claimed for him, Crosland did not present a viable alternative. His insularity was remarkable in a Foreign Secretary. Partly as a result of that insularity, the Crosland coalition was coming apart. In moving from an attack on the deflationary impact of an agreement with the IMF to restrictions on trade, Crosland lost the support of Harold Lever and Shirley Williams. Lever and Williams continued to oppose the IMF terms, but Lever was committed to free trade and was, apparently, unwilling to use threats of intervention in trade in an attempt to modify the IMF's conditions. His devotion to free trade was, no doubt, allied to a perception of the absurdity of the Crosland tactics. For her part, Shirley Williams regarded the import deposit scheme as protectionist and damaging to the Third World. On 30 November, the Crosland camp had a 'disappointing meeting'. Bill Rodgers had abandoned them for Healey. He had perhaps been dissuaded by the preposterous Crosland plan for running down the UK contribution to Western defence. Shirley and David Ennals were undecided since they were now less worried about their departmental budgets.[6] The IMF team had, as they had promised, listened to Treasury arguments and were scaling down their first, admittedly crudely calculated, demands. Of the original Crosland group, only Hattersley was left still standing unreservedly with Crosland.

Callaghan decides

In any case it was too late for alternative strategies. Callaghan had, at last, made up his mind. It was time for a decision. Between early March and early December, roughly the period of Callaghan's residence at No. 10, the value of sterling compared with a range of other currencies fell by about 20 per cent, a depreciation greater than the devaluations of sterling in 1949 and 1967. The message that he had to settle with the IMF finally got through to him at the European Summit on 29 and

30 November. On the flight home, he gave Crosland his definitive conclusion that he had to support Healey. Crosland

> was sad about his conversation with Jim on the flight back. Jim . . . said he would support Denis. Schmidt had taken a hard line . . . 'Although Jim repeated that all the arguments haven't yet been heard, he expects to accept the IMF's terms . . . I inserted arguments to remind him of the growing general opinion against the IMF's terms.'[7]

Callaghan's conclusion could only have been reinforced when, at the request of President Ford, Witteveen paid his secret visit to London on 1 December and, together with Whittome, met the Prime Minister and the Chancellor. Ford, harrassed by Callaghan's pleas, secretly begged Witteveen 'in the interests of the international community', to travel to London 'to persuade Mr Callaghan to support a reduction in public sector borrowing'.[8] The secret that it was President Ford who had asked Witteveen to pay the visit was deeper even than the secrecy of the visit itself. Healey seems to have imagined that Witteveen had come over to stiffen the too flexible Whittome.[9] The real purpose was, more probably, to ensure that Callaghan understood that he had to negotiate with the IMF, not with his friends, and to impress on the Prime Minister that there could be no favours for the UK.

But one illusion appeared to remain in the Prime Minister's mind. When Witteveen arrived at No. 10, he found on the table a copy of the GATT charter.[10] Callaghan, alerted by Shore's paper, threatened Witteveen with import deposits claiming that they were permissible under the GATT. He did not appear to realize that their status under the GATT was irrelevant, once he had decided to support Healey, because the IMF would not consent. Callaghan's pressure for them at Cabinet the following day was despite what he was told by Witteveen.[11] Callaghan probably realized that his support for import deposits was now nothing but bluster, private bluster for the benefit of Cabinet colleagues. Too much time had already been spent on bluster, most of it in public. At least this final bluster was kept secret.

Decision time in Downing Street

At Cabinet on 1 December, ten Ministers who had not yet spoken said they would support the Prime Minister in whatever he thought best. Moreover it was becoming apparent that Healey was making progress in

Accepting the Inevitable

his discussions with the IMF towards a more comfortable conclusion. That evening Crosland, having been warned by the Prime Minister, and having conceded that that must be the end of his opposition, told Hattersley that he intended to switch to reluctant support of the Prime Minister the following day and that Hattersley should do the same.[12]

The following day, 2 December, Healey opened the discussion forcefully by leaving the Cabinet in no doubt as to the facts to be faced. He emphasized that the $1.6 billion drawing on the stand-by had to be repaid. If it was repaid without an IMF drawing, it would leave less than $2 billion of usable reserves. Unless the PSBR was cut from the present forecast of £10.2 billion to £8.7 billion, we would not get the loan and we would not be able to borrow abroad. No one abroad believed that this would be deflationary. Helmut Schmidt might be to the right of Milton Friedman but the world agreed with him. There was not yet a settlement with the IMF, but anything less than he was proposing would not restore confidence even if the IMF did accept it. Crosland's package was quite unsaleable. On the other hand, if the Cabinet accepted his recommendations, we would be able to borrow again, and there would be a safety-net for the sterling balances. He dangled the possibility of import deposits but indicated that they would be unacceptable to the IMF and therefore almost certainly not negotiable.[13] Healey's statement that the world agreed with Helmut Schmidt, even if he was to the right of Milton Friedman, must have dispersed many of the illusions with which so many in the Cabinet had been living for so long. The Cabinet had been enticed into thinking that the UK was leading the world with its economic policies. What Healey had told them was that there were no followers and that they had no choice but to change.

Callaghan then made clear that he supported the Chancellor of the Exchequer. Emphasizing the political and economic uncertainties, and his attempts to persuade Ford and Schmidt, he called for a 'three-legged stool' approach, a cut in the PSBR of £1 billion to £1.5 billion, a safety-net for the sterling balances, and import deposits.[14] The stool, in fact, ended up with only two legs, the cut of £1.5 billion in the PSBR and the safety-net. But it really only needed one leg on which to stand, agreement with the IMF.

For a moment it appeared that Callaghan's intervention had not had the expected effect. Michael Foot gravely informed the Prime Minister that his proposals would not do. He went back to the alternative strategy. Even if that meant defeat for the Government, and a return to

Opposition, it would keep the party whole. This was followed by the little pantomime in which Crosland, warned in advance by Callaghan, made his speech of capitulation, itself an exercise in self-deception. Susan Crosland tells us what he said:

The Prime Minister's statement had significantly changed the situation, Tony said. He remained absolutely unconvinced by the economic arguments which had been used. But his clear political judgement was that, given the position which the Prime Minister had taken, it would not be right to press the issue. If it became known that the anti-deflationists had won a big majority in Cabinet, or even constituted a significant minority, this would ruin confidence not only in currency markets. It could smash up the Party.[15]

Of course it was already known that those whom Crosland lauded with the title 'anti-deflationists' had been strongly placed in the Cabinet. Crosland's leaking to the Press had ensured that. What had now been made clear by the Prime Minister was that the time had come for them to drop their illusions.

After the Callaghan pronouncement, and Crosland's capitulation, the debate in Cabinet continued though the conclusion was no longer in doubt. Barnett says: 'Edmund Dell, as usual, gave the Chancellor the strongest support, saying that without the package we would be swept away.'[16] Or, as Benn reports my words, 'If we have a choice of seeing the Government destroyed by the markets or by ourselves, I think it is better that we should not allow it to be destroyed by the markets.'[17] The difficulty that remained was that Callaghan was still advocating import deposits, and that no decision had yet been made about how the cuts in public expenditure should be distributed between Departments. While the majority had come round to accepting the need for an agreement with the IMF, Ministers were offering their own pack of varieties on the main theme of reducing the PSBR. They were beginning to stake out their own claims for relief from the impact of the cuts by forecasting dire effects on the party. The discussion was becoming muddled and there was a danger that the Prime Minister would be confused in his summing up, thus delaying the inevitable conclusion yet further.

In fact, in his summing up, he spoke only of 1977/8. For that year Healey was authorized to offer £1 billion public expenditure cuts plus an expected £0.5 billion from the sale of the BP shares bought at the time of the rescue of Burmah Oil.[18] He also made a reference to import deposits but without making their introduction a condition of an agreement with the IMF. It was good that he did so because the IMF would have had none of it. He said nothing about 1978/9. Michael Foot insisted on its being recorded that this was simply the view of a majority and that final judgement should be left until the final package was known. Denis warned that he could not be sure that this would suffice.[19] But he could now negotiate with the support of the Prime Minister and hence of a majority of the Cabinet.

Susan Crosland claims that the outcome of this contest was 'a draw between the Foreign Secretary and the Treasury'.[20] Her verdict is reminiscent only of the cricketer who claimed to be not out because, although he had been bowled middle stump, two stumps were still standing. Crosland gave way before arguments by which he claimed still to be unconvinced. His excuse for doing so was that it would destroy the party if the Prime Minister was overruled. He could hardly have imagined that that Government would have survived if it had become known that the Chancellor had been overruled in Cabinet on such an issue at such a time. The truth was that he had been out-argued by Healey and demolished by the facts.

Healey negotiates

With restored spirits and typical bravura, Healey threatened the IMF team with a general election if they refused to accept what the Cabinet was now prepared to offer. Callaghan had not authorized the challenge and the Government was fortunate that it was not taken up for it would certainly have lost any ensuing election.[21] However, with whatever reservations, the IMF accepted the offer. They knew they were getting a good deal more than the predominant school of opinion in the Treasury thought was necessary. Unbeknown to them, and indeed to the Cabinet, they were getting a good deal more than they were offered. They made a sensible judgement and the deal was done. I believe that the Cabinet would have bitten the bullet even if we had not had available £0.5 billion of BP shares with which to ease the pain. When I bought the shares on behalf of the Government in January 1975, I had promised that they would be sold again as soon as convenient. I certainly did not anticipate that the sale might have a role in saving the Labour Government pain, if not actually in saving the Labour Government.

As usual the task of making the detailed cuts was made more difficult by increased expenditure on industrial policy—to fund which it was found necessary to invoke the regulator powers and increase revenue duties on tobacco and alcoholic drinks by 10 per cent, adding rather over 0.5 per cent to the retail prices index. An even greater obstacle lay in the Government's commitment to social security and to the fact that any changes might well need legislation which the Commons might refuse to pass. The greater the political impediments to cutting current expenditure, the more necessary it became to concentrate the cuts on capital expenditure.[22] The final package involved the postponement for six months of all new starts in a wide range of programmes such as roads, health and water and sewerage.[23]

The Expenditure Committee observed that

> The Government is thus itself acting like those industrialists it criticizes for failing to invest. Indeed, even worse, it appears to be cutting capital expenditure and selling off productive capital assets (e.g. BP shares) in order to sustain current expenditure, the classic action of an ailing industrial company.[24]

Eventually, after much debate in three further meetings of the Cabinet, and suggestions of resignation by Callaghan that in the end called the bluff of the dissidents, the detailed cuts were agreed. The end of this stage came at a Cabinet meeting which began at 8 p.m. on 7 December. Joel Barnett recalls: 'We came to the end in a strange mood, of exhilaration at having got agreement, and apprehension, at the consequences for unemployment.'[25] Now all that remained was to agree the Letter of Intent with the IMF.

The Letter of Intent

Donoughue seems to suggest that there was a Treasury conspiracy to deny his Policy Unit a sight of the draft Letter of Intent. As Treasury conspiracies are the meat of a certain kind of journalism, this story will to some have an air of authenticity. The Letter of Intent was a letter from the Chancellor to the IMF making commitments on how he intended to conduct economic policy over the period of the agreement. As the Letter of Intent had to come to Cabinet for approval, as it did on 14 December, and the Prime Minister might well want the Policy Unit's advice on it; as it was to be a public document when agreed; this particular allegation of conspiracy seems to be more the product of an overwrought mind than of actual fact.

Donoughue also tells us that when he saw the draft Letter of Intent, 'The Prime Minister was very severe with Mr Healey over the telephone and secured a number of important changes . . . including the loosening of the ceilings on monetary growth.'[26] The draft letter was, evidently, too tough on the PSBR and on domestic credit expansion, and appeared to rule out reflation before the next election. It even threatened further deflationary cuts. That there were preliminary discussions about the Letter of Intent before it came to Cabinet, we can be certain. But if Mr Callaghan was in fact severe with Mr Healey, we can be sure that Mr Healey replied with his customary courtesy and without reflecting on the trouble he had had during the previous three months in bringing the Prime Minister to a conclusion.

The Letter of Intent was intended to be a constraint. It ruled out import deposits and further exchange controls. It said that 'An essential element of the government's strategy will be a continuing and substantial reduction over the next few years in the share of the resources required for the public sector.' It accepted that 'It is . . . essential to reduce the PSBR in order to create monetary conditions which will encourage investment and support sustained growth and the control of inflation.' The specific measures required were a reduction in the borrowing requirement from its 'unacceptably high' level to £8.7 billion in 1977/8 and £8.6 billion in 1978/9. To help achieve these PSBR targets, public spending adjustments of £1.5 billion in 1977/8 and £2 billion in 1978/9 were to be implemented. This was in addition to the cuts already announced, including the £1 billion for 1977/8 agreed the previous July. The 1978/9 commitment included a provisional undertaking to make a further but unspecified fiscal adjustment of about £0.5 billion at 1976 survey prices if the situation at the time required it. The IMF insisted on targets for domestic credit expansion. DCE was to be progressively reduced from £9 billion in 1976/7 to £7.7 billion in 1977/8 and £6 billion in 1978/9. It was no doubt hoped that this would help with Britain's balance of payments problems. It would also help to ensure that the Government remained committed to its public expenditure targets. The Letter of Intent also said that it was expected that the increase in the sterling M3 measure of money would be between 9 and 13 per cent. This 'expectation' for sterling M3 growth inevitably took on the status of a formal target. Whether as an expectation or as a target, it had already been reinforced by action under the supplementary special deposits scheme.

There has been criticism of the failure of the Cabinet to discuss more fully the IMF figures for limits on domestic credit expansion. Such comments overestimate the capacity of a typical Cabinet to comprehend the implications of such matters as domestic credit expansion. Some matters even this Cabinet, which contained people not uninformed in economic questions, had to leave to the Treasury. It has also been noted that the PSBR, £10.6 billion in 1975/6, turned out to be £8.5 billion in 1976/7, rather than the £10.5 billion forecast on which the Cabinet acted. Some other forecasts of the 1976/7 PSBR had been much lower than the Treasury's. What was unknown at the time either to the Treasury or to outside forecasters was that there had been significant underspending by Departments in 1976/7. This fact, known only retrospectively, casts a curious light on Ministers' desperate struggles against a reduction in their budgets for subsequent years.

There was great concern in the Cabinet about the effect of the Letter of Intent on the level of unemployment. Benn tells us that Callaghan 'said he was disappointed. Ford and Schmidt had let him down and it was the first time in his life that he felt anti-American.'[27] According to Barnett, Peter Shore angrily said, 'There is no will in this Cabinet to tell the IMF to take a running jump, even if unemployment rose to 2 million.' Healey had wanted to do as little as possible in the first year, 1977/8, with more in 1978/9, leaving him free to change 1978/9 later if, having got the IMF loan, the position improved. At that point, we could then tell the IMF to shove off. The only trouble 'was that Mr Whittome and the IMF mission were not born yesterday. They wanted "front-end loading", that is to say more cuts in the first year.' Healey's response to Shore was, therefore, that telling the IMF to take a running jump was precisely what he had in mind but only from the position of strength he expected in 1978 rather than from the position of weakness in 1976.[28] With the exchange of such pleasantries, and with opponents striking Churchillian attitudes, the Letter of Intent was approved by Cabinet. In practice, so dramatic was the turn-round in the market's attitude to the UK economy following the agreement with the IMF that the Letter of Intent proved far less of a constraint on policy than the IMF intended or many in the Cabinet feared.

Statement in the House

On 15 December Healey made his statement in the House. It carried the support of Bill Simon and the departing US Administration. Simon issued a statement in which he described the new UK programme as 'a responsible and sustained approach which represents a sound and realistic strategy for the United Kingdom rather than a one year transitory effort'. So it proved. Healey's Letter of Intent led to formal approval by the IMF, on 3 January 1977, of the £3.9 billion loan, to be made available in instalments.[29] In January 1977, the safety-net for the sterling balances was negotiated. If there was another run on the pound, there were to be medium-term swap facilities, which would permit the Bank of England to exchange sterling for foreign currencies from other central banks. The swap, however, would have to be reversed after an agreed period. It was not an agreement of great significance, but politically presentable.

When Healey made his statement on 15 December, he met less hostility from his back-benchers than expected. Perhaps they were learning a lesson. If you do not like your bank manager, do not let him become your lender of last resort. But no bank manager ever did his client more good than did the IMF to the UK Government in 1976. Unfortunately for the Labour Party, the benefit of the IMF's ministrations was thrown away when Callaghan failed to call a general election in the autumn of 1978.

Notes

1. Crosland 379.
2. Tony Benn gives an account of the reception of his proposals in Cabinet in Benn 663–5.
3. Crosland 380.
4. Benn 663.
5. Crosland 380.
6. Crosland 380.
7. Crosland 379–80.
8. Garritsen de Vries (1985), 472–3.
9. Healey 431.
10. Garritsen de Vries (1985), 471.
11. Benn 672.
12. Crosland 381.
13. Benn 670–1 gives a detailed account of what Healey said.
14. See Benn 671–3 and Barnett 104–5.
15. Crosland 381–2.
16. Barnett 105.
17. Benn 676.
18. See, on the sale of the BP shares, Donoughue 100 and Pliatzky (1982), 156–7. The Policy Unit appears to have misunderstood the significance of this sale.

19. Benn 678–89 and Barnett 105.
20. Crosland 381–2. See also Benn 674.
21. Healey 432. Callaghan 441.
22. See Pliatzky (1982), 155 and 157.
23. Barnett 108 comments that 'The whole cutting exercise in the case of the nationalized industries was in any case something of a nonsense. The cash flows were so large, and implementations of investment plans subject to so much variation, that there were shortfalls in expenditure of many hundreds of millions of pounds every year. We were lopping off one or two hundred million to count as part of our package when, in the event, the net result might well be to simply reduce the size of the shortfall.' He refers to the lack of independence of the major nationalized industries. 'There we were, a small group of Ministers, deciding, over the heads of the chairmen and their boards, that cuts would be made in their expenditure programmes.' Barnett 107.
24. Quoted by Pliatzky (1982), 157.
25. Benn 683–6 and Barnett 105–6.
26. Donoughue 99–100.
27. Benn 687.
28. Barnett 109.
29. SDR 1,950m. was to be made available in calendar 1977 and SDR 1,410m. in calendar 1978. The GAB was to be activated to the extent of SDR 2,860m. and SDR 500m. was to come from the IMF's own resources.

T·W·E·N·T·Y F·I·V·E

The Final Assessment

The Cabinet debates in retrospect

Donoughue commends 'the tremendous political skill of Mr Callaghan in mobilising, encouraging and maintaining unity among his Ministers'. Callaghan did have a problem. He was dealing with a Cabinet which wished seriously to discuss alternative strategies that it would never implement. On the other hand, Callaghan seems to have entertained comparable illusions. In his memoirs he writes:

It would have been best if we could have reached a quick decision, but I knew this would not be possible if we were to remain together, so by instinct more than by rational judgement I decided not to bring matters to a head but to allow time to work and Ministers to become familiar with the problems, with the arguments and with the possible solutions.

He also writes:

For me the issue was not in doubt. We had to repay $1.6 billions on 9 December. We were running a large current account deficit on overseas transactions that we would need to finance in 1977, probably to the tune of a further £3 billions, and oil revenues would not begin to accrue until 1978 or 1979. I accepted the Chancellor's argument that while the IMF loan was necessary, it was less important than the favourable impact its existence would have on the market.[1]

If all this can be taken at its face value, Callaghan knew from the beginning where he stood on the IMF negotiation. At the time, there was considerable doubt as to where the Prime Minister stood. Healey did not know. That, presumably, was part of the strategy. The strategy would, however, have been more defensible if Callaghan had not allowed, without convincing contradiction, frequent reports that, so far from supporting Healey, he was distancing himself from him.

Donoughue commends the 'excellent quality of the ministerial debate'. There must be a question whether any Chancellor has ever had to contend in Cabinet with more extraordinary arguments. Great risks were being taken with the market which might have decided at any moment to withdraw its tolerance of a government that, apparently, preferred to whistle in the wind rather than to accept its responsibilities. The tribute would only be justified if it was appropriate for a Cabinet to discuss dreams and wish fulfilment rather than how to tackle problems in the real world. I intervened from time to time to indicate continuing support for Healey. Indeed he has generously written that I was his 'most formidable ally in the Cabinet'.[2] But Healey himself, with his combative character, debating skills, and remarkable command, would leave nothing to chance and fought every nonsense every inch of the way. He certainly justified Donoughue's reference to his 'remarkable resilience and stamina'.[3] I did not realize that even he was approaching exhaustion, though it was clear enough that uncertainty about the Prime Minister's support was draining his morale.

Help from the friends?

Credit has been given to Callaghan for securing, through his friends, modification of the IMF's original terms. Certainly the IMF's original terms were modified, but we have seen the manner and circumstances in which they had been formulated and have noted the readiness of the IMF team, from the beginning, to soften them if given persuasive reasons to do so. After the event both the German Government and the American Administration squabbled for the credit of having made life easier for the British. Spokesmen for both attempted to gain for their masters some costless credit without the trouble of having earned it by any significant efforts. To claim credit for what would have happened anyhow is the mildest of dishonesty by the standards of international diplomacy.

The German Government professed to believe it had tempered the influence of Simon and Yeo to the shorn British lamb. In fact the German Government made everything more difficult by appearing to be kind when cruelty was the only genuine form of kindness appropriate. It is unclear whether Schmidt, in the end, took a hard line with Callaghan or whether he temporized, leaving it to Callaghan to understand that the settlement had to be with the IMF, not with his friends.[4]

Likewise, those who had inhabited the White House during the last days of President Ford went out of their way, in conversation with British journalists, to explain how helpful they had been in restraining the wilder ideologists of the US Treasury.[5] Callaghan himself concedes: 'in Washington Secretary Simon's influence was paramount, and the President could not deliver beyond repeating his assurance that the United States would move sympathetically on creating a sterling safety net as soon as we had reached substantial agreement with the IMF on the conditions for the loan.'[6]

There are also suggestions that the White House was influenced in the UK's favour by memories of the fall of the Labour Administration in 1931. Indeed, we are led to believe that Lever, on his visit to Washington, convinced the President and the State Department that a refusal of help to the Labour Government would have cosmic repercussions. Under the leadership of Tony Benn, Britain would depart from the Western liberal economic system, Italy would follow, with France not far behind.[7] Oddly enough, the US Treasury held to its course, uninfluenced by what, if one is to believe these reports, was an histrionic performance remarkable even by Harold Lever's persuasive standards.

It may well be true that Simon and Yeo would not have greatly worried if the Labour Government had fallen as a result of excessively tough terms demanded by the IMF. Simon and Yeo would have been aware, as would their colleagues in the White House, that, if it had fallen, it would have been replaced not by left-wing extremists but by a Conservative government. Certainly the defeat of Labour in such circumstances might have caused temporary social disturbance which was better avoided. But the idea that a left-wing government embodying 'the isolationist school in the Cabinet, assumed to be led by Tony Benn' would have succeeded is sheer illusion and it is difficult to imagine that the White House and the State Department were so out of touch as to believe it.[8] At stake in the UK was the survival of the Labour Government, not the survival of democracy, let alone the survival of Western European democracy. The survival of the Labour Government could be secured by the simple device of persuading Callaghan to make up his mind. Eventually, this was achieved with little difficulty and less sorrow.

The political anxieties of the White House could not be a principal concern of the IMF. The IMF had to be satisfied that any agreement it made with the UK Government was sufficiently robust to survive market scepticism. It had to be satisfied that any agreement with the UK would not prejudice its negotiations with Italy. The IMF was negotiating the largest stand-by in its history. It would also be its first two year agreement. If the IMF's Managing Director and staff had allowed themselves to be unduly influenced by the UK's friends into negotiating a package without market credibility, it would have been their reputation that would have suffered. It would have suffered, among others, with developing countries which saw the IMF's resources being diverted to a prosperous developed country that should have been able to look after itself. For this reason, Witteveen and his staff insisted on acting independently.[9] The IMF negotiated what seemed to it an agreement which had a strong chance of surviving the varying moods of the market when once the euphoria created by actually making an agreement had passed.

A major problem in the negotiations with the IMF was the division in the Treasury and the belief among the majority of officials that nothing further needed to be done. This belief strengthened the hands of the Crosland group and justified the hesitations of Callaghan. Eventually even such officials realized, if reluctantly, that something more than nothing would have to be done.[10] These officials appear to have been shocked that, after persuading so many Ministers that nothing needed to be done, there was some delay before those same Ministers could be persuaded to the new position that at least something had to be done. Pliatzky recalls:

I still somehow have in my possession a scrap of paper on which, at one meeting of Ministers and officials in the Treasury, in despair of ever getting agreement on anything, I had the following scribbled exchange of comments with whoever was sitting next to me: 'I think that this Government must be finished.' 'Nearly, but not quite yet? Thursday?' 'Yes, I meant in principle, leaving it to the forecasters to put numbers on it.'[11]

The Labour Government had a stronger self-preservation instinct than these officials may have realized. But if its survival was ever in doubt, the weakness of the official Treasury must bear its share of the blame.

A deflationary world?

One of the influences on thinking at the time was put into words by Peter Shore. He claimed that 'the world was following a deflationary road.'[12] This argument was very much overdone. The world was doing what it was doing and the UK had little influence to change it. But the world economy was growing. It grew quite rapidly in 1976. The prospect was that it would continue to grow, even if more sluggishly, in 1977 and 1978.[13] The world economy may not have been expanding enough to get the UK out of its troubles. The UK could not expect that other countries would put our interests above their judgement of their own. The responsibility for the IMF crisis lay not with our trading partners but with ourselves.

It was inevitable that the UK's acceptance of the IMF terms would have a temporarily deflationary effect on domestic demand though this was likely to be more than compensated for by the growth of export demand. In his statement to the Commons on 15 December 1976, Healey said:

> I do not see a prospect of a fall in unemployment; indeed, I fear that there is likely to be some further rise, but a smaller rise than would have been likely without the adjustments I have described. If unemployment does rise, this will be the consequence not of today's measures which, in sum, will increase employment next year, but of the lower growth now expected all over the world and of other factors I have previously described to the House.[14]

This proved to be a good forecast. The rate of growth in unemployment slowed. Unemployment in Britain, which had risen by around 500,000 in 1975 and 170,000 in 1976, rose by about 100,000 in 1977. In 1978 unemployment fell. Industrial production rose. By 1978, growth in GDP was just over 3 per cent.[15]

The influence of forecasts

Healey writes,

> we could have done without the IMF loan only if we—and the world—had known the real facts at the time. But in 1976 our forecasts were far too pessimistic, and we were still describing our public expenditure in a way which was immensely damaging to our standing in the financial markets.[16]

Callaghan authorized the application to the IMF on the basis of a forecast 1977 deficit on current account of £3 billion.[17] In fact, in 1977, the current account was in surplus. Yet there was no lack of indications that the current account might be about to improve. There had been a marked depreciation of sterling and, despite the arguments of Godley and Kaldor, it was at least likely that after a period there would be an improvement and even a return to balance provided resources were freed to be moved into the balance of payments.[18] In August, *NIER* forecast an improvement in the current balance.[19] In November 1976 it forecast a return to surplus in 1977. '[I]ndeed . . . this happens by the middle of the year.'[20]

The Times described this forecast as 'dangerously optimistic'.[21] Yet it turned out to be accurate. But, as with all forecasts, it was based on imperfect knowledge of the present and speculation about the future. That speculation had to include guesses as to the behaviour and economic performance of our trading partners. It has not been only in the later 1980s that forecasts of the current account have been found to be grossly inaccurate. In his statement to the Commons on 15 December Healey said: 'The current account deficit, which has totalled £1.7 billion in the first 11 months of this year, is likely to fall next year, and there is good hope of reaching a substantial surplus in 1978–79— perhaps as high as £2 billion to £3 billion.'[22] This turned out to be pessimistic. But he did not know it was pessimistic. Both he, and those making more optimistic forecasts, were basing themselves on what they knew of the present which itself turned out to be inaccurate in material respects.

The implication of Healey's argument is that, if only the world had understood how rapidly the UK was returning to balance in its foreign accounts, any funding for the UK's deficits would have been available from world markets unconditionally, including funding for the repayment of money used under the June stand-by. There is less in this than Healey appears to assert. He was no admirer of economic forecasts. He had suffered too much from their inaccuracy in 1974. He believed that now at last he had the fundamentals right. Yet he did not try to convince the market that the forecasts were wrong. Precisely because economic forecasting is so uncertain, he was in no position to substitute any other forecast. He did not try to convince the market that there was no need to go to the IMF. He knew he had debts to repay on the due date.

Moreover, as he also knew, the conjuncture can be changed in unexpected ways by market reaction to policies and declarations.

If Healey was not prepared to rely on the Treasury forecast being too pessimistic, and felt it necessary to go to the IMF, why was the market to take a more optimistic view? Everyone knows that forecasts will be wrong. Ever changing forecasts may not inspire the public with much confidence in the forecasters. But they do not necessarily undermine confidence in governments. Forecasters who do not know where they are are not in a good position to see where they are going. It is for this reason that one measure of successful economic management is independence of forecasting errors. If it was forecasting error that put the UK in the hands of the IMF, it does not say much for the quality of economic management.

Was Crosland right?

It may be said that even if no one else knew that the forecasts were too pessimistic, Tony Crosland did. It was he who argued that every policy was already in place for the achievement of the UK's private economic miracle. Was this not borne out by subsequent developments? Even Healey accepts this view. Crosland, he recalls, 'argued persuasively that the situation was already under control. So in fact it was, but the markets would not believe it.'[23] The same line is taken by Donoughue. He argues that the actual IMF cuts were much less than initially asked for by the IMF and the Treasury, that they were not necessary except for reasons of confidence, that otherwise the economy was already in good shape. He points to the IMF's later 'Portuguese hysteria' which, he claims, shows that they wanted to force the UK through their hoop. He succeeds in finding one index by which the UK's economic performance looks excellent. The UK's money supply figures since 1974 were better than any other major Western country except Germany. He ends by paying tribute to James Callaghan's great personal contribution in resisting the extreme demands of the IMF.[24] In dealing with these arguments, I leave aside the decisive point made by Healey that, in the actual circumstances, we had no choice but to borrow from the IMF and hence had to show some respect for the IMF's conditions.

Public spending in 1976/7 was about 3.5 per cent less than in the previous year. This was probably due to the operation of cash limits which had recently been introduced. It was not yet realized, in these early days of cash limits, what effect they would have on actual levels of expenditure. This was not known at the time of the IMF crisis. It was not known to Tony Crosland. What the Government knew, what the forecasters knew, and what the market knew, were the levels approved. In 1977/8 actual expenditure was about 7 per cent (over £4 billion) below the plans in the January 1977 White Paper, and in 1978/9 the volume of expenditure was estimated to have been about 3.5 per cent (around £2.5 billion) below the level planned in the January 1978 White Paper. These cuts, imposed by the inadequacies of departmental control, exceeded the cuts agreed with the IMF.[25]

The influence of the new system of cash limits continued to operate on the new estimates agreed with the IMF. That influence resulted in a major underspend as compared even with the new estimates. Had Departments known how to control their budgets so that sums voted were actually spent, the Government could have accepted the original IMF proposals without any difficulty. They represented what the Government would actually spend in the years covered by the agreement with the IMF. Instead Ministers persisted in fighting desperate battles for money they would never spend. If one is assessing Crosland's statements or the outcome of the IMF crisis, it cannot be ignored that actual public expenditure was, at that moment, and would continue to be, significantly lower than had been planned and published and would continue lower than the new plans published after agreement with the IMF. One cannot discount the relevance of this major underspending to the rapid recovery of the UK economy, and notably of the current account, after the IMF crisis.

Arguments for being tough: even overkill

We have seen that, during these events, Tony Crosland told Susan that 'Edmund Dell . . . is in a very very reactionary state of mind.'[26] My reputation in Cabinet was illustrated by a remark made later by Harold Lever to Joel Barnett, Chief Secretary to the Treasury: 'Edmund makes you look like a left-winger throwing money away.'[27] What, if anything, justified, at the time and in retrospect, my willingness to go so far with the IMF on its original demands?

Economics is not a matter of science, only of judgement. The judgement now had to include, as an essential ingredient, the opinion of the market. This was especially true for any borrower. If the market was not persuaded, even an IMF certificate of good housekeeping would not suffice for long to save the Government. The autumn of 1976 represented the Government's last chance to get things right after the failure of a series of earlier attempts, all of them politically exhausting. The market clearly had not, been persuaded for long, by the measures of July 1975, nor by the public expenditure cuts of January 1976 and July 1976. This was the fourth attempt to get things right and it had to succeed.

Although Callaghan, and others, regarded me as a political innocent, I was fully aware of the damaging political consequences of these repeated failures and of their effect on the morale of the Government and party. The reputation of both stood low in the country. We needed as much time as possible before the next election if we were to have the least chance of winning it—and although a general election could be three years off, it might be forced on us at any time. We could not afford a further botched job.

I was sure, moreover, that the Government would not break up if Callaghan gave it a firm lead. Here the TUC would help. The last thing it wanted was a Conservative government entrenched with a large majority after the slaughter of Labour in an election. True the TUC did not help during the winter of discontent but by then trade union members were out of control as a result of the 5 per cent incomes policy which could only have been accepted by the Cabinet on the assumption of an autumn 1978 general election.

In short, the argument was for overkill. If it proved to be overkill, we could always add back.

Confidence restored

A year later Hattersley, who alone had stood with Crosland to the end, said in Cabinet that, after all, Healey had been right.

There was a great deal of evidence to support Hattersley's revised view. Many were astonished at the speed with which confidence was resurrected.[28] Between October 1976 and October 1977, the minimum lending rate fell from 15 to 5 per cent, an unprecedented rate of reduction influenced by the desire to discourage capital inflows but one doubtfully appropriate to domestic economic conditions.[29] The pound recovered dramatically. By early 1977, it had risen to just above $1.70.

Contrary to the situation in March 1976, the Bank of England was now able to sell sterling for foreign currency confident that it would not thereby trigger a sterling crisis. Wilson would have been delighted that it had become quite impossible for the Treasury to talk sterling down. The official reserves rose during 1977 from $4.1 billion to $20.6 billion. Once more, in the Treasury and in the Department of Trade, there was concern about competitiveness. But the trend was too strong to be defeated by intervention. On 31 October 1977 a Treasury announcement stated that 'A continuance of foreign inflows on a large scale could endanger continued adherence to the domestic monetary targets'. Sterling, therefore, would be allowed to find its own level. By the end of the year, it had risen to more than $1.90. The earlier attempt to keep it down had damaged the possibility of achieving the M3 target and it was exceeded. But the DCE targets were comfortably met. Inflation, nearly 25 per cent in 1975, registered 15 per cent in 1976 and 10 per cent in 1977. At the end of 1977 the UK was in a strong enough position to respond positively to a request from the IMF not to draw on its full entitlement. The UK could generously allow the IMF to deploy its scarce resources in aid of those whose needs were much greater.

If prizes were to be awarded for these successes, something would go to Callaghan for guiding the Cabinet to a mutually tolerable conclusion, much to Healey for his gallantry in battle against colleagues with whom he largely agreed, a great deal to the US Treasury for sticking to its opinion despite all the political arguments for being kind to a friend, but above all to the IMF for being unwavering in its determination not to be deflected from what it believed to be right both for the UK and for the international economic system.

Thoughts from a distance in time

It remained true that nothing fundamental had been done to improve the UK's poor economic performance. The history recounted here is but an episode in the secular decline of the British economy relative to its principal industrial competitors.

Without claiming too much for the study of history, it may be possible to make some suggestions for the future which emerge from this experience.

An independent central bank

Advocacy of an independent central bank has become fashionable because of the experience of the Thatcher Government in attempting to cope with that most difficult task, the management of the British economy. The argument is no less persuasive for that. Those, including this writer, to whom it appeals should find in this book raw material for their arguments. The Treasury can sometimes be a reliable custodian of the responsibilities of economic management but it has a variety of objectives, some of them political, and it is the servant of political masters. Some politicians regard the independence of a central bank as undemocratic. This is nonsense, as demonstrated by the examples of the USA and the Federal Republic of Germany. An independent central bank would have a remit laid down by Parliament. The remit would probably place price stability at the forefront of its responsibilities. If a government wished to change those responsibilities by subverting the price responsibility, it should ask Parliament for powers and explain why it needs them. It should not have the right in a democracy to undermine price stability by executive action. To do so is a form of theft by Government from its people.

A Grand Coalition?

No government with 34, 38, or even 42 per cent of the poll has the democratic legitimacy with which to confront crises such as that faced in 1974. In some countries, an electoral result such as that of February 1974 would have resulted in a Grand Coalition between the major parties. There were arguments for such a coalition in the UK. Whether or not such arguments would have been persuasive, they were not even heard. There was not the least chance of such a coalition coming into existence. The hostility between the parties, born of ideological incompatibility, was too great. There is no habit of coalition making because the electoral system usually gives victory to one party or another even without a majority of the votes or anything like it. Economic failure, the experience of virtually every British government since the war, leads to defeat. Defeat then congeals party dogma and reinforces the ideological incompatibility of the parties.

On both left and right of the political spectrum, the case for an electoral system which better reflects the inclinations of the electorate is rejected. It is argued on the left that an overall majority of the electorate for 'socialism' would be unattainable, and on the right that it would have been impossible to get an overall majority for 'Thatcherism'. So far as those policies described as Thatcherism are concerned, it is very doubtful if this argument now applies. Policies of fiscal and monetary prudence, often exceeding in caution those that the Thatcher Government found it politically possible to conduct, are today characteristic of most governments in the democratic world. As for socialism, as no post-war Labour government has succeeded in finding a meaning for the word, it seems a pity to sacrifice democratic legitimacy in an attempt to achieve so unspecific an objective.

The limitations of economics

Sir Bryan Hopkin who, from early 1975, was Chief Economic Adviser to the Treasury has written about the period 1973/9:

The understanding of what was going on was imperfect, mistakes were undoubtedly made, and there were some sharp reversals of policy under the pressure of events. The growth rate did slow down and unemployment rose. I do not know that anyone has shown convincingly that an alternative policy was available which would have coped equally well with the problems.[30]

I find this far too complacent. It is of course true, and is part of the argument of this book, that understanding was imperfect and that the international economic contours had changed beyond recognition. What was worrying is how few of the economists giving advice to the Treasury had any appreciation of what the changes in the international contours meant for UK policy. Either they assumed that the world would look benignly on the UK's egregious conduct of policy, and even pay for it without demur, or they tried to shut the world out by advocating protectionist policies which would have been unsustainable. The principal characteristic of the economic advice offered to Ministers was its insularity.

Economics is as much at the mercy of the conjuncture as is politics. And if the conjuncture is too different from past experience, the economics will be even less reliable than usual. Economics, as a science, is still in a state of innocence. The only evidence that it *is* a science is that economists are frequently as rude about their colleagues as scientists are about those who claim priority in their discoveries.

The limitations of policy

Governments show an unwise tendency to exaggerate the effectiveness of policy and underestimate the time-scale even the best policy needs to yield its benefits. The tendency to exaggerate is encouraged by the political cycle. At general elections, governments place before the people evidence of success even where it cannot yet exist. Whatever one thinks of the industrial policies of Labour governments, or the privatization and trade union policies of the Thatcher Government, the idea that they could significantly influence economic performance within the lifetime of one or even two Parliaments is ludicrous. Such policies have to be judged over a very long time-scale.

There is a further danger that governments may be misled by their own propaganda. One of the costs of exaggerating the effectiveness of policy is that it encourages the taking of risks. When Chancellors of the Exchequer begin to believe their own propaganda, the nation, and not merely their own political future, is in jeopardy. The need to make this point is emphasized by the intellectual journeys of Mr Gavyn Davies, an economist who served in Donoughue's Policy Unit at No. 10. He has confessed, speaking for other economists besides himself, that in the mid-1980s 'Many of us believed a miracle had happened.' Only in 1987 did he come to the conclusion that the miracle was a mirage.[31] One value of the study of history is that it helps to eschew belief in miracles.

Early in 1978, during a ministerial visit to Spain, I was asked by a leading Spanish industrialist to explain the British 'economic miracle'. I demurred. Miracles are for the gods. There had been no economic miracle.

Forgiveness?

In February 1977 I delivered my Rita Hinden Lecture. In words described in the *Financial Times* as 'remarkably blunt', I set out my economic philosophy and gave my defence of the attitudes I had taken during the IMF crisis.[32] The lecture could have been held to be in breach of collective Cabinet responsibility. Callaghan saw the text in advance and made no great objection. Healey also saw it in advance, commented that I had not given sufficient credit to the problems the Government had inherited, but again raised no great objection. Indeed, in a friendly spirit, he encouraged me to deliver it if I dared. A few days later,

Callaghan and I had a meeting at No. 10 with Mario Soares of Portugal. Soares had a doleful tale to tell of the state of the Portuguese economy. Listening to it, Callaghan passed me a note. It read: 'Hearing all this makes me feel better—and that I would like to hear a lecture . . . by the Portuguese Edmund Dell.' I often felt lonely in the Labour Government and I was very grateful for the friendly tone of the message. I almost felt forgiven.

Notes

1. Callaghan 434 and 436.
2. Healey 390.
3. Donoughue 93 for these quotations.
4. Callaghan reports on the conversation with Helmut Schmidt at the European Council at The Hague. To the question whether Schmidt would intervene to soften the IMF's terms, Schmidt 'made a temporising reply' which even Crosland could understand as a polite 'No'. Callaghan 438.
5. Keegan and Pennant-Rea report on the White House's supposed intervention 'to calm down the missionary zeal of Simon and Yeo'. Keegan and Pennant-Rea 168. Yet their account also informs us, rather more persuasively, that the long delay in London handed a weapon to the US Treasury. '[T]he longer the British Government procrastinated over terms, the more the US Treasury was able to argue that "these men are not going to change—they're defending those policies".'
6. Callaghan 437. Pliatzky believes that the representations made by Callaghan resulted in a softening of the initial hard line of the US Treasury and greater flexibility in the IMF's negotiating position. He does, however, assert that 'the United States and West Germany would not seek to influence the Fund beyond a certain point or support our application unless we could negotiate terms with the IMF team which they could bring themselves to accept and put to the IMF Board of Directors'. Pliatzky (1982), 154.
7. Fay and Young, 21 May 1978.
8. Keegan and Pennant-Rea 166. Keegan and Pennant-Rea believe 'Scowcroft and Hormats, with support from Kissinger, put the point to the US Treasury that, if the Labour government did fall, there was no guarantee that an administration even less to Simon and Yeo's liking, a left wing government running a siege economy, would not emerge'. In the end Keegan and Pennant-Rea virtually concede the point that Callaghan's solicitations at the White House door had little effect. 'The eventual package was much bigger than Healey, Callaghan or the doves in the Treasury had ever wanted; it is not absolutely clear whether, by fighting long and hard, Callaghan gained all that much. A number of the overseas participants believe that British obstinacy made the Government's credibility in the financial markets that much worse, and that, in the words of one observer, "they played into the IMF's hands".' Keegan and Pennant-Rea 168.
9. Garritsen de Vries (1985), 471.

10. See Keegan and Pennant-Rea 167.
11. Pliatzky (1982), 155.
12. Benn 666.
13. *NIER* (Nov. 1976), 3. See also *NIER* (Feb. 1977), 3.
14. HC Debs., 15 Dec. 1976, cols. 1536–7. The other 'factors' were an expected fall in interest rates, additional employment measures, and industrial aid.
15. *NIER* (Feb. 1979), 23.
16. Healey 433. See also Healey 381.
17. Callaghan 428.
18. In an article in *The Times* of 1 Nov. 1976, Godley questioned the effectiveness of the devaluation that had taken place during 1976 and added, 'as devaluation is proving so ineffective, I find the continued strength of the opposition to protection surprising'. He did accept that there might be retaliation but appeared to believe that protection by the UK would be in the spirit of the GATT.
19. *NIER* (Aug. 1976), 4.
20. *NIER* (Nov. 1976), 4.
21. *The Times*, 26 Nov. 1976.
22. HC Debs., 15 Dec. 1976, col. 1537.
23. Healey 431.
24. Donoughue 93–9.
25. 2.5% when debt interest is brought into account. 'Unknown to us at the time, unplanned shortfall was much bigger than the planned reductions which had brought the government of the country to crisis point.' Pliatzky (1982), 159–61. See also Healey 401. See also the January 1977 White Paper (Cmnd. 6721), the Jan. 1979 White Paper (Cmnd. 7439), and the Mar. 1980 White Paper (Cmnd. 7841).
26. Crosland 378.
27. Barnett 126.
28. See e.g. Pliatzky (1982), 159.
29. The decline was to be largely reversed during 1978.
30. *Financial Times*, 26 Mar. 1987.
31. *Financial Times*, 4 Oct. 1990.
32. *Financial Times*, 14 Feb. 1977.

References

BALL, Sir JAMES (1989), 'The United Kingdom Economy: Miracle or Mirage', *National Westminster Bank Quarterly Review*, Feb.
BARNETT, JOEL (1982), *Inside the Treasury*, André Deutsch, London.
BENN, TONY (1989), *Against the Tide: Diaries 1973–76*, Hutchinson, London.
BLACKSTONE, TESSA, and PLOWDEN, WILLIAM (1988), *Inside the Think Tank: Advising the Cabinet 1971–1983*, William Heinemann, London.
CALLAGHAN, JAMES (1987), *Time and Chance*, Collins, London.
CASTLE, BARBARA (1980), *The Castle Diaries, 1974–76*, Weidenfeld & Nicolson, London.
CROSLAND, SUSAN (1982), *Tony Crosland*, Jonathan Cape, London.
DELL, EDMUND (1977), Fifth Rita Hinden Memorial Lecture, '*The Politics of Economic Interdependence*', Feb.
—— (1987), *The Politics of Economic Interdependence*, Macmillan, London.
—— (1973) *Political Responsibility and Industry*, George Allen and Unwin, London.
DONOUGHUE, BERNARD (1987), *Prime Minister: The Conduct of Policy under Harold Wilson and James Callaghan*, Jonathan Cape, London.
Economic Trends (various dates), published for the Central Statistical Office by Her Majesty's Stationery Office.
FAY, STEPHEN, and YOUNG, HUGO (1978) '*The Day the £ nearly Died*', *Sunday Times*, 14, 21, and 28 May.
GARDNER, NICK (1987), *Decade of Discontent: The Changing British Economy since 1973*, Basil Blackwell, Oxford.
GARRITSEN DE VRIES, MARGARET (1985), *The International Monetary Fund, 1972–78: Cooperation on Trial*, vol. i, ii, iii, International Monetary Fund, Washington, DC.
—— (1986), *The IMF in a Changing World, 1945–85*, International Monetary Fund, Washington, DC.
HAINES, JOE (1977), *The Politics of Power*, Jonathan Cape, London.
HATFIELD, MICHAEL (1978), *The House the Left Built: Inside Labour Policy-Making, 1970–75*, Gollancz, London.
HEALEY, DENIS (1989), *The Time of My Life*, Michael Joseph, London.
HMSO (1976), *Public Expenditure to 1979–80*, Cmnd. 6393, London, Feb.
Institutional Investor (1987), 20th Anniversary Issue, June.

JONES, JACK (1986), *Union Man: An Autobiography of Jack Jones*, Collins, London.

KEEGAN, WILLIAMS, and PENNANT-REA, RUPERT (1979), *Who Runs the Economy: Control and Influence in British Economic Policy*, Maurice Temple Smith, London.

MACDOUGALL, DONALD (1987), *Don and Mandarin: Memoirs of an Economist*, John Murray, London.

MARTIN, PAUL (1988), *The London Diaries, 1975–79*, University of Ottawa Press, Ottawa.

PART, ANTONY (1990), *The Making of a Mandarin*, André Deutsch, London.

PLIATZKY, LEO (1982), *Getting and Spending: Public Expenditure, Employment and Inflation*, Basil Blackwell, Oxford.

—— (1989), *The Treasury under Mrs Thatcher*, Basil Blackwell, Oxford.

SMITH, DAVID, (1987), *The Rise and Fall of Monetarism: The Theory and Politics of an Economic Experiment*, Penguin Books, Harmondsworth.

THIRLWALL, ANTHONY P. (1987), *Nicholas Kaldor*, Wheatsheaf Books, Brighton.

WILSON, HAROLD (1976), *The Governance of Britain*, Weidenfeld & Nicolson and Michael Joseph, London.

—— (1979), *Final Term: The Labour Government, 1974–76*, Weidenfeld & Nicolson and Michael Joseph, London.

Index

Aberdeen 203
accounting officer 139
Adamson, Sir Campbell, Director General of the CBI 106
advance corporation tax (ACT) 38, 41 n., 83
Aitken, Ian 167
Allen, Alf, General Secretary of USDAW 76
Allen, Sir Douglas, Permanent Secretary to the Treasury, subsequently head of the Home Civil Service (later Lord Croham) 70
alternative strategy 123–4, 226, 258, 262, 266–7, 269
Amalgamated Engineering Union 105
Austen, Jane 42

Ball, Sir James 74 n.
Balogh, Lord (Thomas), Minister of State, Department of Energy 116–17
Bank of England 8, 47, 62, 77, 119–20, 134–5, 236, 243, 247
  author as socialist saviour 40
  on company liquidity 82
  on depreciation 135, 195, 198
  on dual exchange rates 127–8
  on incomes policy 123, 162–3
  June 1976 stand-by credit 219–20
  managing the exchange rate 165, 205–9, 213, 234–5, 286
  on managing the money supply 113, 231, 238
  on public expenditure 223, 225
  on reflation 79
  special deposits 10, 36–7, 47, 235, 238, 246 n., 274
  sterling balances 275
Bank of International Settlements 219
Barber, Anthony, Chancellor of the Exchequer (later Lord Barber) 6–7, 10, 24, 30, 35–6, 55, 66, 86, 111, 147, 231
Barnett, Joel, Chief Secretary to the Treasury (later Lord Barnett of Heywood and Royton) 13, 24–5, 85, 122, 134, 140, 226–7, 229, 247, 253, 258, 270, 272, 274
  control of public expenditure 66
  the exchange rate 128, 132
  food subsidies 228
  influence of the General Election on the March 1974 Budget 34
  nationalized industries 276 n.
  supporter of Harold Lever 29, 65, 68, 284
Basnett, David, General Secretary, General & Municipal Workers' Union (later Lord Basnett) 76, 147, 153, 244
Beastall, John, Private Secretary to the Paymaster General 85, 87, 99
Benn, Tony, Secretary of State for Industry, subsequently Energy 17, 28, 38, 40, 82, 167–8, 170–1, 175, 238, 254, 262, 270, 274
  on alternative strategy 124, 182, 195, 226, 258–9, 265–6
  on Concorde 49–50
  considered a threat to Western economic liberalism 279
  on Crosland 252
  on cynicism 49
  on economic policy 34, 65, 183, 253
  industrial policy 88–101; Industry

Benn, Tony (*cont.*):
  Bill 142–3; injecting the public interest into the private sector 88; National Enterprise Board 141–2; 'The NEB is an absolute dream' 95; presentation of industrial policy White Paper 96, 100–1, 142; victories over the Treasury 88, 140
  relations with civil servants 89, 139
  relations with Harold Wilson 91–3, 95, 97–9
  supports flat rate incomes policy 157, 177 n.
  wants author as Minister 23
Bennery 17
Berrill, Sir Kenneth, Chief Economic Adviser to the Treasury, subsequently Head of the Central Policy Review Staff (CPRS) 85
Bispham, J. A. 74 n.
Blumenthal, Michael, US Secretary to the Treasury 256
Bolton Committee on Small Companies 91
Booth, Albert, Secretary of State for Employment 258
Bretton Woods 4, 6
British Aircraft Corporation (BAC) 49–50
British Leyland Motor Company (BLMC) 140–2, 167
British National Oil Corporation (BNOC) 144, 229
British Petroleum (BP) 17, 144, 203, 248, 271–3
British Railways Board 151
Brittan, Samuel 239, 243, 258
Brown, George (later Lord George-Brown) 26
Budgets and Mini-budgets:
  1972 5–6
  1973 7
  March 1974 30–41, 43, 55, 57, 90
  July 1974 76–87
  November 1974 45, 111–14, 116, 118, 147
  1975 121-2, 128, 131–8, 149, 153
  1976 216–17, 222
  1978 241
Budget Committee 32, 111, 131, 135
Budget deficit and balance of payments 63, 126
building societies 46–7
Burmah Oil Company Limited 120, 129 n., 261, 271
Burns, Arthur, Chairman of the US Federal Reserve 221

Cabinet Committees:
  Economic Committee 12, 15, 106, 140, 146, 156, 253
  Economic Committee (Pay) known as ECP 104–5, 148, 150–3, 172
  Economic Strategy Committee 71–2, 124, 145, 151–2, 174, 235, 252, 254
  Industrial Development Committee 49, 94, 140–1
Callaghan, James, Secretary of State for Foreign Affairs, subsequently Prime Minister (later Lord Callaghan of Cardiff) 27, 37, 51, 126, 140, 167, 216, 220, 257, 261, 270–1, 280, 284–5, 287
  as Chancellor of the Exchequer 210
  on doing tough things 188
  on economic policy: believes enough has been done to satisfy IMF 252–3; Blackpool speech 236–7; decides to do deal with IMF 267, 269; distrust of Treasury 247, 249; keeps himself informed 225; not to be bounced 230; sterling balances 214, 255; takes charge 223
  fails to call General Election 275
  feels anti-American 272
  his foreign friends 214, 254–5, 262, 265, 268, 274, 278–80, 290 n.
  on import controls 243, 259, 266, 268
  as manager of Cabinet 226, 262, 276, 282
  a more political government 52
  on Party Manifestos 97

relations with author: appoints author Secretary of State for Trade 212; but friendly 290; considers author as successor to Healey 241; regards author as political innocent 241, 285
relations with Crosland 227–8, 240, 251
relations with Healey 238–9, 247, 272, 276–7
relations with TUC 215, 253
on self-defenestration at time of crisis 213
Cambridge Economic Policy Group (CEPG) 127
capital transfer tax 123
Carr, Robert, Secretary of State for Employment, subsequently for the Home Department (later Lord Carr) 5, 80
Carter, Jimmy, President of the USA 256
Castle, Barbara (later Lady Castle), Secretary of State for Health and Social Services 28, 34, 71–2, 159, 166, 190, 227
  on Cabinet under Harold Wilson 24
  on Tony Crosland 187
  on Michael Foot 46, 150, 168
  on Denis Healey 85, 105, 182, 184
  In place of strife 16, 215
  on industrial policy 94
  on the Left's lack of credible policies 168
  pay beds and the unions 176
  on pension uprating 44–5
  on the social contract 15, 146, 157
  on the social wage 82, 149, 158
  on statutory powers over incomes 175
  on vote-catching by Harold Wilson 45
Central Policy Review Staff (CPRS) 253, 267
Chrysler 27
Clapham, Sir Michael, President of the CBI 38–9
Clarke, Sir Richard (Otto), Permanent Secretary to the Ministry of Technology 88

commodity prices 8, 76, 103, 137, 145–6, 193–5, 234
community land scheme 135
Company liquidity 38–9, 82–3, 87 n., 90, 100, 114, 116
Concorde 30, 49–50, 53 n.
Confederation of British Industry (CBI) 55, 104, 153
  company liquidity after March 1974 Budget 38–9, 82, 114
  import controls 243–5
  incomes policy 106, 155–6, 159–60, 166–7, 169–70
  industrial policy 142–3
Confederation of Shipbuilding and Engineering Unions 49
contingency reserve 184
corporation tax 38, 83, 126
Council for Foreign Affairs 61, 231
Cripps, Francis 65, 124, 126, 258
Crosland, Anthony, Secretary of State for the Environment, subsequently Foreign Secretary 23, 212, 285
  building societies 46–7
  capitulates 268, 270
  the Crosland cabal 258–9, 267, 280
  devolution 51
  Europe 16–17
  IMF debates 256–85
  industrial policy 140, 152
  The Lump 252
  national insurance charge 230
  opposes IMF terms 257, 260–1, 283–4
  public expenditure 183, 187–9, 232
  relations with author 17, 261, 284
  relations with Callaghan 226–8, 240, 251
  rents 48
  Socialism Now 17
  threatens import controls– deposits 260, 262, 265–6
  threatens run-down of UK defence commitments 257, 260–1
  trade unions 45, 152–3, 158
Crosland, Susan 257, 262, 267, 271–2

Daily Telegraph 216
Dale, William, Acting Managing Director of the International Monetary Fund 239
Davies, Gavyn 210 n., 213, 289
Day, Robin, subsequently Sir Robin 156
Dearing, Ron, Under Secretary, Department of Industry, subsequently Sir Ron 89
Dell, Sidney 126
Denmark 54
Department of Economic Affairs 106, 212
Department of Employment 105–6
Department of Energy 37, 143–4, 258
Department of the Environment 47
Department of Industry 23, 39, 88–90, 95, 104, 124, 136, 139–40, 143–4
Department of Prices and Consumer Protection (DPCP) 71–2
Department of Trade 212
devolution 50–2
'disengagement' 4–5
Donoghue, Bernard, Head of the Prime Minister's Policy Unit (later Lord Donoghue) 187, 223 n., 229, 243, 289
  believes Wilson provoking Benn's resignation 98
  on biding one's time 70–1
  Cabinet cabals 226
  on Callaghan 223, 225–6, 277
  on collective Cabinet discussion of economic policy 54, 278
  fed-up with the Treasury 172, 174, 247, 249
  on 4 March 1976 206
  on Healey 190
  on IMF cuts 283
  Letter of Intent 272
  Policy Unit and the economy 120, 213
  Policy Unit and incomes policy 159–74

Economic Policy and the cost of living 14
Edwards, Sir George, Chairman of British Aircraft Corporation (BAC) 49
Electronic Engineering Association 156
Elwyn-Jones, Lord Chancellor 166–7, 170

Employment Protection Bill 153
Ennals, David, Secretary of State for Health and Social Security (later Lord Ennals) 258, 268
European Economic Community (EEC) 16–17, 87, 98, 124, 143, 156, 232, 242, 244, 259
  European Commission 129, 244
  Finance Ministers' Council 25, 171, 197
exchange rates 5, 54, 58, 68, 73, 86, 136, 197, 213, 218, 242
  collapse 205, 207, 239
  competitiveness 84, 118, 196, 204, 222
  in dealing with wage claims 8
  distorting the economy 6
  dual exchange rates 127–8, 136
  floating 4, 6, 8–9, 86, 198, 204, 239
  Kaldor's attitude 126–8, 133
  the snake 6, 197–8, 206, 208
Exchequer, The 47, 48
Expenditure Committee 273

Federal Reserve 221, 235, 256
Financial Times 123, 155–6, 239, 245, 290
Fleet, Kenneth 155
food subsidies 14, 38, 44, 71, 80, 150, 228
Foot, Michael, Secretary of State for Employment, subsequently Lord President of the Council and Leader of the House of Commons 44, 143, 146, 175, 217
  on agreement with IMF 258, 262, 269, 271
  as departmental Minister 46
  as economist 150
  on import controls 194, 226, 253
  incomes policy 104, 166, 168, 170–1
  industrial democracy 82
  Price Code 100–1
  on reflation 72, 81, 183
  relations with CBI 105–6
  relations with TUs 45, 115, 151–3, 158, 227
  social contract 147–8

Ford, Gerald, President of the USA 214, 220, 232, 254–6, 262, 265, 268–9, 274, 279
Forties field 203
foundry industry 136
France 66, 133, 219, 280
Friedman, Professor Milton 231, 270

General Agreement on Tariffs and Trade (GATT) 245, 267, 269
General Arrangements to Borrow (GAB) 237, 246 n., 248, 276 n.
General Electric Company Limited (GEC) 140
Germany, Federal Republic of 57, 59, 66, 133, 147, 186, 237, 248, 249–50, 254–6, 262–3, 284, 279, 288
Gilbert, John, Financial Secretary to the Treasury 25, 46, 85, 128, 134
Giscard d'Estaing, Valéry, President of the French Republic 214, 232
Godley, Wynne 63, 67–8, 126–7, 213, 260, 282, 291 n.
Goldring, Mary 241
Goodhart, Professor Charles 10 n.
Gregson, Peter, Under Secretary, Department of Industry, subsequently Sir Peter, Permanent Secretary, Department of Trade and Industry 89
Guardian 167, 257

Haines, Joe, Prime Minister's Press Secretary 157, 161–6, 168–9, 173–4, 177 n., 217
Hamilton, Adrian 243, 258
Hattersley, Roy, Minister of State, Foreign Office, subsequently Secretary of State for Prices and Consumer Protection 226, 235, 253, 258, 267–8, 270, 285
Healey, Denis, Chancellor of the Exchequer:
  abandons Keynesianism 79, 138
  blames Barber for rising inflation 36, 147, 231
  Cabinet of 2 December 1976 269–70
  claims IMF guidance for economic policy 56-7, 66
  Concorde 49–50
  declining confidence in Treasury advice 40, 125, 179–80
  deflationary views lead to neutral March 1974 Budget 30-2
  disappointed in international co-operation 57, 137–8
  dislikes Treasury's monolithic papers 62
  on exchange rate 68, 84, 195, 198, 207–8
  to the IMF 'on existing policies' 237–8
  inexperience in economic policy 25–6
  influence of forecasts 32-3, 281–3
  June 1976 stand-by and the IMF trap 219–20
  at low ebb 239, 253
  monetarism and the money supply 35, 231
  'The most political Chancellor' 85, 87 n., 180, 239
  navigating between economists 81, 180
  North Sea oil 70, 84
  optimism on the economy 54, 76, 80
  rejects direct action on current account 133, 136, 194–5, 243, 245
  relations with author 15, 35, 78–9, 92–3, 113–14, 124–5, 186, 210, 238, 240, 259, 289
  relations with Callaghan 226, 238, 247, 251, 277–8
  relations with Crosland 188–9
  relations with TUC 134, 147–50, 152–3, 217
  reluctance to publish 33-4, 112–13, 122
  retreat from Heathrow 235–6
  saves government and ejected from NEC 176
  sceptical of Treasury forecasts 32-3, 131
  on Simon and Yeo 221
  social contract 15, 35, 45, 105, 123, 147, 150–1, 154, 158–71
  on sovereignty 137
  tax-pay proposal 216–17

Healey, Denis (*cont.*):
  Treasury demarche 119–21
  a Treasury industrial policy 90, 94, 136, 189–90, 271
  Treasury's 'sado-masochism' 185
  'A triumph for Chancellor Denis Healey' 190
  Whither Healey? 128
Heath, Edward, Prime Minister 3–6, 8–10, 12, 15, 17, 19, 23–4, 46, 94, 103–4
Heffer, Eric, Minister of State, Department of Industry 92, 104–5, 143
Heisenberg uncertainty principle 10 n.
Hercules 217
Heron, Sir Conrad, Permanent Secretary, Department of Employment 46
Hodgson, Sir Maurice 140
Holland, Stuart 90
Hopkin, Sir Bryan, Chief Economic Adviser, Treasury 120, 132, 288
Howe, Sir Geoffrey 156
Husbands and Wives 81

Imperial Chemical Industries Limited (ICI) 26, 140
import controls 19, 120, 123, 126–7, 182, 187, 194–7, 204, 215, 222, 238, 241–5, 251, 253, 259, 266–7
import surcharge–export subsidy scheme 123–5, 128–9, 131–3, 135–6
incomes policy (pay policy) 35, 174, 183–4, 186, 199, 203, 208, 214, 218, 238, 285
  consents under the Pay Code 104–5
  and depreciation 196, 198
  ECP 104, 150–2
  Heath Government's incomes policy 9–10, 11 n., 67, 104–5
  monetarists and incomes policy 35, 37
  official despair 151
  orderly growth of incomes 103
  tax-pay proposal 216–17
  tedium 115
  Treasury proposals 123, 126–7
  under the social contract 14, 106–7, 146–7, 155–76, 209, 215–17
income tax 3, 32, 113, 132–3, 137, 216, 217
Industrial Relations Act 14, 45
Industry Act 143–4
inflation tax 132, 150
In place of strife 16, 43, 46, 103, 215
insularity 268, 289
International Monetary Fund 27, 35, 58, 60, 186, 188, 197, 206, 210, 213, 216, 225
  Committee of Twenty 56, 199
  credit tranches 193, 197, 246 n.
  Executive Board 194, 199
  on import controls 194, 268–9
  Interim Committee 73 n.
  on management of world economy 31, 56–7, 73 n.
  oil facility 199 n.
  UK application September 1976 234 ff.
  UK stand-by application December 1975 191, 198–9, 204
  UK's June 1976 stand-by credit and recourse to the IMF 219–20, 222
  views on UK economy 3–4, 193–4, 218
IPD 49
Iran 80, 118 n.
Italy 54, 57, 219, 256, 280, 281

J curve 68, 195, 222
Japan 57, 59, 66–7, 90, 133, 147, 244–5
Jay, Peter, subsequently UK Ambassador to the USA 236
Jenkins, Peter 257
Jenkins, Roy, Secretary of State, Home Department (later Lord Jenkins of Hillhead) 16, 25, 51, 63, 71, 99, 140, 187, 239
Johnson, Frank 216–17
Jones, Gwynoro, Labour MP 94
Jones, Jack, General Secretary, Transport and General Workers' Union 168, 173, 176
  discourages Michael Foot from resignation 171

dissatisfied with level of
  consultation 14
IMF crisis 257
inflation 76, 147, 149, 215
proposes flat-rate incomes policy 156–7,
  159–60, 169
sanctions against employers 165, 167
suspicious of some Ministers 159–60
tax-pay proposal 217
unreceptive to Benn and Orme 253–4

Kaldor, Nicholas, Adviser to the
    Chancellor of the Exchequer (later
    Lord Kaldor) 79, 130 n., 135
  advocates import controls 124, 127,
    130 n., 195–6, 258–60
  advocates wage subsidy 118
  budget deficit, PSBR, and balance of
    payments 63, 112, 126, 129 n., 132
  company liquidity 11–12, 114
  criticizes Sir Bryan Hopkin 132
  depreciation 126–8, 135–6, 198, 282
  import surcharge–export subsidy
    scheme 127–8, 129, 133, 135
  on incomes policy 126–7
  oil borrowing 116
  opposes IMF terms 258–9
  pay-roll tax 232 n.
  on unemployment 67, 126
  Whither Healey? 128
Keegan, William 206–7, 229–30
Keith, Sir Kenneth (later Lord Keith) 152
Keynes, Lord 56, 79, 231
Keynesianism 7, 13, 18, 27, 56, 64, 183
  against adding to deflationary spiral in
    international economy 35, 55, 57–8
  apparent demise 5–6, 10 n., 236
  depreciation 196, 204
  'Keynesian dissenters' 226
  'We are all anti-Keynesians now' 79
Kitson, Alex 50, 177 n.
Kuwait 163, 167

Lea, David 159
Lever, Harold, Chancellor of the Duchy of
  Lancaster (later Lord Lever of
    Manchester) 29, 140, 187–8, 214,
    227, 284
  advocates economic expansion funded
    by borrowing 27–8, 58–60, 71–2,
    125, 182
  against depreciation 118
  against IMF terms 226
  against import controls 267
  author's undelivered speech 91–3
  building societies 46–8
  criticizes March 1974 budget 34
  debates in the Treasury 62–6, 68
  'The greatest Socialist of all' 215
  on inflation 73
  influence on Healey and Wilson 35, 65,
    126
  June 1976 stand-by credit 219–20
  'a man for ingenious solutions' 28
  participation discussion with oil
    companies 144
  on a 'prosperous disequilibrium' 57,
    74 n.
  Stock Exchange in August 1974 99–
    101
  visits Washington about sterling
    balances 255–6, 279
Liaison Committee between Labour Party
    and TUC 14, 76, 147, 149, 153, 194,
    215
Lloyd, Selwyn, Speaker of the House of
    Commons 111
Lord, Alan, Deputy Secretary, Department
    of Industry, subsequently Second
    Permanent Secretary, Treasury 89
Lump, the (labour only sub-
    contracting) 252, 263 n.
Luton Chamber of Commerce 90

Macdonald, Ramsay, Prime Minister 250
Macdougall, Sir Donald 38, 55, 159, 169
Macmillan, Harold, Prime Minister (later
    Earl of Stockton) 19, 24
Macmillan, Maurice, Conservative
    Minister 24
McMahon, Sir Kit 135, 195, 197

302 Index

Martin, Paul, Canadian High Commissioner 218, 247
Mason, Roy, Secretary of State for Northern Ireland (later Lord Mason of Barnsley) 230
Maudling, Reginald, Chancellor of the Exchequer 19, 26
Meacher, Michael, Parliamentary Secretary, Department of Industry 94
Mellish, Robert (later Lord Mellish of Bermondsey) 44–5, 153, 164, 167
Meriden Co-operative 140
Mikardo, Ian, Labour MP and Member of the NEC of the Labour Party 230
Mitchell, Sir Derek, Second Permanent Secretary, Treasury 85, 198
monetarism 35–6, 112, 127, 182, 230–1, 236, 260
money supply 5, 10, 35–7, 63, 112, 136, 230–1, 234, 238, 283
Morrell, Frances 89, 259
Morris, John, Secretary of State for Wales 48, 50–1
mortgages 46–8
Murray, Lionel (Len), General Secretary of the TUC (later Lord Murray) 76, 146, 165, 167, 169–70, 244, 254

Napoleonic Wars 42
National Enterprise Board (NEB) 17–18, 89, 91, 94–5, 97, 100, 135, 141–3, 190, 228
National Executive Committee of the Labour Party (NEC) 12, 17, 85, 90, 95, 176, 194
National Industrial Relations Court 105
National Institute Economic Review (NIER) 7–10, 74 n., 75 n., 77, 122, 127, 191, 196–7, 204–5, 217–18, 241-2, 283
National Institute for Economic and Social Research (NIESR) 7, 63, 67
National Savings Movement 156
National Union of Mineworkers (NUM) 3, 10, 44, 72, 104, 156, 169

National Union of Railwaymen (NUR) 151–2, 157–8
nationalized industries 18, 30, 107, 114, 150, 229, 276 n.
North Atlantic Treaty Organization (NATO) 257
Netherlands 186, 219
Netherlands Central Bank 219
New Cambridge School 63, 65, 67, 126, 196, 258, 267
Nield, Professor Robert 152
Nigeria 167, 195, 205–6
North Sea oil 25, 51, 63, 68–70, 84–5, 117, 144, 189, 194–5, 204, 243
  participation 16, 49, 144
  petroleum revenue tax 25, 144
Norway 216

O'Brien, Sir Richard 106
Observer 18, 94, 98, 157
oil borrowing 116–17, 118 n.
Old Cambridge School 196
Organization for Economic Co-operation and Development (OECD) 31, 58, 76, 185, 220, 242
Organization of Petroleum Exporting Countries (OPEC) 8–9, 57, 60, 77, 203
Orme, Stanley, Minister of State for Social Security in the Cabinet 226, 235, 253, 258
Owen, Ron 159

Pardoe, John, Liberal MP 249
Parliamentary Labour Party 122, 209, 214, 231, 240
Parsky, Gerald, Assistant Secretary to the US Treasury 220
Part, Sir Antony, Permanent Secretary, Department of Industry 40, 89, 180
Pay Beds Bill 176
Pay Board 104, 107
Pay Code 104, 106
pay policy, *see* incomes policy
Pennant-Rea, Rupert 206-7, 229–30
pensions 30, 44, 215

planning agreements 89–90, 94–5, 140, 142, 215
Pliatzky, Sir Leo, Second Permanent Secretary, Treasury, subsequently Permanent Secretary, Department of Trade 231, 235
  on the control of public expenditure 184
  on inadvertence in managing the exchange rate 206–8
  on July 1976 measures 228
  on Harold Lever 28, 218
  on official advice 74 n.
  on presentation of public expenditure 185
  on relations with the IMF 219, 248–50, 280
Pöhl, Karl-Otto 256
Political Responsibility and Industry 143
Posner, Michael, Deputy Chief Economic Adviser to the Treasury 196
Prentice, Reg, Secretary of State for Education and Science, subsequently Minister for Overseas Development 48, 134, 150, 262
Price Code 100–1, 114–16, 161, 167, 169
Prime Minister's Policy Unit 37, 54, 120, 124, 160-1, 168, 172–3, 216, 273, 290
productivity deduction 39, 114–15
Public Accounts Committee 25, 139
public expenditure 7, 10, 23–4, 28, 30, 33, 37, 44, 58, 61–2, 65–7, 71–2, 81–2, 114, 120–3, 137, 149, 156, 160, 163–4, 168, 170, 174, 181–91, 194–5, 198, 203, 209, 214, 218–20, 222–3, 225–32, 238, 244, 248–9, 251, 253–4, 257–8, 260–1, 270, 273, 281, 283–4
  PESC 232 n.
  shortfall 184, 291 n.
Public Sector Borrowing Requirement (PSBR) 4–5, 30, 32–3, 36, 38, 41 n., 62, 77, 79–80, 86, 111–13, 115–16, 119–20, 123–5, 127–8, 131–2, 137, 142, 187, 196, 203, 222, 229–30, 235, 248–9, 252–4, 257, 260, 262, 266, 269–70, 273–4
Puerto Rico 220

Qatar 60

railways 151–2
real national income 145–6, 149, 154 n., 185
referendum 17, 124, 129, 136, 143, 156, 176
regional employment premium (REP) 77–8, 82
Remuneration, Charges and Grants Act 171
retail prices index (RPI) 37, 71–3, 80, 116, 131–2, 134, 137, 148, 150, 156, 175, 228, 273
Richardson, Gordon, Governor of the Bank of England (later Lord Richardson of Duntisbourne) 8, 120, 135, 195, 197, 219, 225–6, 236
Rita Hinden Memorial Lecture, February 1977 242, 255, 289–90
Rodgers, William, Secretary of State for Transport 235, 258, 268
Rolls Royce 17, 135, 152
Ross, Willie, Secretary of State for Scotland (later Lord Ross of Marnock) 48, 50, 94
Ryder, Sir Don (later Lord Ryder of Eaton Hastings), Chairman of the National Enterprise Board 141–2
Ryrie, Sir William 199

Saudi Arabia 116–18, 163, 167
Scandinavia 186
Scanlon, Hugh, General Secretary, Amalgamated Engineering Union (later Lord Scanlon) 147, 153, 160, 169, 173
Schmidt, Helmut, Chancellor of the Federal Republic of Germany 214, 232, 254–6, 265, 268–9, 274, 278
Scotland 50–1, 117, 234
Scottish Labour Party 50

304   Index

Scottish Nationalism 50, 61
Scottish Trade Union Congress 50
Serjeant at Arms 135
Sheldon, Robert, Minister of State,
   subsequently Financial Secretary,
   Treasury 25, 122, 128, 134–5
Shore, Peter, Secretary of State for Trade,
   subsequently for the Environment 81,
   94, 168, 175, 187, 226–7, 238, 253,
   258–9, 266–8, 274, 281
Silkin, John, Minister for Planning and
   Local Government, subsequently
   Minister for Agriculture, Food and
   Fisheries 226, 252, 258
Simon, William, US Secretary to the
   Treasury 219–21, 239, 265, 274,
   278–9
Skinner, Denis, Labour MP 105
Smith, David 207
Smithsonian Institute 4
Snowdon, Philip 160
Soames, Sir Christopher, Vice-President of
   the European Commission (later Lord
   Soames) 244
Soares, Mario, Prime Minister of Portugal
   (later President of Portugal) 291
social contract 12–15, 33–4, 42, 44–5,
   62–4, 80, 82, 104, 106–7, 115,
   123, 143, 145–53, 155, 157–8, 174,
   257
social wage 44, 82, 148, 149, 150, 154 n.,
   158
Socialism 12, 17, 40, 169, 215, 227, 289
special drawing rights (SDRs) 193, 199,
   199 n.
stand-by credit—June 1976 219–20, 222,
   235–6, 269, 282
sterling balances 195, 204, 206, 209, 214,
   222, 251, 255–6, 260, 269, 275
Stock Exchange 99–101
Stowe, Sir Kenneth, Principal Private
   Secretary to the Prime Minister 238
Sunday Times 58, 239, 246 n.
Short, Ted, Deputy Leader of the Labour
   Party (later Lord Glenamara) 48,
   50–1, 176

The Next Three Years and the Problems of
   Priorities 215
The Politics of Economic Interdependence
   242
The Regeneration of British Industry 88,
   96, 142
The Times 8, 156, 244, 249, 259–60,
   264 n., 282
Thomas, Jimmy 160
Trade Union and Industrial Relations
   Bill 105
Trade Union Congress (TUC):
   'curious statistics' 146
   flat-rate incomes policy 156–7, 159–
     61, 168–70, 177 n.
   guide-lines 106–7, 147, 149, 151–2
   Healey and the TUC 134, 217
   import controls 243–5
   industrial policy 96, 142–3, 189
   Price Code 101, 115
   reflating the economy with wage
     claims 147–8
   the social contract 14, 76, 106–7,
     147–9, 152–3
Treasury, The:
   'Addiction to elementary
     arithmetic' 237
   allegations of tendencies towards
     secrecy 34, 72, 228–30, 272
   Callaghan's distrust 247
   cash limits 184
   company liquidity 38–9, 82–3, 114–16
   December 1974 Demarche to
     Chancellor 119–20, 129
   depreciation 84–5, 195–6, 198, 206–9
   disagreements within 62–5, 68–9,
     83–5, 180, 225, 248–50, 280
   forecasts 32–3, 74 n., 194, 234, 253,
     281–3
   Healey's distrust 40, 179
   Keynesian influence 35, 55, 59, 113
   Labour's valuable contacts with
     TUs 19, 174
   learning economic management 26–7
   looks for leadership 180
   March 1974 Budget 37–8

official Treasury's concern for its reputation 120, 133, 287
official Treasury's lack of enthusiasm for its own policies 133
on not making tough recommendations 74 n.
'One must select one's time' 70–1, 191 n.
presentation of public expenditure 185–6
relations with the Policy Unit 160–6, 172–4, 272–3
social contract 107, 150–1, 161–2, 175
a tendency to bounce 161, 163–5, 173, 226
Treasury's alternative strategy 123–4, 133, 136
Treasury industrial policy 90, 140, 189–90, 228
Trudeau, Pierre Elliott, Prime Minister of Canada 214

unemployment 4–9, 13, 34–5, 43–5, 55–6, 66–7, 72, 76–7, 79, 82–4, 113–15, 122–3, 126, 128, 138, 147–8, 153, 155, 158, 175, 183, 188–9, 191, 194, 197, 199, 203, 213, 215–16, 218, 227, 236, 242, 245, 251–2, 257, 272, 274, 281, 288
United States of America (USA) 47, 57, 67, 125, 133, 147, 209, 214, 219–21, 237, 244, 249, 254, 279, 287

value added tax (VAT) 37, 39, 77, 80, 82, 134, 137, 248
Varley, Eric, Secretary of State for Energy, subsequently Industry (later Lord Varley) 143–4, 151–2, 167–8, 175, 190
Venezuela 258, 261
voluntary aided schools 48

Wales 50–1
Wass, Sir Douglas, Permanent Secretary, Treasury 85, 90, 120
Watt, David 123

Weighell, Sid, General Secretary of the National Union of Railwaymen 157
Weinstock, Sir Arnold (later Lord Weinstock) 140
W. Greenwell & Company 220
Whittome, Alan 247–8, 256, 268, 274
Williams, Shirley, Secretary of State for Prices and Consumer Protection, subsequently Education and Science 40, 72–3, 98–101, 107, 115, 121, 146, 150, 167, 228, 235, 253, 258, 267
Wilson Harold, Prime Minister (later Lord Wilson of Rievaulx) 16, 25, 27, 37, 39, 54, 70, 89, 99, 105, 125–6, 154, 188, 210, 215, 227–8, 286
anger with the Treasury 206
author and Benn 91–3
author as Paymaster General 23–4
best Treasury team ever 25
'A Cabinet rich in experience' 19
devolution 50–1
his ability to count 190
'I too am a Treasury Minister' 48
import surcharge–export subsidy scheme 129, 131–2
incomes policy 103, 156, 159, 161–70, 184
industrial policy White Paper 95–6, 100–1, 142
'A law of British politics' 18
'The leading financial powers reacted in the wrong way' 59
management of Cabinet 24–5, 187
mortgage interest 46
promises author Cabinet membership 23, 212
real national income 145–6
relations with Benn 97–9, 139, 142–3
resigns 175, 209
social contract 14, 103, 156, 159, 161–70, 184
'Think politically' 52
'An unparalleled economic crisis' 42, 71
vote-catching 45, 49

Witteveen, Johannes, Managing Director of the International Monetary Fund 56–7, 199, 236, 248, 268, 280
Worswick, David 67

XYZ 67

Yeo, Edwin H., Under Secretary for Monetary Affairs, US Treasury 220–1, 236, 256, 279
Young Fabian Group 145

Zijlstra, Jelle, President, Netherlands Central Bank and Bank of International Settlements 219

£5-00
Speakers library fund